The Chancellors

The Chancellors

Steering the British Economy in Crisis Times

Howard Davies

polity

First published in 2022 by Polity Press

Polity Press
65 Bridge Street
Cambridge CB2 1UR, UK

Polity Press
101 Station Landing
Suite 300
Medford, MA 02155, USA

ISBN-13: 978-1-5095-4953-5
ISBN-13: 978-1-5095-4954-2 (pb)

A catalogue record for this book is available from the British Library.

Typeset in 11 on 13pt Sabon
by Cheshire Typesetting Ltd, Cuddington, Cheshire
Printed and bound in the UK by 4edge Limited

The publisher has used its best endeavours to ensure that the URLs for external websites referred to in this book are correct and active at the time of going to press. However, the publisher has no responsibility for the websites and can make no guarantee that a site will remain live or that the content is or will remain appropriate.

For further information on Polity, visit our website:
politybooks.com

Contents

Abbreviations

AIFMD	Alternative Investment Fund Management Directive
B-DEM	Bespoke Dynamic Equivalence Mechanism
BEIS	Department for Business, Energy and Industrial Strategy
CBI	Confederation of British Industry
CCC	Committee on Climate Change
CPI	Consumer Prices Index
CST	Chief Secretary to the Treasury
DMO	Debt Management Office
DTI	Department of Trade and Industry
ECB	European Central Bank
ECJ	European Court of Justice
EEA	European Economic Area
EMU	Economic and Monetary Union
ERM	exchange rate mechanism
EST	Economic Secretary to the Treasury
FCA	Financial Conduct Authority
FCDO	Foreign, Commonwealth and Development Office
FSA	Financial Services Authority
FSR	Financial Stability Review

FST	Financial Secretary to the Treasury
GDP	Gross domestic product
GFC	global financial crisis
GVA	gross value added
HAM	High Alignment Model
HMRC	Her Majesty's Revenue and Customs
ICT	information and communication technologies
IFS	Institute of Fiscal Studies
IMF	International Monetary Fund
MOU	Memorandum of Understanding
MPC	Monetary Policy Committee
OBR	Office for Budget Responsibility
PFI	private finance initiative
PRA	Prudential Regulation Authority
PSAs	public service agreements
PSL	private sector liquidity
QE	quantitative easing
R&D	Research and Development
RBS	Royal Bank of Scotland
RPI	Retail Prices Index
SEC	Securities and Exchange Commission
SIB	Securities and Investments Board
SME	small and medium-sized enterprise
SNP	Scottish National Party
TSC	Treasury Select Committee
WTO	World Trade Organisation

Introduction

In 2006, I edited and introduced *The Chancellors' Tales*.[1] It included lectures given at the London School of Economics by the five former Chancellors of the Exchequer then alive: Denis Healey, Geoffrey Howe, Nigel Lawson, Norman Lamont and Kenneth Clarke (I excluded John Major who had served for a short period). Their brief was to reflect on the challenges of running the Treasury.

The period covered ran from 1974 to 1997. Aside from the personal availability, there was a certain policy logic in that it began with Healey's attempt to establish budget discipline and control inflation, after the International Monetary Fund (IMF) visitation in 1976. Healey introduced the monetary framework which Howe made the centre of his policy. The period ended with the 1997 election, immediately after which Brown handed control of interest rates to an independent Bank of England.

Since 1997, five more Chancellors have passed through the Treasury, with a sixth (as I write) now in office. So it seemed timely to assemble their reflections on the role. But, partly because the Covid pandemic ruled out another series of lectures, I have adopted a different technique. Gordon Brown, Alistair Darling, George Osborne and Philip

Hammond, who cover the period from 1997 to 2019, were kind enough to agree to be interviewed. I am very grateful to them, and to the senior officials, special advisers and ministers who also agreed to answer my questions. Where they were happy to be quoted, they are identified in the text and the notes. I have taken the story up to late 2021, though without the benefit of oral evidence from Sajid Javid or Rishi Sunak.

Three pieces of conventional wisdom are often recycled by the Treasury's critics. First, that by international standards it is far more powerful than its counterparts: in most other major developed countries there is typically an economic ministry alongside the finance ministry, and there is often a stronger central policy function around the President or Prime Minister. Second, that the Treasury's 'dead hand', masquerading as public expenditure control, constrains government policy unreasonably and damages investment and innovation. Third, that after a series of missteps, the Treasury's authority is not what it was, and it is riding for a fall.

There may be some truth in the first argument, though a little less since Bank of England independence and the creation of the Office for Budget Responsibility (OBR). But it is not obvious that a single ministry of finance and economy delivers worse policy outcomes. There were several attempts during this period to cut the Treasury down to size, usually driven by the Prime Minister's staff. In a political system where a Prime Minister with a large majority in Parliament has a remarkable degree of power, the existence of a strong alternative centre is a valuable check on 'elective dictatorship'.

The second, the 'dead hand' argument, includes two subvariants, one micro, one macro. The micro case is that the Treasury is 'the bank that likes to say no', always sceptical about new ideas unless they are generated by its own people, and especially suspicious of local initiatives. As one former Permanent Secretary acknowledged, officials are far readier to explain why new initiatives may not work than to generate new thoughts of their own. The Treasury defence is that if it does not train a sceptical eye on wizard ideas for spending other people's money, no one else will, and that, in the long-running Whitehall drama, it is inevitably cast in the role of Scrooge. To mix Dickensian metaphors, Scrooge may not be popular, but where all the other characters are Oliver Twists with their bowls out asking for more, some with bowls already quite full, his spirit is required.

The macro critique is more serious and has gained force during the period under review. In a world where there is a chronic surplus of saving over investment, the Treasury has maintained a version of Mrs Thatcher's household economics, urging successive Chancellors (though Osborne needed little urging) to work towards balancing the books, even when the economy was operating below capacity and real interest rates were very low or negative. So the charge is that UK recovery from the 2008/9 financial crisis was slower than it need have been, and that a similar mistake is in the course of being made as we exit from the pandemic. I review those arguments in Chapters 2 and 3, and again at the end.

The third argument is that, partly because the Treasury has been on the wrong side of history on the second critique, its authority has declined within government and it is a shadow of its former self. Lionel Barber, former *Financial Times* editor, summarized the case in an article in *Prospect* magazine titled 'The Treasury Today: A Devalued Currency?'.[2]

That view, as I hope to show, is misconceived. The Treasury has successfully fought off attempts to diminish its status over the past two decades, continues to attract high-quality staff (if perhaps too few of them) and is as powerful as ever. Successive Prime Ministers have found that fighting the Treasury in the end makes them weaker, and they come to rely on its support. Boris Johnson has followed exactly that trajectory. In macroeconomic policy, the Treasury must now share centre stage with the Bank of

England, but that has in some ways strengthened its hand: 'We would love to help with your spending plans, but the bank manager will not allow it.'

This is, nonetheless, a story of downs and ups for the Treasury as an institution. It took a knock in 1997 when the Bank was set free, but rolled with that punch. It was floored briefly by the financial crisis, but not counted out, performed well at the most difficult time, and reasserted its authority in the recovery phase. It triumphed in the 2014 Scottish wars, but suffered another heavy blow in the 2016 EU referendum, and was then side-lined in the Brexit negotiations. For a time, that looked fatal, and its enemies marshalled their resources for a final assault, but Covid, paradoxically, came to the rescue. It was no time to begin reshuffling the economic deckchairs, and Treasury ministers and officials showed resilience and imagination in devising rescue schemes to keep the productive economy afloat in the storm. So reports of its death proved greatly exaggerated.

In what follows, my aim has been to allow ministers and officials to tell the story themselves, as far as possible, though I am sure they, and readers, will consider that I have at times led the witnesses. Others will consider that, as an intermittent insider, I have delivered a conventional reading, too favourable to the 'Treasury view'. As the saying goes: 'You can take the man out of the Treasury, but you can't take the Treasury out of the man.'

Chapter 1 sets the scene, with a brief review of the UK's economic performance during the period.

Chapter 2 discusses macroeconomic policy, which was defined rather differently in a period when interest rates were set by the central bank.

In Chapter 3, I review the approach taken by successive governments to the control of public expenditure and in Chapter 4, I assess the performance of the Treasury in setting tax policy.

Chapter 5 changes gear and considers the Treasury's unusually public role in the 2014 referendum campaign on

Scottish independence, where its intervention was arguably decisive in determining the outcome. Chapter 6 examines the department's far less successful interventions in the EU referendum campaign – dubbed Project Fear – and explores the Treasury's changing attitude to the European Union, and specifically to Economic and Monetary Union (EMU), through the period. I review the economic implications of Brexit and the Treasury's role in the negotiations leading to the Trade and Cooperation Agreement.

Chapter 7 explores the Treasury's responsibilities for financial regulation and the City of London generally. Those responsibilities were broadened in 1997 after the creation of the Financial Services Authority (FSA). The way the department responded to the Global 2008/9 financial crisis is evaluated, as is the subsequent second reform of the regulatory bodies carried out under Osborne. The specific issues raised by Brexit for the UK financial sector and its access to EU markets are considered.

Chapter 8 reviews the Treasury's attitude to climate change and its economic implications, from initial scepticism, through the Stern Review to the embrace of a net zero target in 2021.

In Chapter 9, I describe the way the responsibilities of the Treasury have evolved through the period and Chapter 10 includes an account of the key individuals, both ministers and officials, who have led and shaped the department over the last quarter of a century.

Chapter 11 concludes with some reflections on the period as a whole, and the challenges the Treasury now faces. My thesis is that the troubles ahead will be more menacing to the institution, and more challenging to its traditional philosophy and ways of working than were the crises of the recent past. The whole basis of the 'Treasury view' needs to be rethought and, if it is to navigate the twin challenges of Covid recovery and climate change, it will need different skills and more people.

1

Economic Performance

Gus O'Donnell, Permanent Secretary to the Treasury from 2002 to 2005, has declared that 'the era of GDP being the unique measure is now over'. He quotes Robert F. Kennedy, who said: 'GDP measures neither our wit nor our courage, neither our wisdom nor our learning, neither our compassion nor our devotion to our country, it measures everything, in short, except that which makes life worthwhile.'[1] And he points out more prosaically that gross domestic product (GDP) as conventionally defined is not well suited for modern service-based economies with larger government sectors. That describes the UK quite well, indeed increasingly so. But even O'Donnell acknowledges that GDP measures 'have a long history and are very useful for making comparisons over time and between countries'.

Using that imperfect methodology, how well did the British economy perform under the five Chancellors whose periods of stewardship we are considering, both in absolute and relative terms? And what can we confidently say about the influence of the government's economic policy on that performance?

The period, like Gaul, divides into three parts. The Labour government was in office from 1997 to 2010, which is a long enough interval to use for comparisons forward and back. The figures are distorted somewhat by including the years of the financial crisis and its immediate aftermath, but if we allow Labour the pre-crisis boom, it is not unreasonable that they should also accept the bust. Brown famously declared that he had put an end to boom and bust, so it would be hard for him to complain. The second period runs from 2010 to 2016. That encompasses the full term of the Coalition government, and the first year of a majority Conservative administration. Osborne was Chancellor throughout. The third period begins with the EU referendum, which marked the beginning of a significant change of trend. The end of that third period is dominated, and distorted, by the Covid crisis, but the four-year stretch from the launch of the referendum campaign to the first Covid lockdown is long enough to have its own distinct characteristics.

1997–2010: The Brown years

The early 1990s had been a turbulent period in economic policy terms, with the chaotic withdrawal from the European exchange rate mechanism (ERM) in 1992. However, underlying economic performance during the long Conservative hegemony, from 1979 to 1997, was relatively good. GDP per capita had fallen relative to the US, Germany and France from 1870 to 1979, if we ignore the war periods, but the trend began to reverse at the end of the 1970s. UK GDP per head was about 23% above the US in 1870. By 1979 the US was 43% ahead of the UK. In 2007 the UK was still behind, but the gap had narrowed to 33%: still a significant discount, but reflecting a steady improvement in productivity throughout the period.

The extent to which this change in trend can be attributed to the policies of the Thatcher and Major governments remains in dispute, and is outside the scope of this book, though most economists would acknowledge that the labour market reforms, privatization (at least in its early stages), a tougher approach to failing firms, and lower marginal tax rates all contributed. The period was also the first in which we began to see the implications of membership of the European Community, as it then was. Nicholas Crafts shows that larger trade volumes have had a positive impact on productivity. He argues: 'In the case of the United Kingdom the gain from joining the EU was probably around 10 per cent of GDP . . . [arising from] a significant increase in competition as protectionism was abandoned.'[2]

There was no sign that the relative productivity improvement was running out of steam in 1997, so in that sense Labour's inheritance was a good one. The economy was expanding, and for some time had been the fastest growing in the G7.

That record was sustained over the whole period from 1997 to 2010. Even though there was a sharp recession precipitated by the financial crisis, as Dan Corry et al. conclude, 'relative to other major industrialised countries, the UK's performance was good after 1997'.[3] Growth in GDP per head averaged what might by historical standards appear a fairly modest 1.42% a year over the thirteen-year period. But that was faster than in any of the other comparable large economies. Germany grew by 1.26% a year, the US by 1.22%, France by 1.04%, Japan by 0.52% and Italy by a remarkably weak 0.22%.

With the exception of Italy and Japan, the differentials are not great, but sustained over more than a decade they become significant. There was certainly an element of catch-up at work. Poor economic governance leading to high inflation, an underperforming education sector, weak industrial management and bad industrial relations resulted in the UK slipping back against comparable countries during the 1950s, 1960s and 1970s. The German *Wirtschaftswunder* and the *Trente Glorieuses* in France passed us by. So once the shackles of poor labour relations and weak competitive dynamics were thrown off, some convergence was to be expected. But Corry et al. reject the argument that growth in the Brown and Darling years was driven mainly by the momentum created by their predecessors.

Some maintain that much of this outperformance was in a sense illusory, and that the productivity improvement was driven by unsustainable bubbles in the financial and property sectors in particular. But the financial sector contributed only 0.4% of the 2.8% annual growth in the market economy and productivity improvements were primarily driven by business services and distribution, through the utilization of new skills and technologies. Financial intermediation accounted for around 6% of gross value added (GVA) throughout the period from 1979 to 2010, only slightly higher than the French figure (5%). Property activity did grow, but from 5 to 8% of GVA. The biggest improvements in productivity are traceable to changes in the composition of the labour force, in other words a higher proportion of workers with higher-level skills, and greater use of information and communication technologies (ICT) capital, which was an important differentiating factor for both the UK and the US vis-à-vis the large European economies. The UK was also more successful than others in attracting inward investment, and foreign-owned firms have long shown higher productivity than their domestic counterparts.

How much credit can the Blair and Brown governments take for this outperformance?

A neutral to negative interpretation might be that they did not reverse the earlier Conservative labour market reforms, and did not revert to a policy of nationalization and support for ailing industries. But there are also positive points. Labour support for 'neoclassical endogenous growth theory', which earned Brown ridicule when he included it in a political speech (in Michael Heseltine's words 'it wasn't Brown, it was Balls'), did carry through into government. They overhauled competition policy through the 1998 Competition Act and the Enterprise

Act of 2002, which gave the Competition Commission stronger powers. International comparisons of competition enforcement now typically score the UK highly.

Labour also prioritized expansion of university education. The proportion of the workforce with a university degree rose more sharply in the UK than elsewhere, from less than a quarter in 1997 to more than a third by 2010. There is room for doubt about whether holding a degree in media studies is a robust proxy for higher workplace skills, and vocational and further education have remained weak areas, but the additional investment in higher education has overall been positive.

It is also likely that tax credits introduced in 2001 and 2003 helped to arrest the decline in Research and Development (R&D) expenditure, which had been a feature of the UK economy since the late 1970s, and there is a strong case for saying that the regulatory changes introduced under Labour, especially in telecommunications, had a positive impact.

There were, however, three negative features, which have become persistent and worrying. The first is that British management scores poorly in international comparisons, well below the US, Japan and Germany.[4] There was a modest improvement in the later years but not enough to change the overall picture. Second, regional differences in GVA and productivity are greater than elsewhere. In Europe the UK is second only to Ireland in the degree of regional inequality. London is far more productive and wealthier than other cities, partly because of the City's remarkable success in establishing and maintaining its position as the largest financial centre in Europe, even outside the Eurozone. London as a global city has grown apart from its hinterland in terms of growth, productivity and social and political attitudes. That growing inequality seems to have been a factor in the Brexit vote, and also in the 2019 election. Third, the performance of the public sector was weak. Measuring output and productivity in the public services is not straightforward, but Corry et al.

conclude as follows: 'UK output growth in the non-market sectors was greater in the Labour period than under the Conservatives, but labour productivity growth fell from 0.6% to zero ... this is consistent with the story that the large increase in public services expenditures led to a fall in productivity in these sectors.'

Nonetheless, the record of the first decade of Labour, with Brown as Chancellor, was quite strong. The economy was the fastest growing in the G7, with rising productivity, high inward investment (though investment was not high overall) and relatively low unemployment by international standards. Also, while the UK share of exports of goods continued to decline, its share of world services exports rose and remained second only to the US.

The UK economy had grown consistently since the spring of 1992: there were 64 consecutive quarters of growth until the second quarter of 2009. That relentless expansion contributed to the psychology of optimism which lay behind the financial market excesses. The global financial crisis (GFC), which began in the summer of 2007, but hit the real economy hardest in 2009, brought this steady progress to a crashing halt.

As we shall see in Chapter 7, Osborne mounted an argument, in opposition and then in government, to the effect that Labour was responsible for the crisis because of the change in regulatory structure introduced in 1997–8, and because of its encouragement of light-touch regulation. Given the global nature of the problems revealed, that does not seem plausible.

But there is a separate point: the crisis may have hit the UK economy harder, and led to more persistent weakness, because of the large increase in public spending after 2000. We discuss the public spending and taxation profile through the period in more detail in Chapters 3 and 4. The particular argument here is that the government's fiscal position was out of balance when the crisis hit. As Corry et al. put it: 'In retrospect, it is clear that public debt levels were too high for the stage of the cycle in 2008 ...

[and] the debt position exacerbated the pain of recession.'
Nicholas Sowels argues that the pre-crisis deficits broke the
government's own fiscal rules, which 'in turn prepared the
way for a substantial deterioration in public finances when
the crisis broke, a deterioration which may take years, if
not decades, to set right'.[5] By contrast, Jonathan Portes
points out that the structural deficit was only around 1%
of GDP.[6] That jumped to 5% over the next two years, but
the 'poor state of the public finances was a consequence of
the recession, not a cause of it'.

Unsurprisingly, Gordon Brown and Ed Balls, then
Chief Economic Adviser in the Treasury, reject the idea
that they had left the UK in a vulnerable position. In his
memoirs Brown asserts the contrary: 'We entered the
crisis with debt and deficits low by historical standards.
There was no profligate pre-crisis spending spree'.[7] But he
acknowledges that there were different views in the official
Treasury. Nick MacPherson, then Permanent Secretary to
the Treasury, 'considered everyone too soft on the deficit and debt'. From the perspective of 2021, the figures
look almost insignificant, but their influence on policy was
important, as we can see from the spending policies of the
Coalition government.

It is reasonable to conclude that, while all Western governments, central banks and regulators should shoulder a
share of the responsibility for the imbalances and financial
excesses that led to the GFC, the particular role of the
spending and regulatory policies of the Labour government does not feature prominently in considered analyses
of its causes.[8] So the thirteen years of Labour governments
from 1997 to 2010 were a relatively successful period
for the British economy, during which its long catch-up
phase, closing the GDP gap with comparators, continued
at roughly the same pace as in the previous two decades.

The crisis was, however, extremely severe. The economy shrank by more than 6% between the first quarter
of 2008 and the second quarter of 2009, and took five
years to recover fully. Unemployment, always a lagging

indicator, rose from 5% to 8.4% by the end of 2011. The government's deficit reached 7% of GDP in 2009 and was still 5% in 2010. Real incomes fell sharply in 2009 and did not begin to rise sustainably until 2015. With household, business and financial debt at 420% of GDP, the UK was the most highly indebted developed country in the world.

2010–16: The austerity years

That was the difficult background against which the Coalition government was formed in May 2010. George Osborne, who had been Shadow Chancellor since David Cameron became leader of the Conservative Party in 2005, was the inevitable choice for 11 Downing Street. The complex negotiations over the leading positions in government led to the appointment of Liberal Democrat MP David Laws as Chief Secretary to the Treasury (CST), soon replaced by Danny Alexander, making him an unusually powerful holder of that post, as one of the 'Quad' of key decision-makers in the government.

The economy had, in fact, begun to recover in the first quarter of 2010, though that was barely perceptible to the electorate while unemployment continued to rise, as it did for another year or more. Although the recovery was steady, without a second recession, triggered in other parts of Europe by the Eurozone crisis, there was no post-recession boom as had typically been seen after earlier downturns. The economy returned to growth, but on a lower trajectory than before. The Institute for Fiscal Studies (IFS) estimated that in the summer of 2018 GDP was 11% higher than it had been at the pre-crisis peak in 2007–08, so the economy was 16% smaller and GDP per head was £6,000 lower than they would have been had growth remained on its pre-crisis trend.[9]

Surprisingly, employment growth remained strong, and there were 2.7 million more people in work in 2018 than a decade before. So average household incomes were higher than in 2008, and household income inequality had fallen a little. But the worst news was that productivity per hour grew by a mere 0.3% a year compared to a long-term trend of 2% a year. Output per hour worked was 18% below the average for the G7, and the current account deficit in 2015 was at a record high of 5.2%. The IFS summary stated:

> The UK economy has broken record after record, and not generally in a good way: record low earnings growth, record public borrowing followed by record cuts in public spending. On the upside employment levels are remarkably high and, in spite of how it may feel, the gap between rich and poor has actually narrowed somewhat, but the gap between old and young has grown and grown.[10]

That may seem to be a definitively negative verdict on the Coalition government's performance. But through an international lens the position looks rather different. The immediate recession hit to the UK economy was large by international standards, reflecting the high relative size of the financial sector. In 2011, growth in UK GDP remained below the average for the other advanced economies. But by the end of 2012 the UK was expanding a little more rapidly than the average, and that remained true until the middle of 2016, except for a brief period in 2015.[11] That average was, however, reduced by the impact of the Eurozone crisis of 2010–12.

Economic opinion was divided on the extent to which Osborne could claim any credit for the recovery. Simon Wren-Lewis has argued that the government's austerity programme unnecessarily cut 1% from the growth rate in 2011 and 2012, while Nicholas Crafts considered that the deficit reduction programme made little difference to the speed of the recovery.[12]

The underlying problem, however, which preoccupied economists and policymakers alike, was stagnant productivity. Productivity has flat-lined since 2010, a performance unprecedented since 1860.[13] As Paul Krugman of Princeton observed: 'Productivity isn't everything, but in the long run it is almost everything. A country's ability to improve its standard of living . . . depends almost entirely on its ability to raise its output per worker.'[14] After 2010, productivity growth slowed almost everywhere in the developed world, but it fell more sharply in the UK than elsewhere in the G7, except Italy. In the last decade of the twentieth century German and British productivity growth rates, measured as the change in output per hour worked, were similar, at about 2.5% a year. In the second decade of the twenty-first century German productivity growth was around 1% a year. The UK rate had fallen to just below 0.4%.

Unpicking the causes of this differential is not straightforward, but two other measures are relevant. The UK has invested a lower share of GDP than Germany. Since 2007, UK investment as a share of GDP has consistently been the lowest in the G7. In the EU, only Greece invested less. UK fixed capital formation was a little over 16%, while German investment was over 20%. And the comparisons on R&D expenditure are even less favourable. The UK typically spends about 1.7% of GDP on R&D, compared to 2.8% in Germany.[15]

So the second of the three periods, from 2010 to 2016, shows a mixed picture: a slow start, a catch-up to roughly the average growth rate of comparator countries, but underlying weakness in investment and productivity, which suggested continuing sluggish growth, unless performance in those areas picked up.

2016–20: The EU Referendum and after

The third period needs some disaggregation. The Covid-related lockdowns beginning at the end of the first quarter of 2020 confuse the picture. It is too early to say how the economy will recover from a highly unusual health-related government intervention. Also, at the end of 2020 the post-Brexit era began, initially with a very large impact on trade volumes with the EU. Exports to the EU fell by 40% in the first two months of 2021, then stabilized somewhat as firms became more accustomed to the new arrangements.

These immediate post-Brexit trade figures are volatile and may be misleading. But we can assess the period from 2016, when the referendum campaign was announced, to the beginning of the Covid recession. The data strongly suggest that there was a significant change of trend. Up to the referendum, UK GDP growth remained above the average of the other advanced economies, except for a brief period around the end of 2011. Since the referendum, UK growth has been lower than the average. The IFS has constructed a 'doppelgänger' of the UK economy, based on a weighted average of the OECD economies that performed most similarly to it up to the end of 2015. The doppelgänger tracks the UK closely, apart from a period during the financial crisis when the UK underperformed. That was not surprising given the UK's, and especially London's, exposure to trends in global finance. But, as the IFS says, 'since 2016 a sustained divergence has opened up between realised GDP and the level implied by the synthetic model'.[16] By the end of 2019 the economy was 2.5% smaller than expected had the predicted pre-referendum growth trend continued. The differential is closer to 3% if one takes account of the unexpected increases in global growth since 2016. The doppelgänger grew more rapidly than before. The IFS acknowledges that 'the estimates from this model cannot provide a perfect indication of what would have happened had the Brexit referendum gone the other way', but they are strongly suggestive. What can we learn about why this change of trend occurred?

The clearest immediate impact of Brexit was a sharp fall in sterling. Between May and September 2016 sterling dropped from €1.31 to €1.11. That suggested a market view that the UK's growth prospects had deteriorated. But contrary to the Treasury's 2016 forecasts, the domestic economy continued to grow, fuelled by an increase in consumer spending financed in part by a dramatic fall in the saving rate, from 10% in the second half of 2015 to around 4% by the end of 2016, and in part by rising nominal wages, which returned to the pre-crisis average of 4% a year. Between 2015 and 2019, unit labour costs in UK manufacturing rose by almost 10 percentage points more than in Germany, negating most of the competitive impact of sterling's devaluation.

The most depressing observation is that productivity remained flat, and business investment was remarkably weak. The UK appears to have lost out in many of the new, high innovation, high productivity sectors.[17] Investment took a long time to recover from the 2008 recession, but it grew by some 10% from 2012 to 2015. Since the referendum, it has dropped to the bottom of the G7 range and by 2019 it was 20% below what it would have been had the post-2008 trend line continued. That change in trend appears to be linked to a rise in economic uncertainty which, in turn, is linked to the referendum result and the consequential concerns about the terms of Britain's future trading relationships with the EU and other countries.[18] It is probable that, as business adjusts to a new set of trading relationships, that uncertainty will diminish, but the future course of investment remains highly uncertain.

The OBR, in its budget report in March 2021, assumes that long-run UK productivity and growth will be 4% lower as a result of Brexit, and that 'around two-fifths of the 4 per cent impact has effectively already occurred as a result of uncertainty since the referendum weighing on investment and capital deepening'.[19] By 2019, UK GDP per head was 88% of the German figure; in 2007 it had been 94%.

So in economic terms, the period ends on a downbeat note. The UK's Covid-induced recession was deeper than average for developed countries, and the immediate recovery a little stronger. But setting that aside, the economy seemed set for a period of sub-par growth, underperforming even a not very challenging set of comparators in Europe. The Treasury can hardly be blamed for that, or for Brexit. All the Chancellors before Sunak were firmly against leaving the EU, as were most if not all the senior officials, however emotionally disengaged from the European project they might have been. It is highly unusual for a sophisticated developed economy to have its economic and trading policy upended on non-economic grounds. The verdict on the Brexit experiment will take years, if not decades, to be handed down.

Beyond Covid

The deep Covid-induced downturn was followed by a strong short-term recovery. GDP fell by a record 9.9 per cent in 2020. The recovery was expected to bring aggregate GDP back to the level at the end of 2019 by the summer of 2022. Will growth thereafter be stronger than before, allowing the two lost years of growth to be recovered? In the summer of 2021 the Bank of England, while optimistic in the short term, saw no reason to believe the trend growth rate would revert to a figure higher than had been achieved since 2009, in other words 1.7–1.8% a year. That would be a disappointing outcome.

In May 2021 the Resolution Foundation, an independent think-tank, and others launched an inquiry into the UK economy in 2030.[20] The premise was: 'The UK's recent past has been marked by stagnant living standards, weak productivity, low investment and high inequality. This makes a new economic approach desirable.' They present a balanced picture of the strengths and weaknesses of the UK as it emerges from recession.

On the asset side of the balance sheet, they identify a fast-growing services sector, especially insurance and other financial and business services, internationally competitive higher education, and a relatively advanced position in the necessary transition to a net zero economy. The existence of a strong political consensus on the latter point is also potentially a trump card. On the liability side, in addition to the poor investment and productivity record already discussed, they list a high degree of inequality, and an unfavourable demographic position, with the population ageing rapidly in the next decade, and Brexit likely to reduce high-skilled immigration from neighbouring countries.

Some of these factors are not susceptible to Treasury intervention. But the report identifies policy weaknesses which are potentially under Treasury control. In particular, they see 'long-run issues with parts of our tax system, such as the relative taxation of capital and labour', and the absence of a coherent approach to carbon taxation. (I discuss the tax system in Chapter 4.) And they conclude: 'The UK also lacks any long-term institutional structure to govern industrial strategy. The ability of sub-national government to manage change has also been weakened, with local authority spending power in England falling by 18 per cent since 2010.' That is important given the evidence across Europe that attempts to 'level up' economic development 'are driven by regions with high human capital and high-quality local government'.[21] The Treasury's centralizing instincts, and suspicion of local government, could be serious disadvantages in pursuing a levelling-up agenda. Critics see 'no sign the government is embracing the co-ordination needed for the moves to have a significant impact – nor any hint of further devolution of policy powers away from the centre'.[22]

The stakes are high. Torsten Bell et al. conclude: 'If the pace of UK underperformance . . . were to continue at the same pace in the 2020s as in the 12 years to 2019, then the country will end this decisive decade with GDP per capita much closer to that of Italy than Germany: 17 per cent lower than Germany and just 6 per cent higher than Italy.'[23] My first job on leaving university in 1973 was as desk officer for Italy in the Foreign and Commonwealth Office, as it then was. At the time, the Italians liked to talk of *il sorpasso* (the overtaking), the moment when their economy would overtake the UK's. That did in fact happen in 1987, but by 2020 we were almost 30% richer per capita, after dismal performance in Italy since joining the euro. For us to fall back to the Italian level would be dramatic. Fortunately, in the summer of 2021 external forecasters expected the UK economy to grow less rapidly than France and Germany in the recovery phase, but still ahead of Italy.[24] That is not, however, a high bar.

2

Macroeconomic Policy

Bank of England independence in May 1997 changed the role of both the Treasury and the Chancellor in macroeconomic policy. In the dying days of the long Conservative regime which began in 1979, a hybrid monetary policy-making model had been constructed, in which the Bank of England gave its interest rate advice to the Chancellor, and could publish it, but the Chancellor made the ultimate decision. The so-called Ken and Eddie show (Chancellor Ken Clarke and Governor Eddie George) ran monthly from June 1993 to May 1997. No other country has operated such a hybrid model. For two years, I chaired the internal Bank committee which prepared the draft advice, and attended the meetings. They were civilized encounters but sometimes with an element of Whitehall farce. On occasions, faced with a carefully crafted letter, representing thousands of hours of work by the Bank's economists leading to a considered recommendation of a quarter point rise (sometimes accompanied by internal Treasury advice saying the same thing), Ken Clarke would open the meeting by saying cheerily: 'Well there's obviously no chance of a rise this month.' He then asked for our views, but only on how long we needed to stay before the Bank team drove out of the Treasury courtyard. Too short a stay, and the waiting press would say our advice had been dismissed without discussion. Too long a stay, and the story would be that there had been a row between the two teams.

That vaudeville act was swept away in 1997, to be replaced by a model of central bank independence worked up in opposition by Brown and Balls, with help from some US policymakers, including Alan Greenspan, and a few Bank and Treasury moles. The model, which was implemented almost exactly as they drafted it, differed from both the US Federal Reserve System (the Fed) and the European Central Bank (ECB) and also from the Reserve Bank of New Zealand, which had been the first to implement an inflation target regime eight years earlier. The architects were sensitive to the complex history of the Bank–Treasury relationship. The Treasury was fearful that the Bank would be overzealous in its pursuit of low inflation, that it had a strong, enclosed, internal culture generating powerful 'groupthink' and that it was too hierarchical, with all decision-making roads leading to the Governor's office. These points were made to me forcefully when the Treasury appointed me Deputy Governor in 1995. There was much truth in that assessment, I discovered.

So unlike the Fed and the ECB, which were left to themselves to define what they meant by price stability, the Bank of England was to operate under an inflation target regime, with the target set by the Treasury. That amounted to instrument independence – the Bank had full control over short-term interest rates – but not target independence. Most independent central banks in other developed countries have the latter as well as the former. The Treasury could change the target if it wished, and indeed has once done so.

The new Bank of England model is distinctive in other ways too. Unlike the Fed, which has a parallel objective of maintaining full employment, the Bank's objectives are hierarchical. Meeting the inflation target is the prime aim, and only subject to that should it contribute to the government's other economic objectives. In that respect it is similar to the ECB. Brown recalls that his initial thinking favoured a model more closely aligned to the Fed, with an employment objective: 'The early papers we put to the Treasury had that idea included. But we could not find a legislative way of implementing a dual target. It involved revising Acts going back hundreds of years.'[1] But while the new Bank is similar to the Fed and the ECB in some ways, it departs from both the other main models in having four part-time outsiders appointed to its Monetary Policy Committee (MPC). That was specifically targeted at the groupthink point. Their power is buttressed by a requirement to publish individual votes of MPC members after every meeting. The Fed publishes 'dissents', while the ECB does not produce a voting record. The latter argues that to do so would put intolerable pressure on the voting members from national central banks, which would be expected by their governments to vote according to the circumstances of the economy of their country, rather than the Eurozone as a whole.

The UK model has been criticized by other central bankers for its excess of transparency. The publication of individual votes creates pressure on members to justify their views outside the meeting. The number of monetary policy speeches emanating from the Bank has escalated dramatically, as each member of the MPC tries to explain and defend their policy positions. That has generated a lot of 'noise' in the system. If monetary policy works through influencing expectations, it is not clear that these conflicting views help. The markets can become confused and on occasion the Governor has found himself in a minority, obliged to defend a position which is not his own.

In spite of these criticisms, the main architecture of monetary policymaking remained intact throughout the period. The original inflation target was set at 2.5% plus or minus 1%. The target was therefore symmetrical, unlike the target the ECB set for itself, of maintaining inflation below but close to 2%. There are strong arguments for a symmetrical target.

The significance of the range was that if inflation moved outside it, on the upside, or the down, the Governor should write an open letter to the Chancellor explaining why and what would be done to return to the target. For many years, the Governor's pen remained capped, causing Mervyn King, in office from 2003 to 2013, to quip that the art of letter-writing was dead. After the financial crisis, letter-writing came back into vogue. But in structural terms, the changes since 1997 have been relatively minor. In December 2003 the centre of the target range was moved down to 2%, when the basis of measurement was changed from the Retail Prices Index (RPI) to the Consumer Prices Index (CPI). The Bank has, since 2010, maintained inflation at an average very close to the target, while the ECB has been well below. The symmetrical target may be partly responsible for that difference. In 2021 the ECB acknowledged that criticism by shifting to a symmetrical approach.[2]

A potentially more significant change, at the end of the period, was the insertion into the Bank's mandate of a reference to climate change. In March 2021, Chancellor Sunak reaffirmed the 2% target, but said that monetary policy should 'also reflect the importance of environmental sustainability and the transition to net zero'.[3] The Bank responded that it would change its approach to corporate bond-buying 'to account for the climate impact of the issuers of the bonds we hold'. There will also be implications for banking supervision. Since at least 2017, when the Network for Greening the Financial System was created, a number of European central banks have been seeking to incorporate climate goals into their monetary and supervisory policies. That has been controversial, with some commentators arguing that an activist approach to climate change would put their independence at risk. At an ECB conference in November 2020, John Cochrane of the Hoover Institution at Stanford argued: 'This will end badly. Not because these policies are wrong, but because they are intensely political, and they make a mockery of the central bank's limited mandates.'[4] The Bank of England is less exposed to that risk, but Sunak's rather vague formulation puts a heavy burden on the Governor's shoulders. Mervyn King sees risks for the Bank's independence: 'Central banks' increasing focus on climate change is particularly odd . . . Most important, the central banks, new and broader ambitions have profound implications for their independence.'[5]

How did Bank independence affect the Treasury? The staffing implications were minor. The Treasury team of officials and economists preparing interest rate advice was small, and already depended heavily on the Bank of England for market intelligence. There is a Treasury observer on the MPC, who needs to be briefed, but he or she is genuinely an observer, except on fiscal policy where the individual may offer a view on the likely fiscal stance. There is certainly no equality of arms on monetary policy between the two institutions, or indeed on macroeconomic policy more generally. As Gus O'Donnell points out, the Bank employs far more economists than the Treasury, and in the Treasury those in the macroeconomic area 'are typically young and lacking in experience. There is an advantage, though. Younger staff have been trained more recently, and are not slaves to some defunct economist.'[6]

When the change was made, it was widely assumed that Brown would find it hard to restrain himself from commenting on interest rates. That assumption turned out to be incorrect. Brown was scrupulous in avoiding public comment on the Bank's policy, whether in Parliament or elsewhere, and his successors have adopted the same self-denying ordinance. We cannot be sure that in their regular lunches the Chancellor and the Governor do not discuss upcoming decisions, but there is no evidence of any attempt to exert inappropriate influence, which – given the voting structure – would in any event be unlikely to have a decisive impact. The Treasury also stopped its previous practice of censoring, or as it used to put it, 'offering helpful drafting suggestions' on, the Bank's publications. There are more examples of Governors commenting on fiscal policy, which is equally inconsistent with the 1997 division of responsibilities. That created tension, between Alistair Darling and Mervyn King in particular. But for the most part the new arrangements worked well. The implicit assumption was that were a loose fiscal policy to threaten to generate inflation above the target, the Bank would react with a rise in interest rates. There was no particular need for active coordination of fiscal and monetary policy. In the meantime, the Treasury benefited from lower long-term gilt rates. For a long time, the British government had paid around 150 basis points more than the German government for its long-term borrowing. That spread narrowed rapidly after Bank independence promised tighter control of inflation in the future.

For a decade this new dispensation caused few problems, though stocking and restocking the MPC was sometimes a challenge. The Treasury has found it particularly difficult to maintain an appropriate gender balance, for which it has attracted criticism. There were lively arguments about the resources the independent members had at their disposal. MPC members also thought the committee met too often: the number of meetings was specified in the legislation, and was later reduced from twelve to eight. But in other respects the new system, even though it had been legislated in haste, has proved remarkably robust.

Signs of strain began to emerge, however, in the financial crisis of 2007/8. When interest rate reductions failed to provide enough stimulus to economic activity, the adoption of quantitative easing (QE) muddied the monetary and fiscal waters.[7] The arguments were expressed most forcefully on the other side of the Atlantic. Charles Plosser, former President of the Federal Reserve Bank of Philadelphia, argued that 'a large Fed balance sheet that is untethered to the conduct of monetary policy creates the opportunity and incentive for political actors to exploit the

Fed and use its balance sheet to conduct off-budget fiscal policy and credit allocation'.[8]

In the UK the potential for confusion about the objectives of policy and the transmission mechanisms of new monetary instruments was offset to some extent by a process of formal approval for QE by the Treasury. So Alistair Darling, in January 2009, authorized the Bank of England to create a new fund called the Asset Purchase Facility, which the MPC could use for the purchase of gilts and corporate bonds. The total amount that can be purchased is set by the Chancellor after a request from the Governor. The initial request was for a ceiling of £150 billion, but there have been successive further increases. By March 2021, the Bank held £875 billion of gilt-edged stock alone.

Formally, the Bank cannot buy gilts directly from the government. That would conflict with the 'no monetary financing' rule. But as the volume of purchases grew in the Covid crisis, the distinction became much less clear. Market participants were well aware that the central bank would hoover up the debt they had bought at auction. The Bank became the purchaser of first resort rather than the lender of last resort. In 2021 the Bank owned more than half of all gilts in issue. And the government's overdraft facility at the Bank, known as the Ways and Means account, was extended without limit.[9]

In practice, the government has not so far needed to draw on the Ways and Means account, but the question of how the MPC determines the volume of gilts it needs to buy has become a serious preoccupation. The Bank has been criticized for putting its monetary policy tools at the service of the government, and determining the volume of QE by reference to the size of the deficit, rather than to what is needed to meet the inflation target. 'The real question', as one commentator put it, 'is whether fiscal sustainability will begin to encroach on an independent monetary policy committee that targets inflation'[10]

Andrew Bailey, Governor of the Bank since 2020, took to the columns of the *Financial Times* in April 2020 to reject a direct link between the size of the government's deficit and the Bank's bond-buying programme. He denied that the volume of QE was in any way related to what the government is going to borrow: 'Using monetary financing would damage credibility on controlling inflation by eroding operational independence.'[11] He emphasized that the MPC remains in full control of how and when that expansion is ultimately unwound. Monetary financing of the deficit would be 'incompatible with the pursuit of an inflation target by an independent central bank'. But as the programme continued, the sceptical voices grew in volume. The *FT* surveyed the top eighteen buyers of gilts in the London market, and found that 'the overwhelming majority believe that QE in its current incarnation works by buying enough bonds to mop up the amount the government issues and keep interest rates low'.[12] They noted that the monthly volumes of Bank gilt purchases tracked the government's deficit very closely through 2020 and into 2021. In essence, they argue that fiscal dominance has taken over monetary policy. What is certain is that, at least in the short run, QE allows the government to run a lax fiscal policy without facing interest rate pressure.

The Bank has tried to dismiss that concern. Andy Haldane, then its Chief Economist, argued in November 2020 that:

> in the current environment the situation is in some respects the very opposite of fiscal dominance. In the face of a huge shock, fiscal expansion has played an extremely helpful role in supporting demand and in helping the MPC return inflation to its target. What we have seen is better described as fiscal assistance than fiscal dominance when it comes to meeting the inflation target. The externalities from expansionary fiscal policy have in that sense been positive, rather than negative, from a monetary policy perspective.[13]

He recognizes that 'these QE actions have been necessary to support the economy and hit the inflation target. But they pose rising challenges to public understanding of the purposes of QE and, ultimately, perceptions of independence.' If the market believes, as it seems to do, that QE is driven by the government's financing needs, then not meeting those expectations could cause yields to rise, which in turn will put further pressure on the government's finances. The OBR calculated at the time of the March 2021 Budget that a 1% rise in rates would add £22 billion to the government's deficit.

In those circumstances, would the Bank of England feel able to respond to the prospect of higher inflation with a timely rise in rates? Charles Goodhart of the LSE thinks not. He believes that a combination of 'massive fiscal and monetary expansion', on the one hand, and 'a self-imposed supply shock of immense magnitude', on the other, will result in 'a surge in inflation, quite likely more than 5%'. Furthermore, he doubts whether central banks will respond: 'Inflation will rise considerably above the level of nominal interest rates that our political masters can tolerate.'[14] Haldane also sees that risk. In early 2021 he noted:

> There is a tangible risk inflation proves more difficult to tame, requiring monetary policymakers to act more assertively than is currently priced into financial markets. People are right to caution about the risks of central banks acting too conservatively by tightening policy prematurely. But, for me, the greater risk at present is of central bank complacency allowing the inflationary (big) cat out of the bag.[15]

In September 2021, the CPI index jumped to 3.2%, requiring the Governor to uncap his pen to explain why the MPC did not plan to react quickly.[16]

There have been growing concerns, too, about the accountability framework for QE, and the longer-term risks to the public finances. The Economic Affairs Committee of the House of Lords was particularly trenchant, arguing that 'the scale and persistence of QE – now equivalent to 40% of GDP – requires significant scrutiny and accountability

. . . The Bank must be more transparent, justify the use of QE and show its working . . . QE is a serious danger to the long-term health of the public finances. A clear plan on how QE will be unwound is necessary, and this plan must be made public.[17]

It is impossible to forecast the future course of inflation with any confidence. But it is clear that the future of central bank independence is in more doubt than it has been for twenty-five years. There are many who argue that, in spite of all the benefits in terms of inflation control and a reduction in growth volatility, it may be that peak central bank independence has been reached.[18] The risk of fiscal dominance, which now looms largest among the threats, is not the only one. The additional burdens loaded on to central banks, especially in the UK, is another. With its responsibility for prudential supervision of banks, and now insurers too, on top of monetary and macroprudential policies, and a leading role in combating climate change, has the Bank of England become too powerful for its own good? Might the Governor fall into the 'overmighty citizen' trap, which enveloped Alan Greenspan in the United States? There is a populist tide which is suspicious of technocratic power, and even their more cerebral political representatives say they have had enough of experts.

In the next chapter I will review the conduct of fiscal policy during the period, but there is an alternative critique of the macroeconomic policy framework which has become more prominent since the financial crisis, and particularly in the Covid pandemic.

That critique maintains that the primacy of the inflation target has already led to suboptimal economic performance, and could seriously hinder further recovery. Simon Wren-Lewis of Oxford University, for example, has argued that 'to continue with inflation as the primary target could jeopardise a macroeconomic policy that focuses on strong growth, and quickly offsets any negative shocks'.[19] He notes that the Fed's dual mandate allows it to prioritize maximum unemployment and look through temporary increases in inflation. Indeed, the Fed has recently reviewed its approach to the target and declared that in future it will adopt an 'averaging' methodology, which allows it to tolerate overshoots to 'catch up' with past shortfalls.

Presenting the new policy, Jerome Powell, chair of the Fed since 2018, noted that, in an environment where inflation expectations are very low, interest rates 'decline in tandem.' As a result, 'we would have less scope to cut interest rates to boost unemployment during an economic downturn, further diminishing our capacity to stabilize the economy through cutting interest rates. We have seen this adverse dynamic play out in other major economies'. To prevent such a dynamic establishing itself in the US, the Fed decided that in future 'employment can run at or above real-time estimates of its maximum level without causing concern' and 'following periods when inflation has been running below 2 percent, appropriate monetary policy will likely aim to achieve inflation moderately above 2 percent for some time'.[20]

The Bank of England argues that the UK inflation target regime, with its focus on inflation at a two-year time horizon, allows it the flexibility to look through temporary overshoots, as it did in 2010. It argues furthermore that since 2010 there has been no undershoot of the target, as there has been in the US and the Eurozone. But, as Wren-Lewis points out, interest rates have been at or close to their lower bound for some time, and the policy tool then available, QE, 'is just too unreliable compared to interest rates or fiscal policy.'

Ed Balls and colleagues at Harvard Business School have argued that in these circumstances a closer nexus between monetary and fiscal policies is required. They recommend that the Governor should be mandated to write to the Chancellor suggesting the scale of fiscal stimulus they think is needed when interest rates are at their lower bound.[21] Support for that approach came from Olivier Blanchard, the former Chief Economist of the IMF, who argues that if interest rates remain lower than the growth rate, and if monetary policy is constrained by the zero lower bound, it makes sense to run fiscal deficits to sustain demand, even if this leads to a further increase in debt.[22]

So far, neither the Bank of England itself nor the Treasury has shown any signs of being interested in amending the policy framework in this way. If the post-Covid recovery is again sluggish, as the post-GFC recovery was, the question of monetary and fiscal policy coordination will rise up the agenda, but the Bank of England will certainly resist any change which puts its monetary policy independence at risk.

3

Public Expenditure

The fiscal policy narrative from 1997 to the Covid crisis is full of exciting twists and turns. Those of a sensitive disposition should look away. We begin with Prudence in a starring role in Gordon Brown's first term. Then followed the expansionary years before Brown moved to Number 10, which were brought to a crashing halt by the global financial crisis and resulting recession. Alistair Darling fought that fire but left George Osborne a difficult inheritance. Osborne's austerity period followed, and by the time of the Brexit referendum the public finances had been roughly stabilized. Philip Hammond began to moderate the austerity language, at least, but his period in office was dominated by Brexit negotiations and preparations. Fiscal policy took a back seat. No sooner had Rishi Sunak found his way to the Treasury coffee machine than the Covid pandemic blew away any plans he might have had. The period ends with the Treasury spending 'whatever it takes' to sustain economic activity. The net result is that by 2021 the public sector net debt to GDP ratio, 37% in 1997, had risen to over 100%.

How effectively did the Treasury steer the fiscal ship of state through these troubled waters?

Brown One: Married to Prudence

Once monetary policy had been outsourced to the Bank of England in May 1997, the Treasury's core business of managing the government's finances reasserted itself.

In the election campaign, Blair and Brown had committed themselves to the spending plans of the Conservative government for the first two years at least. They also undertook not to raise income tax rates, including the top rate of 40%. Labour was still anxious that the electorate might not trust them with the public finances. That was probably an unjustified fear, as the disorderly 1992 ERM exit had seriously damaged the Tories' reputation for economic competence, but it informed the party's economic strategy. In a speech in 1995, Brown declared: 'Labour in government will be the party of wise spenders, not big spenders.'[1] His strategy was based on 'prudent investment for growth'. (Prudence was a woman frequently invoked by Brown and Balls.) And he set out his fiscal rules: 'First, Labour will be committed to meeting the golden rule of borrowing – over the economic cycle, government will only borrow to finance public investment and not to fund public consumption.' The question of when the economic cycle begins and ends was left unclear, and much creativity was subsequently deployed in government to generate flexibility by redefining the start date. The second commitment was another for the cyclists: 'We will keep the ratio of government debt to GDP stable on average over the economic cycle and at a prudent and sensible level.'

After the election, there was some cynicism in the Treasury about these declared commitments. Would the incoming Chancellor be able to resist the pressures in the Labour Party, out of office for eighteen years, to spend on its favourite causes? Previous Labour administrations had foundered on that rock and found the financial markets unsympathetic. But Brown and Balls, with – usually – the support of their nextdoor neighbour, proved to be made of sterner stuff. In Labour's first term, the 'golden rule' was broadly met. Public spending rose, but in line with the Conservatives' previously announced plans. As Bill Keegan of the *Observer* put it: 'The financial markets witnessed a complete reversal of the traditional pattern by which Labour governments were returned to power, spent freely in the first year, then had to devote the rest of the time to "cuts" and trying to repair the damage to their reputation.'[2]

O'Donnell was impressed by the thinking behind the strategy: 'I was greatly influenced by my conversations with Ed Balls. He argued that it was "prudence for a purpose". He and Gordon wanted to end up with a larger state, with more spending on the NHS and more state investment generally, but recognized they needed to build a reputation for sensible fiscal policy first. That was the focus of their first term.'[3]

Terry Burns, Permanent Secretary to the Treasury from 1991 to 1998, is a little more cynical: 'The plan was to give away money near the end of the Parliament. The objective was always to win the next election, and fiscal policy was manipulated to that end.'[4]

Whatever the motivation, the result, in terms of spending control, was impressive. Public spending grew by only 1.7% a year, more slowly than under Kenneth Clarke, and more slowly than the growth rate of the economy. Brown maintained the two-year freeze on spending which he had promised just before the election. So current public spending fell from 37.6% of GDP in 1996–97 to 35% in 2000–01. In spite of the commitments not to increase income tax, revenues were buoyant, partly because the economy grew, partly through fiscal drag, and partly because other less politically sensitive taxes were raised: stamp duties, insurance premium tax, etc. So public sector net debt fell from 42.5% of GDP in 1996–97 to 30.7% in 2000–01. Credibility in the markets was built, as a result, but opinion polls showed a steady increase in the numbers of people disappointed by the government's performance on health and education.⁵ So the pressure for a different approach, and for more public investment, began to grow.

In Labour's first term, that pressure was resisted. It was easier to do so because Brown strengthened central control of spending, and removed previous arbitration mechanisms which allowed departments to take their case for additional spending to a Cabinet committee (sometimes known as the Star Chamber). As Andrew Turnbull, Permanent Secretary to the Treasury from 1998 to 2002, describes it: 'In the Brown spending rounds there were discussions with departments then a period of silence. The department then received what was known as "the Brown envelope", which contained their settlement letter, telling them how much money they had for the next three years and adding various requests for reviews of particular expenditure areas. Other ministers opposed this unilateralism, but ineffectually. So the Treasury became uniquely powerful. Brown then went further and took direct control of some spending programmes, such as the tax credit system and even the science budget. The Treasury on the whole liked that system, and preferred it to the old Star Chamber approach, but it did mean that there was no collective review of spending priorities.'⁶ One consequence of this tight central control was that in the first term the public expenditure outturn was typically lower than projected.

Brown also introduced a regime of targets for departments to achieve, known as public service agreements (PSAs). They were not popular in Whitehall. As Brown himself acknowledges: 'This was seen by many as a Treasury power grab. In reality, it was necessary to assess continually not just whether departments were coming within their budget limits but also whether they were delivering results.'⁷

The tight control on the aggregate of public expenditure did not, however, betoken inactivity on the fiscal front. Even within a tight fiscal envelope, and without increases in marginal tax rates, Brown worked to achieve a degree of 'redistribution by stealth'. He raised a windfall tax on the privatized utilities, which was largely used to fund a 'welfare-to-work' programme, inspired by similar programmes tried in the United States, the source of almost all the ideas prompted by Balls and Brown. The Treasury became far more closely involved in the details of benefit policy than it had been previously. Keegan quotes an official who had been seconded out of the department for a period as saying: 'I have come back to what seems to have become the Department of Social Policy.'[8] Brown was far more interested in working family tax credits than in increases in the minimum wage, which, for younger workers at least, he resisted.

The impact of the tax and benefit changes was significant. One study calculated that all the changes introduced in Brown's first term as Chancellor produced a gain of 17% in the net incomes of the lowest decile in the income distribution, and of only 1% for the top decile.[9] The continued fall in unemployment also helped, but the tax and benefit changes made a material contribution to reducing poverty, especially working poverty.

A less positive development was Brown's increasing enthusiasm for the private finance initiative (PFI), and for public–private partnerships. PFI was a Conservative idea, first introduced by Norman Lamont in 1992, but Brown pursued it vigorously. It offered the promise of increasing investment in public sector infrastructure without breaching any of his 'golden rules'. Some early projects achieved genuine risk transfer to the private sector, and tighter discipline on total project costs. But others struggled to overcome the obvious disadvantage that private sector finance would always be more expensive than borrowing by the government itself. The deal struck to modernize London Underground, known as Metronet, was an egregious example of a project involving additional financing costs for no obvious benefit. By 2009, more than 800 projects had been committed, with a total capital value of £68 billion, and the associated revenue commitments were £215 billion out to 2032.[10] By 2021 we had reached the *reductio ad absurdum* of private finance, when a former Prime Minister, David Cameron, lobbied the Treasury to provide funds to shore up an invoice financing company, Greensill, in which he had a personal financial interest, whose business model was in part to make a turn on payments between the NHS and pharmacies. Brown cannot be held responsible for that turn of events, but his support for private finance schemes embedded that approach across government, with damaging long-term consequences. In his memoirs, he praised public–private partnerships as marrying 'the long-term thinking and ethos of the public sector with the managerial skills of the private'.[11]

From a Treasury perspective Brown Mark One was a successful Chancellor in respect of budgetary control. The Treasury had good reason to fear the arrival of a new Labour government after a long period in the wilderness, and expected upward pressure on spending. Before 2001 that did not happen. Those who were disappointed by Labour's approach were the public sector workers, and their unions, who had expected far more.

Brown Two: Prudence jilted?

The Labour Party manifesto for the 2001 election had one major theme: 'Public Services: Investment and Reform.' Voters heard the investment part of the message, and Labour achieved another large majority, of 167 seats. The 'Prudence with a Purpose' mantra of the first four years had delivered credibility, but the purpose element was still unclear to many of the government's natural supporters. So something had to change, and it did.

Brown argues that what followed was a disciplined and well-planned programme of investment in public services, which delivered better outcomes, yet still within the fiscal rules he had set out. Critics, at the time and particularly following the GFC, argued that his second term's expansionary fiscal policy left the country vulnerable and exposed to the impact of the crisis when it came, and led to a long hangover, which was indeed still not over when the Covid pandemic hit.

The change in policy was clear. Between 2000–01 and 2006–07, public expenditure rose from 35.7% of GDP to 38.8%. Defence spending continued its steady fall: the post-Cold War peace dividend was sustained, in spite of the Iraq war. And the debt interest line benefited from the lower interest rates consequent on Bank of England independence and the resulting reduction in both inflation and the UK's risk premium, falling from 2.7% to 2.1% of GDP. The increases were concentrated in two areas: education and health. Education spending rose from 4.6% to 5.4% of GDP, and the NHS budget went from 5.5% to 7% in the same period – a huge increase in a short space of time.

The latter increase was partly attributable to a kind of bidding war between Blair and Brown. Blair gave an interview to TV journalist David Frost in which he promised to increase spending on health to the European average, as a percentage of GDP.[12] That was a remarkable commitment to a comparator over which the UK government had no control. As one senior official recalls: 'Brown was furious and commissioned a review from Derek Wanless [a former CEO of NatWest Bank] which recommended further increases and allowed Brown to claim the credit.'[13]

Tax revenues continued to rise strongly, partly the result of continued growth. Public sector receipts rose from £385 billion in 1996–97 to £562 billion in 2007–08. But that was not enough to prevent an increase in net debt. Public sector net debt rose from 30.7% in 2000–01 to 36.5% in 2007–08: 43.6% on the broader definition enshrined in the Maastricht Treaty.

Brown is wholly unrepentant about this record. He describes the years between 2001 and 2005 as 'the catch-up period in public spending – when we dealt with the historic and chronic underinvestment in public services' and emphasizes that after 2005 the government announced

that the underinvestment had come to an end. He argues
that the fiscal rules continued to exclude borrowing for
current expenditure, and that much of the increased funding for the NHS was financed by a National Insurance
increase implemented in 2002 explicitly for that reason.
He rejects the criticism that the spending increase had left
the economy in a vulnerable position when the financial
crisis hit. 'The Treasury had maintained its control of the
public purse. We entered the global financial crisis with
debt and deficits low by historical standards. There was no
profligate pre-crisis spending spree.'[14] He asserts that 'the
debate about whether the deficit was too high in 2007 is
over'.[15]

That not-guilty plea is disputed. Nicholas Sowels of the
University of Paris states the case for the prosecution:

> Gordon Brown . . . presided over a massive expansion in
> public spending to improve public services. This expan-
> sion of spending was justifiable in many ways, given poor
> investment in public services during the Thatcher-Major
> years. But it was arguably not sufficiently financed through
> taxation . . . The result was a run-up of public deficits . . .
> which broke the government's own fiscal rules. This in
> turn prepared the way for a substantial deterioration in
> public finances . . . which may take years if not decades to
> set right.[16]

The IFS verdict is more nuanced. It points out that the
eleven years of Brown's chancellorship as a whole 'followed a remarkably similar pattern to the first eleven years
of the previous Conservative government, from 1979 to
1989. The first four saw the public sector move from deficit to surplus, while the following seven saw a move back
into the red.'[17] It acknowledges that Brown had met his
two fiscal rules, albeit by revising the start date of the
economic cycle. (Robert Chote of the IFS wittily observed
that it was not so much a cycle as a stretch limo.) By 2007,
as a result, 'Labour had reduced public sector borrowing
slightly below the level it inherited from the Conservatives.

And more of that borrowing was being used to finance investment rather than the day-to-day running costs of the public sector.' So far, so favourable, but there is a sting in the tail. The global economic circumstances in the years leading up to the GFC had been benign. That, indeed, was part of the problem which emerged in 2007. Financial market participants had become accustomed to an environment in which risky bets always paid off. And during that NICE period (Mervyn King's coinage: non-inflationary, consistently expansionary), 'the vast majority of other leading industrial countries reduced their borrowing by more than the UK. And most also reduced their debt by more. So while the UK public finances were in better shape when the financial crisis began than they were when Labour came to power, the UK was in a worse position relative to most comparable countries.'

The official Treasury comes close to accepting that conclusion. Burns, who was Permanent Secretary at the start of the period, thinks that 'Labour got into trouble when buoyant revenues encouraged them to believe they could go further on spending. Sometimes tax revenues surprise on the upside; sometimes on the down. There are mysterious periods of feast and famine. The windfall of receipts encouraged them to think they had more room to increase spending than they had previously thought. They misled themselves into thinking that the underlying growth rate was higher than it was. They thought population growth would be accompanied by continued growth in productivity, which turned out not to be the case, so by 2007 spending plans were over-egged.'[18] Turnbull, who inherited Burns's office, agrees: 'In the second Labour term they began to lose control. Balls started to fiddle with the date of the start of the cycle, to allow additional expenditure. That put them in a more difficult position than they should have been in, when the crisis of 2008 hit.'[19] O'Donnell, who followed Turnbull, is a little more sympathetic. 'They did enter the crisis with a slightly bigger deficit than they intended. They were too optimistic on income. But in retrospect it does not look too big a deal. The deficit was not unstable in 2007–08.'[20]

The deficit may or may not have been unstable in normal circumstances, but the crisis which began to develop in the summer of 2007, and reached a crescendo in the autumn of 2008, put the public finances under severe strain. Brown had become Prime Minister in the summer of 2007, so Alistair Darling found himself with the job of picking up the pieces.

Darling and the financial crisis

The impact of the recession that followed the failure of Lehman Brothers, and other banks, was severe. The UK economy contracted dramatically, with similarly sharp consequences for the public finances. Public spending rose from 38.9% of national income in 2007–08 to 44.9% in 2009–10, while tax revenues fell from 36.2% of national income to 35%. The short-term result was a deficit of £153 billion in 2009–10, or very nearly 10% of national income. That was the largest deficit since the end of the Second World War.[21] The fiscal impact on the UK was more severe than in most other countries. According to the IFS, the UK 'experienced the largest weakening of its structural fiscal position between 2007 and 2010, and was set to have the highest level of structural borrowing in 2010'.[22] That reflected, in part, the very large contribution made to UK tax revenues by the financial sector, whose profitability was most severely affected by the crisis.

It quickly became clear that no amount of tinkering with the dates of the economic cycle would allow the fiscal rules to be met. Nor was it desirable to meet them. Attempting to maintain the 'golden rule' would have done more damage to the economy and employment. Indeed, the original formulation of the 1998 Code for Fiscal Stability included a *force majeure* clause.[23] So in November 2008 the Treasury published a new fiscal framework, which incorporated a new 'temporary operating rule' committing the government 'to set policies to improve the cyclically adjusted current budget each year, once the economy emerges from the downturn, so it reaches balance and debt is falling as a proportion of GDP once the global shocks have worked their way to the economy in full'.[24] That formulation begged a number of questions, but in the highly unusual circumstances of late 2008 it was better than nothing. It was also strikingly similar to proposals published by the Conservatives two months earlier. In the meantime, as the recession continued into 2010 the public finances took the strain. Most of the increase in the deficit could be attributed to falling revenues, and the operation of the fiscal stabilizers, but the government also cut VAT to provide a modest temporary discretionary stimulus, amounting to around 0.6% of GDP.

These measures seemed appropriate to most commentators at the time, and there was relatively little difference between the policies of the two main parties. But behind the scenes there were lively policy disagreements, between the Treasury and Number 10, and between both of them and the Governor of the Bank of England.

Alistair Darling was in the eye of the storm. He had to devote much of his attention to the problems of the banks (see Chapter 7), but spending decisions could not be neglected. "I thought it crucial to get spending under control, while Gordon wanted more public investment.'[25] The disagreements came to a head in 2009. Brown identified Nick MacPherson, then the Permanent Secretary, as one of the obstacles.

> As I surveyed the response to the recession, I was alarmed. Was I now witnessing this once powerful institution retreating into a shell? Was it shifting away from being the activist department that said 'yes' to innovation and reform, and reverting to its traditional role as the finance department that specialised in saying 'no'?[26]

He tried to move MacPherson to the Cabinet Office, with O'Donnell, who by then was Cabinet Secretary, acquiring responsibility for oversight of the Treasury as well. That scheme pleased no one and was not pursued. Brown then tried to move Darling, but he declined to go quietly and Brown abandoned the idea when James Purnell, Secretary of State for Culture, Media and Sport, resigned from the Cabinet, and talk of a palace revolution was in the air.

So the 'temporary operating rule' remained the order of the day. But it came in for criticism from the other end of town. In March 2009 Mervyn King had told the Treasury Select Committee (TSC) that he had doubts about the idea of a fiscal stimulus at that time; in the May 2010 Inflation Report he called for a 'significant fiscal consolidation' and a more 'demanding path' for deficit reduction.[27] Brown was furious at what he saw as a political intervention, though Darling was relaxed. Pressure from the other direction was not unwelcome to him.

By the end of 2009, Brown's view began to change. As Darling puts it:

> In the early autumn Gordon told me he accepted that we had to show we were mindful of the deficit. He therefore proposed a Fiscal Responsibility Act which would commit us to reducing the deficit by half over a five-year period. In my opinion, such a move was wide open to the argument that you didn't need a law to ensure that you act as you should. In the circumstances, though, I seized on it because it did at least provide me with the equivalent of a fiscal rule, providing a ceiling on what we could borrow and spend. The Act was eventually introduced in early 2010, to almost universal derision.[28]

As the 2010 election approached, the respective parties' approaches to deficit reduction became a significant issue although, as an IFS paper pointed out, 'it is striking how reticent all three main parties have been in explaining how they would confront the task. Their public spending plans are particularly vague.'[29] But there was a significant difference between them. The Liberal Democrats broadly endorsed the plan set out by Darling in the 2010 Budget, which involved elimination of the structural deficit by 2016–17. 'The Conservatives want to start [tightening] earlier and proceed more quickly. They . . . would aim to get almost all the repair job done a year earlier.'[30] Darling could see the argument for faster tightening but, he told me, 'had Labour been elected in 2010 it would have been hard to agree on a policy as tough as the Coalition managed. The politics of the Labour Party would have prevented it.'[31]

The different approaches to deficit reduction were probably not decisive in Labour's defeat in 2010. Brown argued in the campaign that a Conservative government in charge of austerity measures would hurt many different groups, but other factors, including the Iraq war and Brown's personal unpopularity, dominated. The Liberal Democrats, whose views on public spending were closer to Labour than to the Conservatives, might have been expected to moderate the latter's enthusiasm for deficit reduction, but that did not happen, and the Coalition began life with a strong commitment to reducing public borrowing.

Osborne: The austerity Chancellor

That was the title chosen by Janan Ganesh for his friendly biography of George Osborne, published in 2012. It begins with Osborne at the despatch box on 22 June 2010, announcing that 'this is the unavoidable Budget': unavoidable because of the monstrosities of his economic inheritance. 'The world's first industrial nation was flirting with ruin.' But help was at hand, brought by a man prepared to slay 'the demons menacing his country . . . Britain was to pay its way out of the looming devastation with the greatest fiscal retrenchment since the war . . . This was austerity, and here was its author.'[32]

The fiscal strategy Osborne presented was eye-watering, with savings far greater than those envisaged by Darling. There were to be immediate cuts of just above £6 billion, and a fiscal retrenchment of 6.3% of GDP, or roughly £113 billion, over the Parliament as a whole. There would be immediate tax increases, with the rate of VAT going up from 17.5% to 20%, a big rise in capital gains tax, and a new bank levy, but three-quarters of the retrenchment would come from spending cuts, which would affect all programmes other than Health and International Development.

The scale of the fiscal squeeze was broadly welcome to the official Treasury, which was concerned about the risk of a loss of confidence among investors in gilts, and possible credit ratings downgrades. Officials presented three options to the incoming Chancellor: one with an additional £60 billion of savings, which they did not expect him to adopt and, at the other extreme, a much softer strategy, closer to the Darling plan already published. The central option was only slightly more aggressive than the route Osborne chose. So, according to Ganesh, 'far from imposing an extreme and ideological will, the Chancellor went with the grain of mainstream Treasury thinking'. With the benefit of a decade's reflection, that is not quite how officials see it today.

MacPherson, Permanent Secretary at that time, accepts that the Treasury was strongly in favour of fiscal consolidation. 'The UK has a chronic tendency to overconsume, and the banking crisis had destroyed revenue capacity which looked unlikely to come back. The UK could not run a fiscal deficit of 10% of GDP for long with interest rates at 4.5%. So whoever won the 2010 election would have to work on fiscal consolidation. Previous consolidations had typically been achieved through a mixture of growth and inflation, which eroded the real value of the debt, but that was made much more difficult by Bank of England independence. Of course, in theory the government could raise the inflation target, but that would be seen for what it was and the markets would react badly. We were also concerned that the UK would be vulnerable in the event of another crisis, if we had a debt to GDP ratio of 100%

or more. The Japanese have managed quite well with that level of debt, or even higher, but they have captive domestic savers. In our case around 30% of our debt is held by foreign investors. As Mark Carney put it, "we rely on the kindness of strangers".'[33]

But although the Treasury was institutionally sympathetic to the degree of fiscal tightening proposed, there were important disagreements on the composition of the retrenchment. MacPherson saw the decisions to raise personal allowances in 2010 and 2011 as a costly mistake which meant they had even more to do on the spending side. Furthermore, 'the Coalition protected too many spending areas and too many benefits, for example the triple lock on pensions. And it would have been better to go further and faster on the tax side. The result was that the cuts fell very hard on some sectors, such as local authorities, which have no voice in Whitehall.'

External critics were more trenchant. The 'cuts' galvanized the Left, as did the huge increase in student fees, which damaged the Liberal Democrats – who had campaigned on a no fee increase platform – for a generation and would do little for the public finances in the long run, given the scale of the write-offs that will eventually be incurred. (There is a counterfactual history argument which ascribes Brexit to student fees. In killing off the Liberal Democrats' election prospects in 2010 they created the conditions for an overall Conservative majority, which triggered the implementation of Cameron's referendum commitment.) The 2012 Budget, dubbed an 'omnishambles' after the so-called 'pasty tax' was withdrawn, was a low point in Osborne's fortunes. In February of the following year, Moody's downgraded the UK's debt from AAA to AA, citing the country's weak economic performance.

But by the summer of 2013, when the economy was expanding again, Osborne was confident enough in the consequences of his austerity strategy to declare victory. Addressing the critics of his tight constraints on public spending, he asserted: 'The pace of fiscal consolidation has not changed, government spending cuts have continued as planned, and yet growth has accelerated and many of the leading economic indicators show activity rising faster than at any time since the 1990s.'[34] There were strong echoes of Geoffrey Howe's triumph over the 364 economists who had criticized his 1981 Budget.

Some economists bit back. Martin Wolf of the *Financial Times*, a thorn in Osborne's side throughout his term of office, riposted that 'the performance since Mr Osborne took office in May 2010 has been dismal. Over three years the economy has grown by a cumulative total of 2.2% . . . UK performance is dismal even by the standards of other crisis-hit, high-income economies.'[35] At that time, the UK recovery looked weak even by the non-exacting standards of the Eurozone.[36] Wolf quoted assessments that suggested the economy was perhaps 3% smaller than it would have been with a slower deficit reduction strategy.[37] He recognized that 'the politics of this policy may not be too bad for Mr Osborne if the unnecessarily slow recovery becomes a faster bounce-back in the run-in to the 2015 election . . . [but] this has been an unnecessarily protracted slump'.[38]

Wolf's political forecast turned out to be accurate. But he overstated the scale and impact of the deficit reduction. In practice the deficits were much higher than planned, largely because growth was weaker. As an IFS paper pointed out in 2015: 'The scale of the UK's consolidation since 2010 has been only slightly greater than the Euro area average and leaves the UK with a cyclically adjusted Budget deficit well above the euro area average.'[39] As growth was slower than expected, Osborne did not respond with further tightening and instead pushed out the date at which budget balance would be achieved. The result was that even after five austere years there was more pain to come following the 2015 election. The Conservatives promised that further consolidation would come entirely from controlling spending. The prospects for public sector pay, and for unprotected areas of spending (i.e., outside health and education) looked bleak. The IFS suggested that Act 2 of this fiscal drama 'could well be considerably tougher and bloodier than the opening act'.

Osborne did not survive beyond Act 2, scene i. The EU referendum brought his chancellorship to a premature end, though not before he had set the fiscal course for the Conservative government elected in 2015. His Budget in July 2015 broadly maintained the steady deficit reduction profile of the Coalition years. The highest-profile measure was a big increase in the minimum wage, whose impact on earnings was offset by a reduction in tax credits for the working poor. Employers were to carry a higher burden, but with the promise of a lower corporation tax. The potentially adverse impact on jobs became submerged in the many changes in economic circumstances attributable to Brexit and Covid.

We might conclude, therefore, that Osborne's fiscal policy was, *pace* Martin Wolf, moderately successful in stabilizing the economy. The deficit was reduced from £87 billion in 2010–11 to £27 billion in 2015–16. Growth revived nonetheless, at a rate comparable to much of the rest of Europe, though not to the US. And his party won an overall majority at the next election, without the benefit of a fiscal giveaway beforehand.

That achievement was obscured by the result of the 2016 referendum. Was that result influenced by the austerity programme? A 2018 paper by Thiemo Fetzer of Warwick University argues that it was: 'The rise of popular support for the UK Independence Party, as the single most important correlate of the subsequent Leave vote in the 2016 EU referendum, along with broader measures of political dissatisfaction, are strongly and causally correlated with an individual's or an area's exposure to austerity since 2010.'[40] Until 2010 the welfare system acted to offset growing income differentials. After the Coalition's cuts, it ceased to do so. And exposure to those cuts affected voting intentions decisively, so that 'the referendum could have resulted in a Remain victory had it not been for austerity'.

It is hardly a surprise to find that Osborne rejects that conclusion. 'Pensioners voted in large numbers for Brexit', he argues, 'even though they had been protected by the triple lock. And the disaffected in marginal towns had been suffering for a long time. That did not start under the Coalition government. The long-term impact of the global financial crisis and the resulting recession had affected them more than any cuts in public expenditure. It was not austerity "what done it". Even the Red Wall problem was not caused by austerity: Balls lost his seat in 2015.'[41]

His own considered verdict, recollected in tranquillity? 'Austerity was oversold. I was too macho about it.'

The Hammond years

When Philip Hammond moved into Number 11, in July 2016, fiscal policy was not at the top of his in-tray. Brexit dominated the immediate agenda, and would remain his principal preoccupation for the three years of his appointment. But when Theresa May gave him the job, 'we had a short discussion about our shared views on fiscal discipline and the need to get the deficit down still further, and our similarly shared view that the targets my predecessor had set were probably not realistic or achievable. And we agreed that I would go away and look at re-setting how that was going to work.'[42] That apparent early agreement did not last: 'We had some difficult conversations during our time in office together, some of them over fiscal issues.'

His thinking was close to Osborne's: he had been his Shadow Chief Secretary:

> I would have said I was a continuity Chancellor . . . There was no bit of George's policy that I felt was alien to me . . . [but] I'd observed things that George had done that he couldn't really back away from, but which hadn't quite worked out as planned . . . the balanced budget target didn't look incredibly realistic at the time. It would have meant a further round of squeeze, particularly on welfare,

which would not really have been deliverable either politically or legally . . . So, I think we made a virtue of necessity in announcing a different timescale.[43]

And as he assessed the position over the summer, the balance between continuity and change began to switch. 'Although I bought into Osborne's principles, I thought he had got into a macho political posture in relation to the deficit', he told me. 'It is now obvious that he had lost the Conservatives a lot of popular political support which affected the referendum result. So I wanted the objective to be to get closer to fiscal balance, but not necessarily the *"schwarze Null"* [black zero – the German balanced budget law] as the Treasury called it.'[44]

The resulting reformulation was announced in the autumn statement of 2016. One important change, which the IFS had recommended, and the official Treasury welcomed, was the move away from two 'fiscal events' a year to one. 'George liked two opportunities to pull rabbits out of hats. He liked the platform a fiscal statement gave him. When I took over I said I would be less good at pulling out rabbits, but maybe better at picking up balls from the back of the scrum [a reference to one of Johnson's *bons mots*]. Boris took umbrage and did not forgive me that joke. He has a thin skin.'[45]

The statement also reformulated the fiscal rules. There were three. (Fiscal rules generally appear with a couple of friends for company.) Overall structural borrowing would be below 2% of GDP by the end of the Parliament. The debt to GDP ratio would be falling by the same date, and the government would run an absolute surplus by the middle of the 2020s. Within the spending totals there was also a cash cap on welfare spending, as proposed by Osborne in the past. The 2017 Budget made an unpromising start. Hammond proposed an increase in national insurance payments for the self-employed, a measure the Treasury and the IFS had advocated, but which turned out to be inconsistent with the 2015 manifesto. 'Nobody, but nobody – special advisers, civil servants – looked back through the legislation [Osborne had legislated the previous year in a way which was interpreted as amending the manifesto commitment] to see what we had actually promised. And it was genuinely a surprise when, during the budget, Laura Kuenssberg [BBC political editor] first tweeted that this appeared to breach a manifesto commitment.'[46] The increase was withdrawn.

The embarrassment for the government was considerable. Hammond offered the Prime Minister his resignation, which she rejected. 'She gave me a bollocking, then supported me. It was the only time she was on my side! She was very difficult to deal with but had an old-fashioned view of loyalty.'[47] Hammond still believes it would be right to make the change, as the concession costs the Treasury a huge amount of revenue, but 'there will be forceful opposition from White Van Men and their friends on the Conservative benches'.

The fiscal rules were not changed in the three years Hammond spent in the Treasury, but he did not meet them, partly because revenue increases were abandoned, and partly because economic growth disappointed in the years following the referendum. The current spending balance was negative to the tune of over £11 billion in 2017–18, and only slightly positive in the following year. Public sector net debt fell slightly as a proportion of GDP, from just over 83% to 81%, and was set to fall further, but only because of the way the government accounts for the unwinding of the Bank of England's Term Funding Scheme.

Hammond was at the Treasury rather longer than he expected. Had May secured a bigger majority in the 2017 election he would have been dismissed. His relationship with Nick Timothy (one of the Prime Minister's joint Chiefs of Staff), in particular, was hostile. The weak result, widely attributed to a botched manifesto commitment on the costs of social care, led to Timothy's departure, and Hammond's reconfirmation in office. But Boris Johnson's victory in the leadership of election of July 2019 led to his replacement by Sajid Javid.

Javid's short-lived rules

Javid was Chancellor for just over six months, the shortest tenure since Iain Macleod, who died after a month in office in 1970.

His period covered the chaotic final months of the 2017 Parliament, when much government business was put on hold while Parliament agonized over Brexit, and eventually collapsed into another election. But public finances are eternal, and, as part of the election manifesto, Javid reconfigured the fiscal rules, which were in any case bound to be breached. He was also in a government led by a Prime Minister with, apparently, a very different approach to public spending from his two predecessors. In an interview during the election campaign, Johnson said: 'I remember having conversations with colleagues in the government that came in in 2010 saying I thought austerity was just not the right way forward for the UK.'[48] There is no contemporaneous evidence to support that claim. Since returning as an MP in 2015, he had consistently voted in support of austerity policies, particularly the cuts in benefits,[49] though as Mayor of London he did argue his corner for more generous funding for the capital.

Osborne does not recall Johnson as a dissenting voice on the government's fiscal policy. His view on his claim to have been one is, in a sense, more indulgent. 'Boris Johnson has no idea at all about budgets and fiscal policy. When I dealt with him on London's budgets he did not know the difference between £10 million and £100 million, though his spending ideas were not ridiculous. As Prime Minister, he will not know if the Treasury is imposing cuts or not.'[50]

Against that background Javid was bound to find imposing fiscal discipline a challenge. Nonetheless, in November 2019 he announced a trinity of new targets:

- a commitment to balance the current budget (excluding capital expenditure) in three years' time and implicitly to remain in balance thereafter;
- a limit on net public investment of 3% of GDP;
- a trigger for debt interest costs of 6% of tax revenues, beyond which the government must reassess its borrowing plans to ensure debt does not rise further. (That reflected a growing view internationally that with very low interest rates and sluggish investment, governments could afford to run higher deficits than had previously seemed prudent – unless interest rates began to rise).

Since the new rules were not presented alongside a budget, there was no evaluation by the OBR. So the Resolution Foundation produced a hasty assessment, describing the current spending rule as 'a modest loosening on the previous approach'.[51] New spending commitments announced in September of that year were accommodated, with modest room for more within the target. And the revised investment ceiling would allow an almost 20% increase in capital spending, taking it back to levels last seen in the 1970s, though the 6% trigger for reassessing borrowing plans might well prove to be a constraint on the investment plans.

Unfortunately, when the rest of the manifesto was published later in the month, the rules looked fragile. A second Resolution Foundation review concluded that 'the Conservatives already look highly likely to be on course to break their new rules before the ink is dry on them'.[52] The manifesto spending commitments left very little headroom against the achievement of the fiscal targets set, only about a sixth of the average forecast error over a three year period: 'This suggests an 86% chance of the rule being broken based on the experience of previous forecasts.'

Furthermore, the forecasts did not account for the additional costs consequent on higher borrowing and the departmental costs associated with the promised recruitment of armies of doctors and nurses. The imprudence of these proposals was only matched by the rival promises made by Labour. The dismal conclusion was that the government elected in December 2019 would face difficult choices: 'Raise taxes further, return to austerity, renege on manifesto commitments or abandon their new fiscal rules at the first hurdle.'[53]

Rewriting fiscal rules as circumstances change has been a regular feature of the past twenty-five years, and longer. Sometimes receipts surprise on the upside, and spending on the downside, though more often the reverse is true, but there has usually been a central plausible scenario which would allow the targets to be met. By 2019 that was no longer the case. In their election manifesto Labour presented a fiscal case based on the world being other than it is, and the Conservative proposals were frankly implausible. Perhaps one factor was that, as one Treasury official put it, 'we now have a Prime Minister who does not believe in arithmetic'.[54] The consequences of this false prospectus had not been seen before its author, Sajid Javid, was removed from office, and all previous fiscal bets were called off by the Covid-19 pandemic.

Sunak: Covid-19

Rishi Sunak took over as Chancellor in February 2020 in unpromising circumstances. Javid refused reappointment in Johnson's reshuffle, saying that the conditions – a joint team of special advisers managed by Dominic Cummings in Number 10 – were such that 'no self-respecting minister could accept' them. Sunak was his instant replacement, an internal promotion, as he had been Chief Secretary since the previous July and had defended the November spending plans as 'sensible fiscal management'.

We shall never know whether Sunak as Chancellor would have taken a materially different approach, as his budget in the following month was dominated by the government's first attempts to respond to the Covid-19 pandemic and its public spending implications, especially for the NHS. The details of the many spending and subsidized lending initiatives which emerged from the Treasury during the longer than expected lockdowns would unbalance this narrative, and in any event it is far too early to assess the consequences. But even the first response, which would subsequently be massively expanded, was seen as a significant departure from the fiscal policies pursued, with varying degrees of enthusiasm and rigour, over the previous two decades.

The fiscal loosening implied by the announcements in March 2020 amounted to 1.5% of GDP. Some elements were driven directly by the health consequences of the pandemic, but there was also a boost to public investment. That was welcomed by Martin Wolf, as a marked contrast to the post-financial crisis cut in investment, which he characterized as 'a classic bit of Treasury idiocy'. He saw it as more than a short-term expedient. It was a 'repudiation of what the party stood for under David Cameron and George Osborne. Gone are austerity and small government: this is now a party of high spending and big government. Its programme is "welfare nationalism".'[55] The OBR noted that it was the largest fiscal loosening since 1992.

The next twelve months saw further spending commitments on furlough schemes, universal credit and a wide range of business support programmes both general and specific, together with massive expenditure on vaccination and test and trace programmes, with varying degrees of success and cost-effectiveness. MacPherson described the NHS Test and Trace scheme, estimated to cost £37 billion, as 'the most wasteful and inept public spending programme of all time' – high praise indeed.[56] The consequence, according to the OBR, would be net borrowing of 16.9% of GDP in 2020–21, with the debt to GDP ratio rising rapidly towards 100% of GDP, a level not reached since the aftermath of the Second World War.

As the lockdowns continued, interspersed with periods of relative normality, the fiscal implications became ever more severe. The 2021 Budget gave an idea of the scale of the damage done to the public finances. The OBR estimate of net borrowing for 2021–22 came in at 10.3% of GDP. Sunak began to sketch out a process of fiscal consolidation in the outer years, with the most eye-catching measure a rise in the main rate of corporation tax from 19% to 25%, the first increase in the rate since 1974. (Osborne had reduced it during his time in office from 28% to 19%.) The increase was offset in the short term by a rise in investment allowances, to 130% of expenditure. Such consolidation as was promised came on the revenue side, with a projected freezing of personal allowances, but no forecast cuts in public spending, apparently underpinning Johnson's promise that 'we will not go back to the austerity of 10 years ago'.

The consequences for public borrowing would in any other circumstances have been alarming to investors in the government's debt. Net debt as a proportion of GDP was forecast to rise to 110% in 2023–24, before dropping back to 104% in 2025–26. And commentators mainly took the view that the forecasts were optimistic. Taxes would rise to 35% of GDP, the highest percentage since the 1970s. The IFS noted that the November 2020 spending review had cut £10–13 billion from departmental spending plans and that the budget included an additional £4 billion cut not mentioned in the speech. Its assessment was that for 'unprotected' departments (i.e., excluding the NHS, education and defence) there would be a 3% real-terms cut in 2022–23. So unless further increases are conceded 'for many public services the first half of the 2020s could feel a lot like the first half of the 2010s'.[57] In summary: 'The Chancellor's medium-term spending plans look implausibly low.'[58]

Why did these remarkable and unprecedented figures not alarm the financial markets? In the past, profligate British governments have been disciplined by buyers' strikes in the gilt market or, in 1976, by the IMF. (I recall shrinking to the side of an ill-lit Treasury corridor as the IMF delegation marched through the building, like a bureaucratic version of a scene from *Reservoir Dogs*.)

One proximate answer is that the principal buyer of gilts during the year was the Bank of England, through its QE programme. By March 2021, the Bank was the largest holder of government bonds, bigger than all foreign investors combined. A second is that, at a time of low interest rates globally, attributable to an excess of savings over investment opportunities, highly indebted governments, even in countries with a worse record for fiscal discipline than the UK, found it easy to fund themselves. The UK was by no means alone. The Eurozone's fiscal rules were abandoned, and the US embarked on a huge stimulus programme, far bigger than anything envisaged in London. A third is that conventional fiscal orthodoxy had been turned on its head, partly because of the second factor. In its October 2020 Fiscal Monitor, the IMF said:

> Governments need to scale up public investment to ensure successful reopening, boost growth, and prepare economies for the future. Low interest rates make borrowing to invest desirable . . . scaling up of quality public investment can have a powerful impact on employment and activity, crowd in private investment, and absorb excess savings without causing a rise in borrowing costs.[59]

As the stuttering recovery from Covid developed in 2021, the gloomiest predictions proved excessive. Government borrowing came in rather lower than feared. The OBR attributed the improvement to 'both stronger-than-expected receipts (thanks largely to a faster-than-expected economic recovery) and lower-than-expected spending (due to the faster-than-expected unwinding of Covid-related government support)'.[60] As a result, borrowing was £26 billion lower than forecast at the time of the budget. But the overall prospect remained of a severe deterioration in the public finances.

How did the official Treasury regard the prospect? Have they been converted to the new relaxed view of deficits?

The answer is 'up to a point'. Treasury officials are attuned to disappointment. The UK economy rarely surprises on the upside, and officials remain preoccupied by the very poor productivity performance, and the stubborn resistance of business investment to the stimulus of very low interest rates. They are also trained to highlight downside risks. The OBR points out that, while at current rates the cost of servicing the elevated level of public debt is at a historic low of 2.4% of total spending, the fiscal position is highly sensitive to any rise in rates. 'To illustrate this risk, the 30 basis point increase in interest rates that has happened since we closed our forecast on 5 February would already add £6.3 billion to the interest bill in 2025–26 . . . All else equal, that would be enough to put underlying debt back on a rising path relative to GDP in every year of the forecast.'[61]

Officials say 'there is no single institutional view. Ministers decide. The bias in the building is still towards "austerity", though the word and the policy have been oversold. Much of the so-called austerity was not real. Debt remained high. The Treasury would have done it differently with more tax rises, earlier. Would that have choked off the recovery? Probably not. Local authorities bore the brunt of the spending cuts, leaving them enfeebled which is costing the government now. On debt, the IMF has changed its view on how much debt is sustainable and we are influenced by that.'[62]

There was no significant dissent about the spending packages put in place by Sunak to cope with the impact of the lockdowns. 'He has done the right things, particularly the furlough scheme. It was a word nobody used until the Treasury reinvented it. His crisis management has been good. He is fundamentally a 1980s fiscal conservative who sees it as the Chancellor's sacred duty to balance the books and is desperate to make a start on consolidation, but is also part of a populist government which wants to please its red wall voters. That is an incoherent mixture. The government appears to have a large majority, but in practice does not have one for tough fiscal measures.'[63] Sunak himself underlined that point in the summer of 2021, as the economy began to revive after the Covid shutdown. There will be 'absolutely no return to austerity' he said.[64]

'The PM and Chancellor do not agree on economic policy, and the electoral cycle is precisely wrong given the timing of Covid. The time when taxes need to be raised will be in the run-up to the next election. We will probably need to raise taxes in 2023 or 2024 which the government will not wish to do. An earlier election would be helpful from that point of view.'[65]

'We have looked at past fiscal consolidations, which have mainly been achieved through a mixture of growth and inflation. It is hard now to believe that rapid growth will come to our rescue. Inflation could emerge, which would reduce the real value of the debt, but the independent Bank of England is supposed to prevent that happening. Could we tell the Bank to aim for a higher target? Yes, in theory, or it could choose to adopt some version of average inflation targeting, as the Fed has done – though that looks like an underhand way of raising the target range. So the way out of the current impasse is not clear.'[66]

'Perhaps devaluation will help to square the circle, though it is dishonest. In the EU referendum people voted to be worse off, and only part of that impact has fed through so far. They are likely to feel the rest of the impact through a devaluation. In those circumstances the Bank would care less about inflation and allow the devaluation impact to pass through, as it did after the financial crisis. There is a risk that the UK will look a bit sick, and be vulnerable to changes in market sentiment compared to other European countries, though Italy, Spain and France will also struggle.'[67]

'There is a second underlying problem. It seems that the population wants to rebalance public and private spending. The Conservatives are no longer targeting a smaller state, as they did in the 1980s, and again from 2010 to 2019.

They judge that people want more of the kind of things the public sector can provide, from improved healthcare, through social care to aircraft carriers. It may be that we are moving towards a situation in which public spending will be more like 50% of the economy than 40%, as is the case in France and parts of Northern Europe. But that is against all the Party's instincts. And it is not clear how it can be financed.'[68]

Part of the answer emerged in September 2021, when the government announced, and passed through Parliament the next day, a new Health and Social Care Levy set at 1.2%, 'based on National Insurance Contributions', but also applying to people working above state pension age and to dividend income.[69] The additional revenues, estimated at £14 billion in a full year, are hypothecated to the NHS, to allow it to catch up on treatments delayed during the pandemic, and subsequently to social care, offsetting the impact of the imposition of a cap on individual payments for residential care, announced at the same time. The overall impact, as the IFS noted would be 'to raise the tax burden in the UK to the highest ever sustained level'.[70]

Will this turn out as predicted? In a speech in 2014, MacPherson pointed out that for a long period 'the share of national income accounted for by taxes and national insurance has remained stubbornly stable: 36.4 % in 1985–86 and 34.9% in 2012–13 . . . Perversely, over the last decade when we have witnessed the biggest economic and financial crisis in generations, the tax take has been more stable than ever.'[71] He speculates on why that might be so: public choice, with taxpayer resistance setting in above a certain point? Domestic arbitrage between taxes and international arbitrage between jurisdictions? Or diminishing returns delivered by poor effectiveness on the part of the tax authorities?

Whatever the reason, the prospect of a sustained rise in tax revenues as a proportion of GDP looks problematic. Commitments by successive governments over recent years to freeze large parts of the tax system give the Treasury even less room for manoeuvre than it had in the past. The structure of the tax system, and the prospects for reform, are therefore crucial, so it is the subject to which we now turn.

4

Tax Policy

The task of stabilizing the public finances is greatly complicated by two so-called 'triple-locks', on taxation and pensions. The Conservatives committed in the 2015 election campaign not to change the basic rate of income tax, the main VAT rate or the National Insurance rate. Indeed, the incoming government passed a law to that effect, and the commitment was renewed in the elections of 2017 and 2019. Since those three taxes, taken together, generate about 65% of government revenues, the commitment puts great pressure on the other sources of revenue. Sunak made much in his March 2021 Budget of his proposed increase in corporation tax, but the tax as a whole raises only 7% of revenue, so a massive percentage increase would be needed to make a serious dent in the deficit. The Health and Social Care Levy technically does not breach the commitment, but it is arguably a National Insurance increase in all but name. The pensions triple-lock commits the government to raising the state pension each year by the highest of 2.5%, the inflation rate and the increase in average wages. Since the unusual circumstances of the Covid pandemic would have delivered a rise of over 8%, following the rise in wages in the recovery, the lock was suspended for a year in an announcement alongside the new Levy, but it remains in place for the longer term.

It is no consolation to the Treasury to learn that the commitment was devised 'on the hoof' in the heat of the election campaign. Ameet Gill, David Cameron's head of strategic communications, confided later to the BBC that it was made 'just to fill a vacuum' in the news flow on a particular day. 'It was probably the dumbest economic policy that anyone could make, but we kind of cooked it up on the hoof a couple of days before [the election] because we had a hole in the grid and we needed to fill it.'[1]

That was perhaps the most egregious example of a political gesture constraining the development of a rational tax policy, but there have been many others. The Mirrlees Review of the UK tax system, sponsored by the IFS, concluded in 2011 with a damning verdict. While recognizing that 'there is a need to operate within the bounds of what is politically feasible', it nonetheless concluded: 'There is a better way to make tax policy. There are taxes that are fairer, less damaging, and simpler than those we have now. To implement them will take a government willing to be honest with the electorate ... [and] willing to put long-term strategy ahead of short-term tactics.'[2] Three years later Paul Johnson of the IFS returned to the same theme in another paper: 'Tax without design'.[3] He noted that 'few of those aspects of the system in most need of reform have been tackled. The need for reform, and a clear strategy for reform, remain as pressing as ever.'

Successive Chancellors in this period, especially Brown and Osborne, came into office with plans, developed over a lengthy period as Treasury Shadows, to make changes to taxes. Some, but by no means all, of those plans were implemented. Taken together, they left the tax system in no more robust or logical position than it was when they started.

Labour and tax: 1997–2010

Brown was the most tax-active of the six Chancellors in the period under review in this book. In his first term he gave a decent burial to mortgage interest relief, though that relief, long hated by the official Treasury, had been under sentence of death since Margaret Thatcher began to reduce it in the 1980s. In his first term he also imposed a windfall tax on the privatized utilities, whose pay excesses, allied to monopoly pricing power, had made them vulnerable to attack. The latter raised around £5 billion, which was largely used to finance a 'welfare-to-work' programme. It was undoubtedly popular at the time, though it is notable that it has not been repeated since. (A similar proposal featured in the doomed 2019 Labour manifesto.) In other areas Brown used the tax system as a policy tool. He introduced a climate change levy, the landfill tax, the aggregates levy and air passenger duty, but none raised substantial sums.

Brown's most fundamental change was the introduction of the Working Families Tax Credit, inspired by the US system. The overall impact remains controversial, and there is now a gradual change from tax credits to universal credit, but Brown argues that it had a decisive effect on child poverty. He developed a concept of 'progressive universalism', which he characterized as 'a floor of basic social rights for all, but with more support to those most in need'. The Child Trust Fund – a tax-free savings account for children – was badged under the same heading. (It was abolished in 2011. The Share Foundation estimates that 2 million accounts have been lost to the intended beneficiaries.[4]) Brown also introduced, and subsequently increased, the winter fuel allowance. That has survived, though it attracts much criticism as a poorly targeted benefit.

He was far less successful with his changes to income tax. In 1999, he introduced a 10p rate on the first £1,500 of taxable income, trumpeted as 'the lowest starting rate of tax for over forty years'.[5] The overall impact was not enormous, and a similar effect could have been achieved by differential changes in the tax-free allowance, but it was of material benefit to some low earners. In his last budget, Brown decided to reverse course and abolish it. The reasons were political: 'I believed that sooner or later – probably sooner – the Conservatives would fight an election on cutting the basic rate to 20p [so] I believed it the right time to kill the income tax issue for good.'[6] The reaction was very hostile. Taxpayers on low incomes lost more from the abolition of the 10p rate than they gained from the cut in the basic rate. So in May 2008 Alistair Darling implemented a large increase in the personal allowance to compensate the losers. Brown acknowledges that 'a mistake had been made and rectified – but at a price: 'Abolition of the 10p rate was an error I made in a rush to boost tax credits.' That episode vividly illustrated the difficulty of making apparently rational changes, which leave a small minority of taxpayers worse off.

Darling resolved the short-term problem he had inherited, early in his term of office. Thereafter, his tax changes were driven by the financial crisis and its consequences. He cut the main VAT rate from 17.5% to 15% for just over a year to stimulate spending in the depths of the recession. But by late 2009, the focus switched to tax increases to begin the process of fiscal consolidation. In November of that year he announced an increase in the top marginal rate from 40p, where it had remained since Nigel Lawson's dramatic reduction in the 1988 Budget, to 45p, then in April 2010 he raised it further, to 50p on taxable income above £150,000.

Darling also introduced popular additional tax measures targeted at the banks. The bankers' bonus tax imposed an additional 50% tax on bonuses above £25,000 (paid by the bank rather than the individual) and, according to Darling, 'brought in far more money than we anticipated'.[7] In addition, he introduced a levy on banks based on balance sheet size, not profitability. The latter has been sustained for over a decade, though introduced as an emergency measure. Both measures met Darling's own criterion for changes which can be implemented relatively easily: 'The only popular tax in this country is the tax that somebody else pays.' Otherwise, as he acknowledges, his time in office was dominated by the financial crisis and the need to react to it, with little bandwidth available for fundamental reforms. 'Any ideas that I might have had about tax reform in the early days were put aside because of one crisis after another.'[8]

Coalition and Conservatives: 2010–21

In opposition, George Osborne criticized the Labour government for its lack of an overarching tax strategy. He maintained that there had been 'not a single speech by either this Chancellor [Darling] or his predecessor on the principles underlying tax reform'.[9] He praised the 1978 Meade Report, and the work of the Tax Reform Commission under Michael Forsyth. That Commission bemoaned the complexity of the system: 'The general trend for the UK's tax system in recent years has been towards more complexity and less certainty, which is gradually making the UK a less competitive location for industry.'[10] Osborne declared that, in office, his tax policy would be guided by four principles set out by Adam Smith: taxes should be efficient, certain, transparent and fair.

Furthermore, the UK should have a tax system which was internationally competitive, which means 'a broad tax base with low tax rates'. In particular, 'if British business is to compete effectively then the rate of corporation tax needs to come down'. And the mechanism of tax policy implementation should be changed: 'We need to fundamentally change the way we make tax law in this country.'[11]

Responding to Forsyth's criticism of the complexity of the tax regulations, Osborne acknowledged that 'our tax code is probably the most complex in the world. It is

certainly the longest – we overtook India for that dubi-
ous honour following last year's Finance Bill. The size
of Tolley's tax handbook [the tax professional's bible]
has doubled over the last ten years.' And he pledged to
do something about stamp duty, which 'has become a
barrier to home ownership', by lifting the threshold and
taking 90% of purchases out of stamp duty altogether. His
overall approach would, as we have seen, be to achieve a
significant fiscal consolidation and a smaller state, but at
the same time he undertook to mount 'a programme of
lasting tax reform that gives Britain the tax system it needs
to meet the long-term challenges of our age'.[12]

Osborne was more active in his approach to tax policy
than his immediate predecessor had been. Before his last
budget in March 2016, the OBR calculated that he had
made 585 separate tax policy changes; at that budget
he made 50 more. The consequence was that Tolley's
Handbook grew from 17,795 pages to 21,602 pages
during his term of office.[13]

The biggest change of heart came in relation to stamp
duty on house purchase, which was raised several times
under Osborne, reaching the extraordinary level of 15%
on buy-to-let properties costing over £1.5 million. The
system also became extremely complex. In evidence to the
TSC in September 2020, Philip Booth of the Institute of
Economic Affairs argued that Osborne's changes to property taxation 'were just dreadful from the point of view of
any kind of reasoned public finance analysis'. He pointed
to the fact that 'there are something like 16 different rates
of stamp duty now . . . all of which have to be defined
and large numbers of pages of regulation to try to decide
whether one particular property goes into one category
or another'.[14] Witnesses to the Committee also pointed to
a plethora of changes to pension taxation, leaving savers
uncertain and confused, and to the complex distinctions
between employment, self-employment and company-
owner management, where people doing very similar
things and paying different rates of tax were highlighted.

(That was the issue which Philip Hammond attempted to tackle in his aborted reform of National Insurance in the Budget of 2017.)

In one area Osborne did attempt to deliver on his promise. The Treasury published a corporate tax road map in 2010, which followed the principles he enunciated in 2008.[15] Gemma Tetlow of the IFS praised it in evidence to the TSC: 'The corporate tax road map, which set out a plan to lower the rate but broaden the base of corporate tax was an area in which there did seem to be a clear strategy that was followed through.'[16] The headline rate of corporation tax was reduced, from 28% to 19% during his time in office, and Osborne was able to claim that the UK had by 2016 become one of the lowest tax jurisdictions in the OECD. It is ironic that this one area where strategy was clear was turned on its head in Rishi Sunak's first budget in March 2021, when he announced that from 2024 the rate would rise again. Osborne said that would send the message that 'Britain isn't a very enterprising place'.[17]

Paul Johnson's overall verdict to the TSC was damning: 'It is hard to discern a set of principles underlying tax policy over the past decade . . . If there is an agenda there, it has certainly not been set out, and it is a good example of making it very difficult for people to manage their finances.' But in Johnson's view the absence of a clear direction of travel was nothing new. 'This has been true forever . . . in terms of Treasury strategy on tax. In every other bit of government, you have Green Papers, White Papers and strategies . . . We have never had such a thing for tax policy, and I think we are desperately in need of it.'[18]

In its recommendations in March 2021, the TSC took the same view and recommended that 'the government should draw up a draft strategy for consultation'. The strategy should include principles for neutrality, fairness, environmental objectives and compliance costs. The Committee did not, however, support calls for a new tax commission which, it thought, 'is unlikely to be able to achieve any-thing that the Government could not do anyway by setting out its tax strategy and by following its tax policymaking process'.[19]

There is no sign that the government plans to deliver such a draft strategy. Treasury officials are sceptical that anything useful would be achieved thereby. They have a point. It is easy to say that a strategy is needed, but behind the difficulty of establishing a set of implementable principles are strongly held political views for and against particular taxes and reliefs. The most serious attempt in recent years to address those difficult issues and identify changes which might deliver a fairer and more efficient tax system came in the Mirrlees Review of 2011.[20]

The Mirrlees Review

The review was launched in 2009 by the IFS and funded by the Nuffield Foundation and the ESRC. It took evidence over two years. James Mirrlees, a Nobel Prize-winning economist, chaired a distinguished panel. In presenting the conclusions, he was realistic about the improvements that might be made. He accepted that while economists can easily produce rational arguments for change, 'tax policy is created in a political process'. He was also sympathetic to the difficulties governments face, in that any substantial change, however logical, inevitably creates losers as well as winners, and he noted 'some genuinely encouraging aspects of tax policy over the past 30 years'. In particu-lar, he acknowledged that the taxation of savings and mortgages, and some elements of corporate taxation, have improved, largely through the expansion of in-work sup-port for low earners, initiated by Gordon Brown. And by international standards the UK system contains rel-atively few loopholes for unscrupulous tax-avoiders to exploit. The cost to the government of tax collection is not excessive.

But even taking account of these pleas in mitigation, the charge sheet Mirrlees presented was damning. He identified seven major flaws in the UK system:[21]

- there are serious disincentives to work for many people with relatively low potential earning power;
- there is a lack of communication and coherence between income tax and national insurance, and between personal and corporate taxes;
- the treatment of savings and wealth transfers is inconsistent and inequitable, resulting in a discouragement of saving;
- there is no coherent approach to environmental taxes, which damages our ability to address climate change, in particular;
- the current system of corporate taxation discourages business investment and favours debt finance over equity finance;
- taxation of land and property is inefficient and inequitable. Housing tax is heavily transaction-based. Council tax is based on 30-year-old property valuations, and is regressive;
- extensive zero-rating of VAT helps people with particular tastes, rather than being targeted at those with low resources.

Mirrlees presented a comprehensive package of reforms designed to address the weaknesses. Over the decade since the review was completed, almost nothing has been done to respond to the critique. Is that because the Treasury rejects the criticisms, or because the political stars which might allow fundamental reform to be advanced have not been aligned?

In an attempt to answer that question, the Institute for Government has published a series of 'sons of Mirrlees' reports. The first, in January 2017 – *Better Budgets: Making Tax Policy Better* – focused on the tax policymaking process, which, it argued, 'is not fit for purpose'. There is a need for more challenge of the Treasury's proposals, and Parliament needs to improve the quality of its scrutiny. It listed the problems which have resulted from the practice, which Chancellors love, of pulling rabbits out of the hat on budget day, without adequate preparation or consultation. Brown's costly income tax error, discussed above, was one such. Osborne's 'omnishambles' budget in 2012 was another. 'Secrecy is justified partly on the basis of the need to prevent market-sensitive information from leaking out and the need to prevent forestalling in advance of a tax change – but it also applies to many decisions that are neither market-sensitive nor where there is real forestalling risk.'[22] The scope for consumers to stockpile warm pasties ahead of a tax increase is limited.

A second report was published in July 2019: *Taxing Times: The Need to Reform the UK Tax System*. That report set the problems identified by Mirrlees in the context of the budgetary challenge which British governments will face in the coming years, 'as an ageing population puts additional pressure on publicly funded health and adult social care, and increases pension costs'.[23] (The Covid crisis has accentuated that challenge.) It argued that the current system is not up to meeting those demands. Total tax revenues have remained broadly flat as a share of national income in recent years, and are unlikely to be buoyant in the future, as some sources of revenue are challenged – fuel duty being the most obvious example. So tax reform is likely to become a more pressing issue.

A third report attempted to identify the reasons for the obvious lack of progress on the reform agenda over the last two decades. *Overcoming the Barriers to Tax Reform* is primarily based on a series of interviews with past Chancellors and Treasury officials, asking the question 'Why is tax reform so difficult?'[24] The exercise was carefully managed, and the interviewees were honest and frank in their assessments. The conclusions were depressing.

Why is tax reform so difficult?

Edward Troup, with a background as a tax practitioner, was a Special Adviser to Kenneth Clarke, and later worked under Brown and Darling. He became Director of Tax and Welfare in the Treasury in 2010, and was subsequently the head of Her Majesty's Revenue and Customs (HMRC). His view is that the Mirrlees Review had very little impact on Treasury thinking, and 'was always going to struggle'. 'Treasury tax teams would just roll their eyes when somebody came in and talked about Mirrlees.' Momentum for reform only emerges 'if it looks like the revenues are falling off a cliff'. When presented with proposals for change, ministers ask 'Why should I do all this damage to this machine which intimately connects with 30 million individuals and five million businesses? Because you say it would look neater or arguably more economically efficient in a way you can't quite measure.' Troup is damning about the ability of the Treasury to construct workable reform proposals. When he joined the Treasury as an official, 'nobody in the Treasury really knew anything about tax as I knew it, as a subject which involved the translation of broad policy thoughts into legislation and the administrative challenges of turning policy into collected tax'. And it is getting worse: 'The skills experience has depleted over time.' So he is 'pessimistic about the prospect for good tax policy outcomes in the future'.[25]

Lord (Nick) Stern is similarly pessimistic. In 2004 he was asked by Gordon Brown to carry out an internal review of the tax system, with a strong team. They covered a lot of ground, including a critical review of property taxation, but almost no consequences flowed. A very small set of numbered copies were produced for internal circulation and nothing was ever published. One major problem was that Brown had been Chancellor for seven years, so any recommendations were bound to be seen as critical of his stewardship so far.[26]

MacPherson agrees that the Treasury finds tax reform hard. 'It's politicians who come up with radical ideas, while the Treasury tends to come up with lots of reasons for not doing them.' And although Brown and Osborne, at least, had a strong understanding of the system, and crucially the parliamentary majorities for change, they did not match up to Nigel Lawson as a tax-reforming Chancellor. According to MacPherson, 'politics has become far more managerial than ideological. The conventional wisdom is "we don't want to upset small interest groups".'[27] As a result, 'there has been a run of "tinkerers" rather than big-picture thinkers as Chancellor'.[28] But MacPherson is resigned to living in this second-best world. 'You just have to try and get revenue where you can. So although it's nice to have – you don't want a totally incoherent tax system because that's inefficient – I think hankering after the perfect tax system is a waste of time.'[29]

Gus O'Donnell's view is similar but, perhaps because he led a review in 2004 which recommended the merger of the Inland Revenue and Customs and Excise (see Chapter 9), he has more personal capital invested in the problem. He is frustrated by the lack of impact on tax policy made by economic thinking and economists. 'I wanted strength in Treasury's tax policy and capacity ... If you think about the allocation of economic resources, the biggest misallocation is the Bank of England devoting millions and millions of economists to only one thing. Let's take half of them and put them into tax policy.'[30] The scope for improvement is great, and the answers are not complex. 'We know what to do, but it never happens. Mirrlees sets it out, but almost no change has been made, indeed we may have gone backwards. On property taxation we certainly have. There is no economic case for transaction taxes on property, but in recent years they have risen and risen.'[31]

Osborne, who was responsible for the large rises in stamp duty, says he wanted two higher rates of council tax, to increase the yield from property taxation (and pay for a cut to 40% of the top rate of income tax), but the Prime Minister would not let him do it, so his only alternative was to increase stamp duty.[32] Burns recalls that the council tax was a very rare example of a tax not designed and developed by the Treasury itself. It was introduced in haste by Michael Heseltine to replace the Community Charge (poll tax) in 1991. But the Treasury cannot evade responsibility for its most glaring fault – that it is effectively capped at too low a level. There was a choice to be made at the outset as to whether the tax bands would be national or local. 'The Treasury wanted, as far as possible, to have national bands ... because otherwise people with quite modest houses in London would have ended up with council taxes as high as people in very big houses somewhere else in the country. The need to have a national system and to get around the London problem led to the band system we ended up with.'[33] The Johnson government's new majority, which is heavily dependent on Red Wall seats in the North of England, rather than on traditional Tory voters in London and the south-east, may make this problem easier to resolve.

All the former Chancellors and senior officials concur with two points. Tax policy reform will always take a back seat, given the risks and the inevitable resistance from losers. The only ways the resistance can be overcome or at least minimized, are by lowering the overall tax yield for a time, or perhaps by introducing a set of overlapping reforms which involve gains and losses for different classes of taxpayer. The former solution is not likely to be attractive, given the budgetary challenges governments are likely to face for the foreseeable future. The second is theoretically possible, but changing a range of taxes at the same time compounds the risk of error and of lost revenue.

The second point on which all agree is that, given the risks and political and popular resistance, Chancellors are unlikely to embark on fundamental reform, however logical, unless there is a strong incentive to do so – in other words, unless there is a 'burning platform', a serious prospect that the government will not be able to raise enough tax revenue to fund its commitments.

Andrew Turnbull believes we are approaching that point. 'What we're trying to do is run public services on a kind of north European level on tax rates that are much lower, probably 10% of GDP lower.'[34] As a result many public services are 'creaking' and will continue to do so unless more money can be found.

Burns sees that problem as exacerbated by the fact that a number of taxes on which the government has heavily relied in recent decades are no longer buoyant. Tobacco duty is an obvious example, but the most worrying is fuel duty. In 1993 Norman Lamont introduced a Fuel Price Escalator whereby the cost of fuel would be increased each year by 3% above the rate of inflation. But since the protests of 2000, the escalator has been in abeyance and the last increase of any kind was in 2010. Fuel duty has been frozen in nominal terms, amounting to a real-terms cut of 17%, and forgone revenue, compared to indexation, of £6 billion a year. In the medium term, by the 2040s, if the government's climate change commitments are met, about £30 billion of tax revenue will be lost. Current Treasury officials see that as the most serious problem they face. Fuel duty is a highly regressive tax which is little understood. Carbon taxation is also regressive, but will be more obviously so, while a new progressive tax will be politically difficult for a Conservative government.

Darling agrees that 'it's becoming increasingly difficult to see how we will raise the money we need because of the demographic challenges we face, as well as people's expectations generally for public spending'.[35] He believes it will be necessary to increase tax on global enterprises like Amazon and Google, but until very recently it has not been possible to agree a coordinated approach with other jurisdictions. Troup thinks that reflects a longstanding Treasury weakness: 'international engagement on policy is under-explored'.[36] The G7 agreement in June 2021 to increase taxation of multinationals, and set a minimum corporate tax rate, brokered by the UK in the chair, is a positive sign that the importance of international agreement is recognized.[37] The practical consequences are yet to be seen, but could be significant.

Darling also believes that 'we have to think of some way of taxing accumulated wealth'. The Baby Boomer generation have accumulated capital on a massive scale, and are also beneficiaries of much public spending, on pensions and healthcare, 'which is funded by, generally speaking, their less well-off children and grandchildren'.[38] That phenomenon has been thrown into sharper focus by the Covid crisis, where the costs have fallen hardest on younger workers in precarious jobs, who have suffered disproportionately from public health measures taken to protect older citizens. But inheritance tax is a fragile and unpopular instrument. Only 4% of estates pay any inheritance tax. And wealth taxes have a poor record when tried elsewhere. Macron abandoned the French version. A report by an ESRC-funded Wealth Tax Commission recommended a one-off levy as a method of paying at least part of the cost of the Covid impact on the public finances.[39] A 1% levy on wealth of over £2 million per person would raise £80 billion. The loud political silence which greeted the recommendation suggested that this is an idea whose time has not yet come.

So we are approaching a 'burning platform' moment, with a Treasury which is acknowledged to be weak in tax policy expertise, and with a poor record at implementing reform. The problems identified by Mirrlees are almost all present today, and some – like property taxation – have got worse in the decade since his report. For the past twenty-five years, Chancellors have followed O'Donnell's witty injunction to 'be very very careful about doing things until you really understand what they are . . . don't just do something, stand there!'[40] That will not be wise advice in the next few years.

There are, however, signs that the debate on how best to raise the revenues needed to sustain a more active state, which seems a likely consequence of Covid, and indeed of the changed complexion of the Conservative Party, is developing. The new Health and Social Care Levy tries to harness public support for the NHS to overcome hostility to tax increases. The cost is another element of complexity in an already confusing system. The simplest and fairest solution, raising income tax, was too direct an attack on the tax lock for the government to contemplate. The result is a further tilt of taxation against working-age people and in favour of pensioners. As the IFS point out: 'The government could have easily achieved its aims without adding the complexity that comes with having a third tax.'[41] Once again, Tolley's handbook will gain more pages.

I return to the future challenges on macroeconomic, fiscal and tax policies in Chapter 11. But the Treasury has also navigated other treacherous waters in the past twenty years, notably two referendums and a financial crisis, all of which have raised issues central to the department's concerns.

5

Scotland: Saving the Union

Although the Treasury was under the control of Chancellors from north of the border from 1997 to 2010, the Scottish question did not loom large for most of the period. In his memoirs, Brown makes only passing reference to the 1997 devolution referendum which delivered a majority in favour of the creation of a Scottish Parliament, with the power to vary the basic rate of income tax. While Chancellor, Darling was more preoccupied by the fate of the Royal Bank of Scotland (RBS) than by the politics of the country itself.

The Barnett formula, introduced before the 1979 general election by the then CST, Joel Barnett, as a temporary solution to allocate funding to the UK's nations, provided a stable basis for public spending decisions affecting Scotland. Spending per head in all the devolved nations remained higher than in England, which occasionally rankled with English backbenchers, but when public spending is growing in real terms, as it was after 2001, the formula causes spending to grow slightly slower in percentage terms in the devolved nations, creating an effect known as 'Barnett convergence'. It was eventually revised in 2016, in part to address perceived inequities in funding for Wales, but remained essentially intact throughout the period, as far as Scotland was concerned.

The 2011 elections to the Scottish Parliament, in which the Scottish National Party (SNP) won an overall majority for the first time, lit the fuse which led to the 2014 referendum, which posed a different problem to the Treasury. The SNP manifesto for the 2012 elections included a commitment to hold a referendum on independence, and in early 2012 the Westminster government offered to legislate to facilitate a vote, providing it was 'fair, legal and decisive'. The Edinburgh Agreement of October 2012 described the framework, and the date was later set for 18 September 2014.

There were many issues at stake in the campaign, including migration and border controls and the overriding question of national identity, but economic questions quickly came to the fore, and the Treasury was thrust into the centre of the debate on four questions: the future trading relationship were the Scots to choose independence; the prospects for its financial sector and especially its banking system; the fiscal viability of an independent Scotland; and – which by a distance became the most significant question – the currency that an independent Scotland would use.

In Westminster, the Treasury coordinated the work which set out the case for the Union. Nick MacPherson, Permanent Secretary at the time, in a speech reflecting on the experience in January 2015 (1), asked rhetorically why the work was done in the Treasury, rather than the Cabinet Office or Scotland Office?[1] His answer was:

> Partly because the Treasury has the analytic capacity necessary to lead a project such as this. Partly because of previous experience. It is not a coincidence that Sir David Ramsden led the work on the five economic tests on the Euro in 2003, and also played a leading role in the Scottish analysis programme. But mainly because the Chief Secretary and Chancellor were determined to play a leading role in the Referendum Campaign and, cohesive organisation that the Treasury is, officials were quick to respond.

Macpherson may be too modest. A former colleague notes: 'It was a remarkable episode, driven by Nick's passionate commitment to the Union. He is not the laid-back cynic he sometimes appears. He turned HMT into a campaigning organization.'[2]

MacPherson himself continues: 'The Scotland analysis was an extraordinary logistical feat. Fifteen papers were produced, running to 1,400 pages. Eight Departments contributed. The project was run by a standing Treasury team of six officials, though during the course of two years' work some fifty officials contributed to the analytical work.' It is hard to think of another time when the Treasury's heavy artillery has been deployed on such a scale against a single target. The conclusions were clear, and clearly inimical to the independence cause. They may even have been fatal to it.

The Treasury's institutional commitment to free trade shone through. It saw the erection of a border along the line of Hadrian's wall as a threat to the very high volume of trade between England and Scotland, 70% of whose exports go to the rest of the UK. Any impediments to that trade would be a threat to the prosperity of both countries. Those impediments were assumed to arise from the fact that, in leaving the UK, Scotland would simultaneously have left the EU, with uncertain prospects of rejoining. Because of the potential read across to the position of an independent Catalonia, Spain was unwilling to support any reassuring words from the Commission on a reapplication for membership from Edinburgh. (In a post-Brexit referendum that argument would need to be presented in a rather different way.)

The analysis of the implications of independence for the Scottish financial services sector were similarly damning. Financial services account for more than 8% of Scottish employment, and the lion's share of the customers of Scottish institutions are elsewhere in the UK. Financial regulation has remained a matter reserved to the Westminster government, and Scottish firms have been regulated by the

Bank of England and the FSA or its successors. That has given overseas regulators and customers reassurance. An independent Scotland would need to establish new regulatory agencies quickly.

Furthermore, and most importantly, the global financial crisis showed that the backing of a powerful central bank, with a large balance sheet, was a crucial factor in financial stability. That simple point had been lost during a long period when banks did not fail; 129 years separated the collapse of the Bank of Glasgow in 1878 and the run on Northern Rock in the autumn of 2007. Investors had paid little attention to the link between the scale of a global bank and of its potential lender of last resort. The failure of two large Icelandic banks in 2008, each of which had a balance sheet more than twelve times Icelandic GDP, showed that in bank rescues size does indeed matter. The Icelandic central bank and government were too small to rescue their banks, most of whose activities were in the London market. As Mervyn King, when Governor of the Bank of England, pointed out, big banks are 'global in life but national in death'.[3] The support obligation for a bank falls back on the 'home' central bank, not the host regulators in the countries where much of the business is done. The rescue of RBS itself cost £45 billion in 2008, a sum which would almost certainly have been beyond the resources of the Scottish Reserve Bank, and a Scottish government.

The two large Scottish-registered banks, Halifax Bank of Scotland and the Royal Bank of Scotland, were both enormous in comparison to the Scottish economy. The disparity was not quite on an Icelandic scale, but big enough to be a market problem. RBS was obliged to say, during the campaign, that in the event of a Yes vote it would seek to redomicile in London. Lloyds (by that time the owner of Halifax Bank of Scotland), Clydesdale Bank, TSB and Tesco Bank said the same. The implications for jobs in Scotland might not have been great in the short term, but the psychological impact would have been considerable,

and over time there would have been economic consequences beyond the moving of a collection of brass plates.
Edinburgh's position as an international financial centre
would have been at risk.

The fiscal arguments were especially contentious.
Scottish Nationalists have long argued that Scotland is
entitled to a larger share of North Sea oil revenues than a
simple allocation based on population or GDP would suggest. A Scottish Fiscal Commission paper published in July
2013 argued by analogy with the experience of Norway
that Scotland would use oil revenues to establish a fund on
the lines of Norges Bank which would sustain Scotland's
fiscal position in the long term.[4] The Treasury, by contrast,
argued that a newly independent Scotland's fiscal deficit
would have been some 6.5% of GDP in 2016–17, based
on the current oil price, more than three times as high as
the overall UK deficit, and that were Scotland to become
independent at that time it would have the largest deficit
of any advanced economy. Furthermore, unhelpful demographic trends – the number of Scottish pensioners is rising
more rapidly than the average for the UK – looked likely,
according to the Treasury, to put pressure on social spending and widen the projected deficit. But, as MacPherson
said, 'it was the currency issue which ended up having the
greatest resonance'.[5]

The future currency arrangements for an independent
Scotland had long been one of the most awkward policy
questions for the SNP. For a time their policy was to join
Economic and Monetary Union. That view survived up
to the point at which EMU actually existed. Had the UK
decided to join, Scotland could have separated from the
rest of the UK without changing its currency. While it
would have needed its own central bank in due course, as
a member of the Eurosystem, the European Central Bank
would have been its monetary authority and, after the
creation of the Banking Union in 2014, its banking regulator also, which would have partly addressed the financial
services question described above. The UK Treasury's

conclusion that it was not in the country's economic interests to join EMU, published in June 2003, was seen as a defeat for Prime Minister Tony Blair, and indeed it was, but it also forced the SNP to rethink its currency strategy.

The Scottish government's Fiscal Commission considered four options: the continued use of sterling, the creation of a Scottish currency, either pegged to sterling or floating, and membership of the Euro.[6] In 2013 the Scottish government published *Scotland's Future*, which argued that retention of sterling, with shared ownership of the Bank of England, was in the best interests both of Scotland and the UK as a whole. There would, the publication acknowledged, need to be complex shared arrangements for the oversight of financial stability, and a Scottish Monetary Institute 'working alongside the equivalent UK authority on a consistent and harmonised basis'.[7]

In a disarmingly frank way, the publication revealed a number of the devilish details which would need to be worked through. While it asserted that the arrangements were in the interests of both future countries, it was not clear why the rest of the UK (dubbed 'RUK' in Scotland) should be attracted to such a complex structure, which would distort the processes of monetary policy, financial stability oversight and financial regulation, for no very clear benefit.

The reaction to these proposals in London was not positive. Three former Chancellors weighed in. John Major said it would require the UK to underwrite Scottish debt. Brown said it would create a 'colonial relationship' between Scotland and Westminster. Darling noted that voters in the rest of the UK might well choose not to be in a currency union with Scotland. And developments in Europe were again not helpful to the SNP. The Eurozone crisis, and especially the travails of the Southern European countries, had demonstrated the problems of a currency union without a common fiscal backstop. The euro survived, but only by means of huge interventions by the ECB, the European Commission and the IMF. The SNP appeared to be proposing a home-grown version of the euro arrangements which had so recently been shown to be deficient.

The question came to a head in early 2014. The Governor of the Bank of England, Mark Carney, in what was then an unusual intervention in a political debate, but which turned out to be the first of many such interventions on his part, issued a dark warning about the SNP's idea, warning that policymakers 'would need to consider carefully what the economics of currency unions suggest are the necessary foundations for a durable union, particularly given the clear risks if these foundations are not in place'.[8] A currency union implies ceding sovereignty over tax and spending decisions, which was not envisaged in the plan outlined in *Scotland's Future*.

The stakes were raised further two weeks later. In a speech in Glasgow on 13 February 2014, Osborne delivered a Valentine's Eve message to Alex Salmond. He argued that 'the pound isn't an asset to be divided up between the two countries after break-up as if it were a CD collection'. (The Spotify generation, who voted Yes in large numbers, must have been mystified by this antediluvian reference.) 'The value of the pound', he underlined, 'lies in the entire monetary system underpinning it . . . It is a system that is supported by political union, banking union and automatic transfers of public spending across the United Kingdom. A vote to leave the UK is a vote to leave these unions and those transfers and those monetary arrangements.' His conclusion was that 'there's no legal reason why the rest of the UK would need to share its currency with Scotland', so that 'if Scotland walks away from the UK, it walks away from the UK pound'.[9]

'He would say that, wouldn't he?', was the political response in Scotland. Those who were disposed to be suspicious of statements from the British government may not have been swayed by the hard line taken by Osborne. But there was a twist. It was not just Osborne the Conservative politician issuing this warning; it was the view of the official Treasury. He referred to the 'rigorous and objective analysis the Treasury had done' and went on: 'Alongside this analysis I am also taking the exceptional step of publishing the internal advice I have received from the Permanent Secretary to the Treasury, Sir Nicholas MacPherson.'

Osborne was not the only person in Whitehall who considered the publication of officials' advice to be an exceptional step. Others used different language. One senior official who was in the Treasury at the time described it as 'the most extreme politicization in the Treasury's history'.[10] Jeremy Heywood, then the Cabinet Secretary, tried to prevent publication, but his advice was ignored by the Treasury. One reason for Heywood's concern was that had the vote been lost, he planned to ask MacPherson to lead for the UK on the departure negotiations – the role played by Michel Barnier in the Brexit negotiations. For his personal views on the currency question to be in the public domain would have made that an awkward choice.

MacPherson and Osborne are well aware of the risks they ran. Both are unrepentant. MacPherson thought Westminster did not take the threat posed by the referendum seriously enough, and that it was right for the Treasury to take the lead as it did. The Cabinet Office had opted out. 'I published that advice because I regarded it as my duty. The British state's position was being impugned. Demonstrating that the political and official state were completely aligned would further strengthen the credibility of the Government's position.'[11] He acknowledged that some 'argued that the Treasury was bluffing' (a charge that would be levelled at the institution again before the EU referendum in 2016, with more force), but was 'absolutely certain that the UK would not have entered into a formal currency union with Scotland had the latter voted for independence'.

Osborne had taken the same view. The currency was the key issue in his mind. He was convinced that for Scotland to use the pound after independence was not a viable option, but the SNP continued to claim they would be allowed to do so. 'So I had to find a way to prove that I would not allow it. I made a series of speeches in Scotland, but eventually came up with the idea of publishing the Treasury advice.'[12] Did that go too far? 'Maybe, but the UK government ultimately exists to keep the UK together. The survival of the British state was a paramount objective. So it was justifiable to do whatever it took to keep the state intact. The Chancellor is one of a very few people responsible for the integrity of the state. The Governor of the Bank of England is another. So it was right for us to speak as we did.'

Was the intervention successful? Did the currency issue influence votes decisively?

Alistair Darling, who subsequently led the Better Together campaign in Scotland, is in no doubt that it did: 'It was the economics what won it. The Treasury's work on the currency, the Institute of Fiscal Studies analysis of public spending and Mark Carney's interventions all influenced swing voters, especially younger women, who were particularly concerned about the impact of independence on their finances. There were groups of voters who were instinctively nationalists but were worried about the risks. The economic arguments influenced them strongly.'[13] That view is borne out by post-referendum polling. Lord Ashcroft Polls carried out a large-scale survey shortly after the vote, asking Yes and No voters which issues most influenced them. Of No voters, 57% named the pound as one of the two or three reasons for their vote. That was, by a distance, the most mentioned concern, above the NHS at 36%.[14]

Brown takes a different view. He believes the No campaign was struggling, and risked defeat, until a positive vision of a new devolution settlement, which he promoted, was put to the electorate – what came to be known as 'the Vow'. Two weeks before the vote, one poll showed a lead for the Yes campaign. He promoted a new vision which would lead to 'faster, fairer, safer and better change' than the nationalists could offer. In his view it was the Vow, rather than the economics, 'what won it'. 'The Vow worked in the context of a more patriotic case put squarely to the public. While economic arguments mattered, the Scottish people could not bear to see themselves as unpatriotic.'[15] Brown acknowledges that 'the documentation was good and the economic analysis was excellent, but they overdid it. The framing given by George Osborne alienated people. The referendum was about national identity and pride in Scotland. People feel more Scottish than British now, and aggressive economic arguments just reinforce them in their identity.'[16] That may be so, but the Ashcroft Poll asked a prompted question to identify the most important reason for the No vote: 27 % identified with the notion of 'a strong attachment to the UK and its shared history, culture and traditions', 25% with the idea that 'a NO vote would still mean extra powers for the Scottish Parliament together with the security of remaining part of the UK, giving the best of both worlds' (roughly the proposition behind the Vow), while 47% endorsed the proposition that 'the risks of becoming independent looked too great when it came to things like the currency, EU membership, the economy, jobs and prices'.[17]

So the evidence seems to suggest that, in Osborne's demotic phrase, 'the Treasury played a blinder'. Could it repeat the trick in a second Scottish referendum, to which the SNP government elected in May 2021 is committed? The Johnson government insists that the 2014 referendum was a once-in-a-generation vote which cannot be repeated for decades. But it may be difficult to refuse demands for a second vote indefinitely. Brown believes there will eventually be a second vote and that the currency issue will not be decisive when it happens. Osborne is also not so sure that the same tactic would work a second time, for three reasons. "First, it is hard to play the same card again. Second, the SNP will see it coming and will try to avoid the currency issue featuring in the campaign, and, third, after the EU referendum and the Brexit negotiations, the border issues will be crucial, and may come to dominate other arguments.'[18] It would also be heavily ironic were a government led by Brexit supporters to lead with an argument based on economic logic, against an SNP evoking identity politics, and the need for Scots to take back control of their own affairs.

The experience of 2014, when the Treasury and the Bank of England both successfully entered the political arena, had consequences which went beyond the immediate vote. Both institutions were emboldened by that success to intervene in the EU referendum just two years later. The consequences were rather different.

6

Europe: The Ins and Outs

'Ask almost any Whitehall official which government department is the most Eurosceptic, and they would say it was the Treasury', wrote Chris Giles, the economics editor of the *Financial Times*, in 2016.[1] In his history of the UK in Europe, *Britain Alone*, Philip Stephens, discussing the run-up to Black Wednesday in 1992, writes: 'Senior Treasury and Bank of England officials were equally reluctant to engage with their continental counterparts. The idea of building strong personal ties with the Europeans defied the Treasury's 'we-know-best' instincts. It saw itself as a cut above mere continentals.'[2] When I joined the Treasury in 1976, on secondment from the Foreign Office, I had just returned from a posting in Paris, where I was the only member of the Embassy staff to vote 'No' in the 1975 referendum on EEC membership. I found the Treasury was a home from home. There was none of the Diplomatic Service's romantic attachment to ever closer union.

Yet by the time of the 2016 referendum the Treasury had become Public Enemy No. 1 of the Vote Leave campaign. Jacob Rees-Mogg accused it of behaving 'disgracefully' during the campaign: it 'came out with nonsense' and damaged its reputation.[3] As Peter Oborne put it in *The*

Spectator: 'George Osborne has now converted the Treasury into a partisan tool to sell the referendum.'[4] How did this transformation come about? Surely one politician could not achieve it in a few months? Did the Treasury as an institution change its mind, or, as one senior official puts it, was the Treasury's view on Europe 'totally consistent throughout, it was just that the nature of the question changed'?[5]

Black Wednesday in 1992, when sterling dropped out of the Exchange Rate Mechanism, was an enormous policy failure, for which the Treasury could not evade responsibility. The Treasury had moved to what might roughly be called a monetarist approach in the late 1970s, but found it increasingly difficult to identify a secure policy anchor during the 1980s. Various monetary targets, for the growth of broad money £M3, or PSL2 (private sector liquidity), were tried, but Goodhart's law, that when a measure becomes a target it ceases to be a good measure, was regularly proved valid. That led the Treasury to be attracted to an exchange rate link. '*The Joys of Floating*', Terry Burns said at the time, 'is a short book.'[6] So in spite of the poor record of sterling stability in the past, and the experience of painful devaluations, the Treasury welcomed John Major's decision to join the ERM in 1990.

But the humiliation of being ejected in 1992, without an alternative policy waiting in the wings, increased the Treasury's enthusiasm for handing anti-inflation policy to the Bank of England. John Major rejected the idea, but it was achieved when Gordon Brown arrived in 1997. The 1992 debacle left the Treasury suspicious of foreign entanglements, and extremely reluctant to put themselves again at the mercy of the Bundesbank. Alan Budd, the Treasury official most closely involved in the talks to persuade the Bundesbank to reduce rates and therefore the pressure on sterling, invoked a German analogy: 'I felt as if I knew what it's like to be a German general at the end of the war, with defeat after defeat and people coming into the room with more bad news.'[7]

The euro: failing the tests

Central bank independence was one of the preconditions of joining the euro, and some interpreted the 1997 change in that context. The policy of the incoming Labour administration on EMU was less than crystal clear, reflecting different views in the party leadership. The manifesto began uncontroversially by saying that 'any decision about Britain joining the single currency must be determined by a hard-headed assessment of Britain's economic interests'. It noted that there were 'formidable obstacles' in the way of membership and that there must be 'genuine convergence ... without any fudging of the rules'.[8] Since the UK met few of the criteria at the time, the drift seemed clear. But it went on to say that "to exclude British membership of EMU forever would be to destroy any influence we have over a process which will affect us whether we are in or out. We must therefore play a full part in the debate to influence it in Britain's interests.' The punchline was that we would only join if the people approved in a referendum. At the time, euro membership attracted about 20% support in opinion polls, which made that prospect remote.

But, although the manifesto was lukewarm, there were those in the party, like the Foreign Secretary Robin Cook, who saw euro membership as 'inevitable' for the UK, if we were to remain at the heart of Europe. And the Prime Minister himself consistently refused to rule out membership: 'Even if [taking Britain into the Euro] is unpopular, I will recommend it if it is the right thing to do.'[9]

The Treasury under Brown was clearly in the driving seat in developing the policy. When Labour was elected, the UK was taking part in the preparations for the single currency at the European Monetary Institute in Frankfurt. I sometimes deputized for Eddie George at those meetings; he was conspicuously unenthusiastic about the idea, as indeed were a number of other European Central Bank

Governors at the time. In spite of that, the Bank of England played a constructive part in the practical work. Indeed, the working group which developed the plans and designs for the euro notes was chaired by the head of the Bank's printing works. While we had an opt-out, secured by John Major at the Maastricht negotiations in 1992, we were still in theory eligible to ask to take part in the first wave, originally due to take place in 1997, but postponed until 1999. A series of papers were published by the Bank covering all the practical changes that would be needed for a successful transition. Those papers were so thorough and authoritative that they were widely consulted elsewhere in Europe.

In October 1997 Brown confirmed that Britain was not ready to join in the first wave, but that 'if, in the end, a single currency is successful, and the economic case is clear and unambiguous, then the Government believes Britain should be part of it.'[10] The rejection of first-wave membership was not a surprise. Brown's assessment was made against the background of the five tests which he had set out in February 1997, and which formed the basis of the Treasury's analysis in 1997, and again – more decisively – in 2003.

It has often been asserted that the tests were devised in the back of a taxi in New York, by Ed Balls. That is not quite true, but not far off. They had been devised as the theme of a speech Brown was about to make in New York. But in a taxi on the way to the venue Balls persuaded Brown to release them to the British press, to forestall what they feared might be a more positive policy formulation from Blair. So a call was made to Robert Peston, then at the *Financial Times*, who obligingly 'bigged up' the story. The five tests dominated debate on the euro for the next six years and produced the outcome that Brown wanted. They ensured that the eventual decision would be 'made on the basis of the national economic interest, and one that would be controlled by the Treasury'. But for Balls, they meant more. 'I also knew they would help me in my task to persuade Gordon Brown that joining the single currency was a bad idea, and should not become the litmus test of whether he was sufficiently modernising, progressive and pro-European.'[11] Balls had been firmly against the idea since the ERM debacle, and published a Fabian pamphlet titled *Euro-Monetarism: Why Britain Was Ensnared and How It Should Escape.*[12]

Although Brown had ruled out joining in the first wave, within government the debate rumbled on. Peter Mandelson remained in favour of membership, as did other influential ministers such as David Simon, the former Chairman of BP. Blair himself seemed uncertain of his own mind. Jeremy Heywood recalled being told by Jonathan Powell (Downing Street Chief of Staff) that the Prime Minister was less positive about joining the euro than was his Chancellor.[13] But after the five tests announcement, the Treasury did little work on the subject, and Balls told Heywood that 'the Treasury has no intention of applying the tests any time soon'. To force the pace, Blair told the Commons in February 2001 that a decision would be taken within two years. His plan was to hold a referendum in June 2003 if the five-test assessment produced a positive answer.

The work was politically led by Balls himself and, on the official side, initially by Gus O'Donnell as Managing Director of Macroeconomic Policy and International Finance. When O'Donnell became Permanent Secretary in 2002, Dave Ramsden replaced him. It was a massive exercise. Eventually there were eighteen 'preliminary' documents plus the 'assessment' itself. Given the declared views on the euro of the principal authors, the outcome may seem to have been a foregone conclusion, but the work was certainly thorough, more so than research produced by the finance or economy ministries of any country which joined.

The five tests were, arguably, four separate assessments plus an overarching summary judgement. The first was whether the business cycles and economic structures of the UK and the core continental economies were sufficiently compatible that the UK could live permanently with Eurozone interest rates. The second asked whether there was enough flexibility to cope with potentially different business cycles. The third assessed whether joining EMU would promote inward investment, while the fourth considered the impact on the competitive position of the UK's financial services industry, particularly the wholesale markets in the City. The final portmanteau test was: 'Will joining EMU promote higher growth, stability and a lasting increase in jobs?[14]

In retrospect, a sixth test might have been relevant: would a decision not to join the euro put the UK at the margins of the EU, reduce its influence on other policy areas, and strengthen the position of those arguing for withdrawal from the Union itself, and from the single market, which could seriously damage the UK's economy? At the time, withdrawal from the single market seemed so unlikely that the possibility was not considered.

The conclusions of the work were not favourable to a decision to join. Just one of the five tests was unambiguously met – the financial services test, where entry into EMU was deemed to provide greater potential for firms and markets in the UK to capture the benefits of the further EU integration that was expected to follow the introduction of the single currency. Ironically, given the negative tone of the rest of the assessment, it can be seen that London continued to capture a large and growing share of mobile EU financial business from outside the euro area, at least until the 2016 referendum. It seems unlikely that the City would have had even greater success within the Eurozone. Participation in the single financial market was crucial, however. The inward investment test also produced a broadly positive conclusion, but it was hedged around. It was argued that more overseas investment would be attracted, 'if sustainable convergence is achieved'.

The conclusions on the other three tests were negative. The convergence test was 'not met', because 'there remain structural differences with the euro area, such as in the housing market'.[15] The detailed papers argued that house prices in the UK had been more volatile than in the core continental economies, and that consumption was more sensitive to changes in house prices. Interest rates set for the Eurozone as a whole might be inappropriate for the UK housing market in one of its regular bouts of exuberance. One of the detailed papers, *Modelling Shocks and Adjustments in EMU*, explored the risks. As Ramsden said later: 'This is the paper that everyone who did join the Euro should have read. When they had the Euro crisis, it played out, as in Ireland: cheap credit, inflation, housing boom. We mapped it out and said it would happen to un-converging countries.'[16]

The result of the flexibility test was also a fail, even though the Treasury believed that UK labour market flexibility had improved markedly since 1997. The key assumption was that inflation volatility 'is very likely to increase inside EMU', and that the rest of the EU needed to make much more progress on flexibility. In the interim, 'we cannot be confident that UK flexibility, while improved, is sufficient'.[17]

These two conclusions drove the final assessment on the fifth, essentially summative test. In spite of the progress made over the intervening five years, the verdict remained the same as in 1997: 'A clear and unambiguous case for UK membership of EMU has not at the present time been made and a decision to join now would not be in the national economic interest.'[18]

Ramsden's characterization of the process was that it was 'a classic technocratic civil service exercise', putting both sides of the argument so that policymakers could decide. That is not the way it appeared to those in the Prime Minister's entourage, or the Cabinet, who thought the political argument needed to be given greater weight. And Ramsden himself acknowledges that the euro decision was 'for some people the high point, and for others the nadir of Treasury control'.[19] Heywood's account recalls the extraordinary secrecy under which the work was conducted. The Prime Minister was refused access to the working papers, and when the work was finally presented to Number 10 staff they were given a few hours to read almost 2,000 pages of analysis, and told that the conclusions, and indeed the drafting, were simply not up for discussion. The Cabinet was given even less time. Heywood and Stephen Wall, the Prime Minister's Foreign Office Private Secretary, and the official keenest to keep open the option of joining, negotiated minor changes which suggested that there had been more movement towards convergence since the 1997 assessment, and which might allow a different conclusion to emerge in the future. But the option was in practice closed down for the Parliament, and effectively for the Blair premiership, though as a face-saving gesture he did get the Treasury to agree another review with the 2004 Budget. That review did not take place.

By this time there was little external pressure to join. Business sentiment in favour, which had been quite significant during the 1990s, had softened. As Director General of the Confederation of British Industry (CBI) in the 1990s, after the ERM failure, I reflected in my speeches and lobbying the support of a good number of large companies for entering the single currency. (I had by then grown out of my youthful enthusiasm for splendid isolation.) Much of that support was rooted in the view that the British government had shown itself not to be competent to run an effective independent monetary policy, following the rise in inflation to double figures at the end of the 1980s and the collapse of ERM membership. Bank of England independence, which delivered effective compliance with the inflation target, created the price stability craved by businesses. So the 1997 change, which some had interpreted as a preparatory step towards euro membership, in effect proved to be an alternative to it, which had always been Balls's intention.

Was this a Treasury win over the Prime Minister, and the Cabinet? It seemed so at the time, but Robert Peston, a commentator and at times almost a participant in the story, concludes differently:

> I'm persuaded that Blair was not in the end unhappy about the outcome, in the sense that a referendum on the euro would have been utterly unwinnable in the subsequent years, when economic conditions were expected to be considerably less benign than in the UK. [Popular support for UK membership peaked at 33% in 2003, according to the opinion polls.] That said, he remains livid to this day at what he saw as a blatant affront to his stature and authority by Brown and – even more exasperating for the Prime Minister – also by Balls.[20]

Balls himself acknowledges that 'it was one of the more heavy-handed and un-collegiate things that I was ever involved in, but it was a difficult time and we weren't in the mood to compromise'.[21]

The euro decision set the UK aside from the core of the EU, with long-term consequences. The Treasury's approach was rational, but arguably a short-term analysis. It is true that other countries did not perform a similar exercise, but in the other initial joiners the political imperative to be at the heart of Europe dominated the arguments on asymmetric shocks and optimal currency areas. So, did the Treasury's approach confirm the UK as a semi-detached member of the EU, and lead inexorably to the 2016 vote to leave? O'Donnell rejects that narrative: 'The blame attaches to those who thought the way to construct Europe was through a single currency, rather than making the difficult decisions on fiscal policy. They created a flawed system. But in any case, our decision not to join did not necessarily lead to the exit. It would have been perfectly possible to maintain a stable group of countries which co-existed with the Eurozone.'[22]

Semi-detachment

Another decision, made around the same time, also had a major impact on public sentiment a decade later, possibly an even greater one. When the EU expanded to the East in 2004, existing member states were able to apply temporary restrictions on immigration from the expansion countries. The UK and Sweden alone chose not to do so. The government was a principled supporter of free movement, and the Treasury favoured it on economic grounds. The Home Office estimated that about 50,000 migrants would come to the UK from Poland and elsewhere. The eventual total was well over a million. The impact on growth was positive, but there was pressure on public services in areas which attracted large numbers of new arrivals,[23] and – though the economic backing for the argument was thin to non-existent – allowed UKIP, and the Brexit branch of the Conservative Party, to claim that British workers were losing jobs and income as a result. Hammond, reflecting in 2020 on how the UK came to a hard Brexit, concluded: 'If you were to take a single decision in this whole saga that has led to where we are now, it would be Tony Blair's decision not to impose transitional controls in 2004.'[24]

That problem was one for the future, and most of the Treasury's day-to-day preoccupations were not much affected by the EU. With a domestic anti-inflation policy and a floating pound, the Commission's impact on its work was normally modest. The EC did produce assessments of the UK's fiscal position from time to time, but, with no commitment to joining the Stability and Growth Pact, they were otiose. Brown, as Philip Stephens puts it, 'understood the logic of British membership of the EU, but would never be comfortable with the consensus politics at the heart of EU policy-making ... [He] framed his regular trips to Brussels for meetings of finance ministers as win-or-lose, claiming supposed victories for British policy and belittling the initiatives of European colleagues.'[25]

From time to time, however, the EC strayed into taxation policy. Commission proposals for a withholding
tax on savings were seen as a serious threat to the City,
and the government expended significant political capital
before an agreement on information sharing was reached
in early 2000. On tax, as one senior official put it 'there is
an institutional bias towards conflict. The Treasury hates
discussing tax with anyone, not even the Prime Minister,
and certainly not the Commission.'[26] Financial regulation
could also be a source of tension. Some elements of the
Financial Services Action Plan, completing the single financial market, cut across domestic regulation. But there were
also areas where the Treasury found Europe a useful ally
against domestic petitioners. The structure (rather than the
level) of VAT was one such. 'At times it has been helpful
to hide behind Europe on VAT, which allows the Treasury
to resist special pleading from interest groups who want
a reduced rate for favoured goods and services.' Another
was the state aid regime, which imposed a tight constraint
on ministers who wished to splint up lame ducks. The
Treasury's longstanding bias towards creative destruction,
and resistance to anything which smacks of an industrial
strategy and picking winners, found a powerful ally in
Brussels. Perhaps most importantly, the Treasury is an
instinctive supporter of free trade and believed the single
market increased competitive intensity and therefore productivity growth.

During Alistair Darling's time as Chancellor, European
policy did not loom large. The EU was not central to the
resolution of the GFC, where the G20 and its emanations
were the critical fora for decisions. There was one sizeable
impact, however. The competition commissioner, Neelie
Kroes, imposed very tough conditions before approving
the bailouts of RBS and Lloyds. In the case of RBS, they
proved hugely more expensive than expected. The bank
was obliged to dispose quickly of Direct Line insurance,
Sempra (its commodities business) and Worldpay, all at
bargain prices and all of which subsequently increased

significantly in value as the economy and the financial system recovered. It was also obliged to dispose of five percentage points of market share in small and medium-sized enterprise (SME) lending. At the time, the net cost of that disposal was estimated to be zero. The eventual cost was around £3.2 billion.[27] So the financial cost to the Treasury as shareholder was enormous, certainly over £10 billion including the impact of the other disposals, but the scale only emerged over time.

When the euro crisis erupted in 2010, the Treasury's instinct was to stay out of it as far as possible. There was some financial help for Ireland, for domestic political reasons, but the government chose not to participate in decisions on the Eurozone as a whole, and caused some resentment by its running commentary on the structural problems it saw. There was a natural tendency to see the crisis as justification of the arguments the Treasury had made in its eighteen papers, but 'we told you so' is never a well-received message. Cameron found the crisis difficult, as he had promised Eurosceptics in his party that he would not agree to any further transfer of powers to the EU centre without a referendum, and the crisis clearly required more central powers. However, Liberal Democrat opposition to the idea of a referendum allowed him to argue that whether or not the changes triggered his undertaking, the question was moot while he did not have a Conservative majority in Parliament.

The EU referendum: Project Fear

In spite of occasional irritants, the EU remained, for the most part, at the margins of Treasury concerns until 2013, when Cameron committed to a referendum on UK membership. Osborne was opposed to the commitment, as was Kenneth Clarke, but William Hague at the Foreign Office was in favour. Cameron had been in the Treasury as a special adviser when sterling fell out of the ERM, and had watched John Major suffer at the hands of the Eurosceptic 'bastards'. He saw a referendum as an attempt to stop the Conservative Party 'banging on' about Europe, which was not high on the list of voters' concerns. As leader of the opposition, he promised a referendum on the Lisbon Treaty, but that fox was shot when Brown's government ratified it before the 2010 election. Under the Coalition arrangements, Cameron was unable to fulfil his referendum commitment. The Liberal Democrats were opposed. But the result of the 2015 election, which delivered the Conservatives a small overall majority, removed any excuse for delay, and the opponents of membership on the backbenches were not slow to demand a timetable for the vote. That election victory proved pyrrhic for Cameron himself, and for his Chancellor.

The preliminary step was a promised renegotiation of the terms of British membership. The detail of what was achieved played little or no part in the referendum campaign, as the efforts to secure concessions on immigration and free movement were largely unsuccessful. That was not a central Treasury concern. The department's interests centred on seeking assurances that non-members of the Eurozone would not be disadvantaged by further moves towards integration. That was thought to be important for the City, and some assurances were received which, in another future, might have had some value. There was to be an 'emergency brake' on financial regulation emerging in the Eurozone which might have an impact on non-members, for example.

Armed with this modest package of reforms, Cameron launched the referendum campaign on 20 February 2016 by announcing that the vote would take place on 23 June. One official recalls that, 'as soon as the government began to talk seriously about a referendum, the official Treasury became seriously concerned. Nick MacPherson wandered around asking whether it would be so bad if we left, but he didn't really mean it.'[28] George Osborne, though he had internally opposed the referendum commitment, and argued strenuously against it with the Prime Minister, eventually toed the government's line and –recognizing that the result could easily be close – determined to use the Treasury to support the Remain campaign as far as it was possible to do so. The success of the economic arguments, and particularly the role played by the official Treasury in the Scottish campaign, offered a promising example to follow.

Osborne commissioned an assessment of the economic consequences of the long-term impact of remaining a member of the EU compared to the alternatives. The analysis used what they described as 'a widely adopted gravity modelling approach, which distinguishes the specific effect of EU membership and the alternatives from all the other influences that determine trade and foreign direct investment. The consequences for productivity and Gross Domestic Product are then estimated.'[29]

The paper analysed the consequences of three potential alternatives to continued membership:

- membership of the European Economic Area (EEA), like Norway
- a negotiated bilateral agreement such as that between the EU and Canada
- World Trade Organisation (WTO) membership only, without a specific UK–EU agreement.

The conclusion was that, in each case, 'the UK would be permanently poorer if it left the EU'. That sentence was printed in bold type just in case the casual reader missed it. The impact was presented as the annual GDP loss per household after fifteen years, an unusually demotic device for a Treasury paper. The numbers were stark, ranging from an annual loss of £2,600 under the EEA scenario to £4,300 for a bilateral agreement (the eventual outcome) and £5,200 under the WTO option. There was also a calculation of lost tax receipts, which would fall by £20 billion, £36 billion and £45 billion a year, respectively. It was helpfully pointed out that £36 billion is more than a third of the NHS budget and the equivalent of 8p on the basic rate of income tax.

Furthermore, it was argued, more tendentiously, that the new settlement negotiated by Cameron included substantial economic reform proposals for the EU as a whole, which could increase UK GDP by a further 4%, or another £2,800 for every household in the country. Without the UK in the EU those reforms might not happen, so the cost of exit should be seen as correspondingly greater.

That latter argument might be thought to be over-egging an otherwise well-mixed pudding. The Treasury included a range of external forecasts, most of which showed an impact on GDP over three to five years ranging from –3% to –8%, and some of which assumed a stronger relationship between trade flows and national income than applies in the Treasury model, predicting a bigger drop in GDP, up to 10% in some cases. Widely cited work by Nicholas Crafts estimated the positive impact of EU membership on UK GDP as being around 10%.[30] The Bank of England took a similar view.

The economics profession would not have lived up to its disputatious reputation had there been no dissenting voices. Among them, Patrick Minford, long a Brexit supporter, painted a different picture.[31] Researchers at the Centre for Business Research at Cambridge have subsequently argued that all the estimates of the economic cost of Brexit are overstated, that the positive impact of EU membership is not well established and that the gravity modelling approach produces exaggerated results.[32] It may eventually be possible to determine how close the Treasury forecasts were to the outturn, though there are many other factors to consider, and the Covid-19 pandemic will make the data hard to interpret. But the OBR still assumes a reduction in UK productivity from leaving the EU of 4%.

The April 2016 long-term assessment was not the Treasury's last word on the subject during the referendum campaign. In his introduction to the long-term study, Osborne promised that a future government publication would assess the short-term economic impact. That promise was fulfilled in May with the release of a second piece of Treasury analysis, undertaken by a team under Dave Ramsden, and endorsed by Charlie Bean, who had been Deputy Governor of the Bank of England for monetary policy from 2003 to 2013.[33] The paper was not discussed extensively with officials, as the May document had been. The conclusions of the second paper were even more dramatic, perhaps even melodramatic. 'A vote to leave would represent an immediate and profound shock to our economy', Osborne intoned. The economy would move swiftly into recession, with an increase in unemployment of around 500,000. GDP would be 3.6% smaller, inflation would rise, partly because of an immediate devaluation of sterling, house prices would be hit and public borrowing would rise. Some in the Treasury were suspicious of it, and thought the numbers had been manipulated. For example, the forecast conveniently included two consecutive quarters of −0.1% growth, followed by a recovery, allowing Osborne to make the recession claim.

On the back of this analysis Osborne promised an emergency budget, if the vote was to leave, to tackle what he described as a £30 billion 'black hole'. That might include a rise in income and inheritance taxes, and a cut to the NHS budget.[34] The last point was clearly a response to the Leave campaign promise to divert £350 million a week of reduced spending on the EU budget to the health service. The budget was characterized by one official as 'an Osborne special. He did the work on his own: the official Treasury was not involved.'[35] These late interventions in the debate were attacked by the Leave campaign. Boris Johnson referred to 'the agents of Project Fear' who were trying to spook the electorate. In fact, the term was first used by Alex Salmond in a Scottish referendum debate with Alistair Darling, but it attached itself more durably to the EU campaign.

The Treasury had once been again drawn deeply into partisan territory, and this time the warnings did not work, so what may have been a sin looks as if it was also a mistake. Why did the Treasury get drawn so far into the controversy? Did it go further than its constitutional position allows? Why did the arguments not resonate more with the electorate? And has the episode damaged the institution in the longer term?

Osborne says that 'The Treasury's role in the EU referendum was driven by three things: (1) The Scottish precedent, which suggested that it was important to begin with careful presentation of the economic case, and then to overlay the political arguments. (2) The five tests precedent. Ramsden led the work on both exercises. (3) At the 2015 general election I had been successful in arguing that Labour's plans would be too costly. The electorate responded well. All that suggested that an economic line of attack might work well again. So I asked the Treasury to get to work immediately after the 2015 election. The medium term forecast they produced in early 2016 still looks spot on, in its estimates of the impact on growth and productivity. It identified all the big issues, including the border problems. It was an excellent piece of work.'[36]

Officials take a similar view on the long-term paper. MacPherson noted that 'it was good and has stood the test of time. There probably will be a Brexit hit to the economy of 3–4%.'[37] Another sympathizes with Osborne's predicament: 'He was opposed to the referendum and understood the risks better than others in government. He was never complacent about winning it. He almost sacrificed his career by resigning on principle, which was odd for a man who did not have very many principles.'[38] Balls, like Osborne himself, sees a clear link between the Scottish referendum work and the EU papers. 'In the Scottish referendum Osborne asked the Permanent Secretary for his view on the currency issue, which was then published. Once that Rubicon had been crossed, the referendum advice was bound to be seen also as the Treasury's institutional view, which was potentially damaging.'[39]

The second paper, and the emergency budget associated with it, divides opinion more sharply.

Osborne himself acknowledges that 'the short-term analysis of the immediate impact of the vote, published just before the vote, was not so good. It forecast an immediate recession and an immediate rise in unemployment, which didn't happen. It was accurate in forecasting a 15% sterling devaluation. It was unrealistic in that it assumed no monetary policy response from the Bank of England, because the Treasury does not seek to prejudge what the Bank will do, but that was in practice an unrealistic assumption.'[40]

Officials now, with the benefit of hindsight, are even more damning. The emergency budget is unanimously seen as a mistake. 'By the time that appeared we were in a panic', says one. 'The Chancellor had to say something, but had nothing to say on migration, which turned out to be the central issue. So what else could he talk about other than the impact on the economy and public spending? The fundamental problem is that there should never have been a referendum or, if the issue was to be put to the people, there should have been two votes, one on the principle and another on the deal that would follow departure.' A third is more critical of the Chancellor. 'Project Fear was a real disaster for the Treasury. And it was George Osborne's fault. The long-term impact study was good, but not the short-term threats published just before the vote. It was a mistake and was used by Osborne in a way that damaged the institution's credibility.' Another is a little more philosophical. 'The Treasury has been damaged, but mainly because it was on the losing side. Politicians were not prepared to make the positive case for Europe until it was too late. The late appearance of very positive economic views on membership was unlikely to compensate for years of criticism. It is fair to recall, too, that the Treasury was not on its own. The Bank of England also did too much in the campaign, for which it suffered. Mark Carney liked being on the public stage.'[41]

The external criticisms were severe, and some from past Chancellors hurt. Nigel Lawson, reincarnated as a fervent Brexit supporter, said: 'I am sorry that the Treasury officials and even economists who I have a high regard for from the past have been made to prostitute themselves in the cause of a political campaign.'[42] Boris Johnson said the Treasury's unemployment figures were 'a hoax'. Ian Duncan Smith said the Treasury was 'the worst thing we have in Britain'. It was obsessed by short-term thinking and should be broken up. When he left government, he 'breathed a sigh of relief that I never have to deal with those people again.'[43] In that particular case, the feeling was mutual.

It is not yet clear, and may not be for some time, whether the reputational damage suffered from this unhappy episode will have lasting consequences. It is encouraging that there has so far been no revival within government of plans to split the department, which have intermittently been considered in the past (see Chapter 9). But the association with Project Fear left the Treasury (and the Bank) in a weakened position when the Brexit negotiation process began. Osborne resigned, and was cast into outer political darkness by Prime Minister May.

Brexit and after

The period immediately after the vote was a time of high anxiety. Cameron had not allowed any contingency planning work to be done. He thought it would leak and be seen as a sign of weakness and uncertainty about the result. So as the markets reopened on 24 June the Treasury was extremely nervous. That nervousness was compounded by the disappearance of the Chancellor, who was absent without leave until some time on Monday, as the pound fell sharply. Fortunately, the Bank, though as hostile to

Brexit as the Treasury, had done some contingency planning of its own. Governor Carney took to the airwaves. In a book published in 2021, he recalled: 'As I said in a televised address to the nation on the morning after the Brexit referendum, we are well prepared for this.'[44] The Bank had built buffers, reserves and contingency plans across the financial system. Sterling continued to fall, but there was no wholesale panic, and markets cleared. As one official commented, through gritted teeth, 'it was Carney's finest hour'.

Philip Hammond took over. He had voted Remain but, like the new Prime Minister, was not seen as a strong Europhile. One official describes him, in terms of his European attitudes, as 'an odd case. He was appointed Foreign Secretary by Cameron in 2014 as one of his many failed attempts to appease the anti-Europeans in the party. Hammond had been listed as one of four cabinet members likely to vote Leave. He had some unusual views on the European institutions. He wanted to scrap the Parliament, and appoint non-Europeans to the ECB, to make it properly independent. But his views mellowed as Foreign Secretary and when he came to the Treasury he tried, throughout his time there, to get the government to focus on the downsides of a hard Brexit, ultimately without success. He wasn't influenced by the Treasury at all. That was his view on appointment, but officials thought it made sense and were happy to back him.'[45]

Hammond recognized that the Treasury 'was . . . severely bruised by . . . being painted as the villain of the referendum campaign'.[46] It thought that 'what they did was produce, objectively, the analysis they were asked to produce, based on the assumptions they were given. Perhaps naively they were rather shocked to find that they were then placed firmly in the spotlight, centre stage.' But Hammond and his officials were aligned in one important respect: 'There was never any doubt that the overwhelming majority of people in the Treasury saw a hard Brexit as an economic catastrophe, as did I – a potential catastrophe to be averted.' Hammond's clear objective from 2016 until his departure when Johnson became Prime Minister, was to deliver as 'soft' a Brexit as possible. He thought 'there was still an opportunity to curtail the economic damage and to deliver Brexit in a way that ... minimised the disadvantage.'

But, in sharp contrast to the previous two decades, the Treasury was not in a strong position to influence the government's policy. In the initial stages, the negotiations were led at the UK representation in Brussels, headed by Ivan Rogers, a Treasury man, albeit one the Foreign Office regarded as acceptable. As Permanent Secretary Simon McDonald put it, 'Ivan never struck me as the essence of the Treasury'.[47] In any event, he was quickly undermined by the Brexit advocates, as a Remain supporter who could not be trusted, and he resigned in January 2017. May set up a new Department for Exiting the European Union, in Hammond's view 'a ludicrous notion, absolutely ludicrous', to lead the talks. And neither Hammond himself, nor the official Treasury, were consulted on the key policy pronouncements which set the tone for the negotiations. Hammond was 'completely stunned' by the Party Conference speech in October 2016. 'I had no idea that she was going to describe Brexit in the hardest possible terms.' He left very soon after the speech for the IMF meetings in Washington, to find a serious run on the pound developing. 'I blame her closest advisers ... If the Treasury had seen the speech, the Treasury could have told them that this is liable to cause destabilisation in markets, because at that stage the markets had not priced in a hard Brexit. They had assumed the trade relationship would continue much as before.'[48]

The government did row back from the extreme position taken then, and Hammond credits David Davis with helping to achieve that. There was agreement, eventually, to a transition period. But the Treasury's impact on the changes was modest. The economic analysis of the impact of different forms of Brexit, produced at the end of 2017, was less influential than it might have been, because of the hangover from the emergency budget published shortly before the referendum. The Treasury 'very much didn't want to be in the forefront'. It was 'very insistent that there should be a cross-Whitehall economists group so that it couldn't be read as a Treasury exercise ... We always knew the analysis was correct, but we were very, very careful about how we presented it to the public and to Parliament, because we didn't want to go through the 2016 experience again.'[49]

After the fall of the May government in July 2019 and the election of Boris Johnson as party leader, Hammond left the Treasury. Sajid Javid, his replacement, had been placed fourth in the leadership election. He was another lukewarm Remainer in the referendum campaign. Whether Javid would, given a free hand, have supported his predecessor's 'soft Brexit' policy is moot. Under Johnson the focus shifted to preparing for a limited or no deal. 'On my watch, the Treasury is ready to play a full role in delivering Brexit', the *Sunday Telegraph* reported him saying.[50] Hammond had been reluctant to commit significant funds to 'no-deal' preparations, though some ferry contracts with boatless companies were signed. Javid, by contrast, began to spend serious money. The Treasury's influence on the outcome in the next six months, while Parliament failed to reach a consensus, and a further election was held, was small.

Surprisingly, after the election, Rishi Sunak, who had served as Chief Secretary under Hammond, replaced Javid, when the latter refused to have his special advisers managed by Dominic Cummings in Downing Street. Sunak had advocated leaving the EU on a number of grounds. He believed the country would be 'freer, fairer and more prosperous' outside the EU. 'Nationally, only five per cent of businesses export to the EU, yet all businesses are stifled by excessive EU red tape', he argued. 'Canada, South Korea and South Africa all trade freely with Europe without surrendering their independence ... As one of Europe's largest customers, I see no sensible reason why we could not achieve a similar agreement.' (That happy outcome has proved rather difficult to achieve.) Furthermore, 'we must have control of our borders and we can only do that outside of the EU . . . It can't be right that unelected officials in Brussels have more say over who can come into our country than you', he told his constituents in Richmond.[51]

Sunak's views could not have been further from the conclusions of the Treasury papers on the economic impact of leaving. But officials nonetheless respected his intellect and hard work, and he had won plaudits as Chief Secretary for efficient decision-making. Oddly, perhaps, for someone who had worked at Goldman Sachs and a hedge fund, he showed little concern for the implications of Brexit for the City of London. One senior official said that, in spite of his time at Goldman, 'he doesn't understand much about the European financial markets, and doesn't care much. His view is based on his time as a market guy at Goldman. He has a West Coast mind-set and sees markets as global, with Europe as a small thing, and EU regulation as an irritant at best. Of course Goldman Sachs can organize itself to cope with whatever the regulatory environment might be. They can move business and people wherever, and have no particular allegiance to London or the UK.'[52]

In practice, however, Sunak played little part in the final negotiations. That was partly because the Prime Minister retained tight control under David (later Lord) Frost, and partly because the Covid crisis consumed most of his time from March 2021 until the end of the year. But Sunak was also little interested in the trade talks. He is an enthusiast for Freeports, which was the main point in the negotiations which concerned him. That, again, ran counter to the long-held Treasury new that Freeports cost tax revenue and influence only the location of economic activity, not its quantum.[53] He expended no political capital on financial services and the potential for equivalence designations. That surprised and disappointed foreign firms in the City. Instead, he launched a series of reviews designed to explore deregulatory options for a future outside the EU. (See Chapter 7.)

Officials expected the economics of Brexit would become clear soon after the UK finally left, and that their forecasts would be proved correct. But Covid has confused the picture, perhaps permanently. It is hard to know how much of the recession of 2020–21 can be attributed to Brexit. The post-referendum devaluation delivered an inflation shock, estimated at 2.9%.[54] The longer-term impact of Europe on the Treasury and the UK economy depends on two things. Will relations with the EU stabilize with a return to the trade flows before Brexit, or will the new restrictions impose a severe penalty on trade? And, second, will the Treasury's own forecasts of the impact of leaving be borne out in practice? If there is some permanent trade disruption, which seems likely, and a hit to productivity and growth of 4% or more, as the OBR assumes, then that will greatly complicate the recovery from Covid and the government's ability to stabilize the structural deficit. In the meantime, officials acknowledge that the bruising experience of the referendum and its aftermath has damaged the Treasury, and won it some enemies with long memories.

7

Financial Regulation and the City of London

The 1997 reform of financial regulation, which created the Financial Services Authority from nine legacy regulators, was a side-dish to the main course of Bank of England independence, but the consequences were far-reaching, and controversial.

The origins of the regulatory change were rather different from those of the central bank independence plan. The latter was seen as a means of bringing the UK up to date with international best practice. The US Federal Reserve had made interest rate decisions since the Treasury–Fed accord of 1951, and the Bundesbank had been independent since its formation in 1957. Central bank independence was a precondition of Euro membership so it had spread across Europe in the 1990s. In the UK it brought the added benefit of reassuring the markets that New Labour would not preside over another bout of inflation. Loss of confidence among investors had been the rock on which earlier Labour governments had run aground. Blair and Brown were determined to avoid that fate.

The change in regulatory structure had quite a different justification. In opposition, Labour had reached the view that the self-regulatory system implemented by the

Conservatives in 1987 was no longer appropriate. The Securities and Investments Board (SIB) provided a thin statutory overlay, but was well short of the power and reach of the US Securities and Exchange Commission (SEC), which policed the markets aggressively. It was widely accepted, even in the City, that the 1987 system was overcomplex and balkanized. Reform of some kind was expected whoever won the 1997 election.

But what kind of reform? Darling, the Shadow Chief Secretary, rather than Brown, was in the lead. 'We considered the possibility of putting everything into the Bank, but thought that would be too risky and would create an institution which would be too powerful. Also, the Bank had had a series of failures in the previous decade.'[1] The most dramatic was the collapse of Barings Bank in February 1995 as a result of the activities of a rogue trader in Singapore. The subsequent report into the failure made unpleasant reading for the Bank of England.[2]

As a result, in the two years before the 1997 election, the Bank, under Eddie George as Governor and me as his Deputy, appointed in 1995, was engaged in a process of overhauling its banking supervision departments. (The key external adviser was John Tiner of Arthur Andersen, who later became CEO of the FSA.) The Bank recognized that the somewhat informal processes revealed by the Barings report had to be tightened. Supervisors had not followed up on warning signs about the bank's Singapore business. It also acknowledged that there were deficiencies in the oversight of markets as a whole, and of financial stability. To demonstrate a commitment to enhanced cooperation with other regulators, it was agreed that the Deputy Governor would join the SIB as a nonexecutive member, and that the two organizations would jointly produce a Financial Stability Review (FSR), whose first edition was published in 1996.[3] I ran that project.

Over time, the FSR had a major impact on central banks and regulators internationally. The first of its kind, it was rapidly followed by many others. By 2011 around eighty central banks were publishing a similarly named report.[4] But, while the FSR was widely emulated across the world, insofar as its objective was to stake out the ground for the Bank of England, and defend it against encroachment by other bodies, it was a failure. The incoming Labour government decided to remove the responsibility from the Bank of England and hand it to a new 'super-regulator', which was eventually named (by me, in fact) the Financial Services Authority.

The Financial Services Authority

Brown was determined to implement central bank independence as quickly as possible, so he summoned the Governor over the weekend immediately after the election to give him the news about interest rate policy. Unsurprisingly, that conversation went well, but there were differences of opinion within the Treasury about how the decision on supervision should be communicated. Some thought it would be wise to consult on the future structure of regulation, rather than making a snap decision on a complex issue. So the two sides of the coin were separated, and George did not immediately appreciate that the condition of independence was the loss of supervision. In the minds of Brown and Darling the Bank had an unfortunate ancestry of acting as 'mother hen' to the City. (Mervyn King, then the Chief Economist of the Bank, took a similar view, and had communicated it to the Labour team.) They wanted the new monetary authority to be seen to be independent of City interests, acting in the interests of the economy as a whole.

The circumstances of this poor handling, blamed variously on Brown himself and on Permanent Secretary Terry Burns, who was sensitive to the Governor's likely reaction, have been described in detail elsewhere.[5] Brown blames his Permanent Secretary: 'Unfortunately, in his exchanges with Terry Burns, Eddie seemed to form the impression that the change would not happen quickly, or perhaps not at all.'[6] There was a difficult forty-eight-hour period while the deal was debated. Burns pointed out that in the weeks before the election a selection committee chaired by him had been looking for a new chairman for the SIB as Andrew Large's term of office was about to expire. I was asked to put myself forward, but I declined. A year on, the SIB had persuaded me that its role in a two-tier structure, loosely overseeing the three self-regulatory organizations, was at best frustrating. The strongest candidate was Steve Robson from the Treasury itself, but he ran a large part of the organization extremely well, was popular with ministers of both parties as a result of his intellect and aggressive pursuit of their objectives, and was not an obvious choice for a role with a public profile and a need to negotiate sensitively with rival authorities. So the search had not identified a plausible successor who wanted the job.

George had two principal concerns about losing supervision. There was a reputational problem with other central banks internationally. The freemasonry of central banking is strong: most of the major central banks then took the view that banking supervision was part of their core business. They were aware of threats to remove that responsibility in a number of countries and were determined to fight them off. For the Bank of England to concede the loss of supervision without a fight would be seen as a betrayal of the fraternity, which might have unfortunate consequences for important international central bank relationships. George's second concern was for his staff. A Bank 'lifer', he felt a strong affinity with, and affection for, the institution. What would happen to 'his people' if they were hived off into another unnamed authority under different and unsympathetic management?

Over the weekend of 17–18 May there was a stand-off. Brown wanted to make his announcement, including the transfer of supervision, early in the following week. George was considering his position at the other end of town.

Brown's team reflected on their next move. Their conclusion was to ask me to leave the Bank of England to become, in the short term, the new SIB chairman. I would then use that vehicle to assemble the new regulator, which for a time would be known as the Super-SIB. That would fill the chair vacancy, and would also part-resolve the second of George's concerns, as he could say that his people were being taken into the promised land by one of their own. It also, incidentally, cleared the way for Mervyn King to become Deputy Governor for Monetary Stability, which made good sense.

I did not know Brown well at that point. We had met a couple of times over dinner in the Governor's flat before the election, when he and Tony Blair had invited themselves in to discuss the Bank and its views on the economy. They had, however, kept their powder dry and did not reveal their plans for independence, and certainly gave us no hint of their ideas on banking supervision or financial regulation more generally. I had also, three years before, when Director General of the CBI, spoken alongside him at a huge Burns supper hosted by Strathclyde Regional Council. Burns suppers involve an incontinent number of speeches and recitals. I made one or two mild jokes at his expense, which seemed to be appreciated by those present – who by that late stage of the evening were disposed to laugh at anything – with one notable exception. I was clearly guilty of a form of *lèse-majesté*, and in his own kingdom to boot. So I had no reason to expect preferment.

Geoffrey Robinson, then the Paymaster General and permanent host of late night rendezvous of the Brown clan in his apartment on Park Lane, says he 'was consulted as to who would do the job. Howard Davies was the name that kept coming to mind.' Robinson says it struck him that I 'had not just the intellectual capability but also the managerial competence that would be required to integrate the difficult [sic] organisations'.[7] Since we had never met, I was not hugely flattered by that judgement, and in any event he added that 'there was not a surfeit of alternative candidates'.

I was in Buenos Aires, speaking at a long-planned conference on monetary policy. So it was that, as I sat on the platform next to President Menem of Argentina, my 'minder' – an Argentine of German extraction called Erika – thrust a note in front of me which read: 'Very urgent – call Mr Braun at once.' I scratched my head. I did not know any Mr Braun. Could the message be intended for the Bundesbank man, who was fascinating the audience with a lecture on the central bank's role in the *Wirtschaftswunder*? It was not until I slipped off the platform at the coffee break that the realization dawned: the Chancellor wanted a word. I spoke to Burns first, who told me what the ask would be. On my next call, Brown duly asked. I said I was honoured, flattered and humbled, but would need a little time to reflect.

Over several long phone calls, Eddie George and I concluded that the choices were stark: either we both accepted the deal on offer and agreed to run the two institutions, or we both resigned. For him to resign while I took on the new regulator would look peculiar and would do nothing to stop the change. And it would be eccentric for him to resign at the moment when the Bank secured its monetary independence, an outcome for which he had quietly lobbied throughout his career. Yet the opposite course made little sense either. If I refused the new position, it would be taken by someone else who might have less interest in sustaining the Bank's culture and approach, and in looking after its transferring staff. Furthermore, if an outsider were brought in, the change would be bound to look more like a damning verdict on the Bank's past stewardship. So the logic was that either we both said Yes, or both said No – and the Ayes had it.

So I called Mr Braun back and accepted his offer, then returned overnight to face the music. When I walked back into the Bank the following morning, I was nervous. Would my acceptance be seen as a betrayal of the institution?

I need not have worried. When I entered the Parlours, where the Governors worked, Eddie was lying in wait, with a small picture frame in his hand. In the frame was a defaced dollar bill on which he had written: 'This buck I hereby pass to Howard.'

The Governor's second concern – the attitude of his central bank colleagues – was, however, not alleviated by my appointment. At a meeting of the European Monetary Institute (the precursor to the European Central Bank charged with the preparations for the euro) in Frankfurt a few days later I explained the changes to my colleagues. To a man (they all were), they asked why the Bank had not refused to agree the change. I explained that a new government, with a large majority, had parliamentary approval for the transfer of functions. We could not resist such a clear democratic mandate. That was regarded as an irrelevant detail. Central banks answered to a higher authority, themselves.

In fact the practice of separating banking supervision caused little difficulty. George recognized that the Bank's position was weak. As he told the Court: 'If the Bank drew attention to its great record in supervision, it would be laughed out of court. The perception was that the Bank had been asleep on the job more often than it should be.'[8] Over time, the monetary and supervision parts of the Bank had grown apart. It was agreed that when the dividing line between the transferring supervision divisions and the rest was drawn, there would be an 'exchange of prisoners'. In other words, people who found themselves in an area due to transfer to the FSA, but whose past career suggested they were more suited to the remaining areas of the Bank, could apply to stay behind, and vice versa. Around 450 staff moved, and about a dozen asked to stay behind, with about the same number applying to board the supervision boat before it floated away. The numbers who could claim experience in both supervision and monetary policy were very small.

In practice, we were left to ourselves to organize the new body. Although Brown and Balls had prepared a detailed blueprint for the Monetary Policy Committee, when I asked the Chancellor what he had in mind for the new Authority, he said, 'what I have in mind is that you should pull it together'.

The problematic point turned out to be the nature of the Bank's continuing responsibility for financial stability, and especially the Lender of Last Resort function. Reporting to Alistair Darling, Burns and I attempted to negotiate a deal acceptable to George. It was not easy. The outcome, a Memorandum of Understanding (MOU) between the Bank, the Treasury and the FSA, seemed superficially clear, but it betrayed long-held prejudices of the Bank and the Treasury.[9] The Bank was concerned about any loss of control to the Treasury, so insisted that it should retain responsibility for overall financial stability, but was worried about being asked to rescue a bank which it had not supervised and about which it knew too little. What if something which presented as a liquidity problem was in reality one of solvency? Since the supervision was being done elsewhere, they would not know the answer to that question. The Bank's balance sheet would then be at risk.

The Treasury, by contrast, feared that the Bank would wish to rescue banks which should, in their view, be allowed to fail. That had been the experience in past banking crises. The Bank had rescued a number of non-systemic banks in the secondary banking crisis of 1973–75 and, an episode which still rankled in the Treasury, had bailed out Johnson Matthey bank in 1984, without telling the Chancellor in advance. In his memoirs, Nigel Lawson recalls that this crisis erupted during the IMF meetings, but 'no-one had seen fit to mention it to me' and eventually he was 'given only a few minutes to decide whether or not to give an open-ended guarantee of taxpayers money in support of a rescue about whose wisdom . . . I was far from convinced.'[10] After the fact, he examined the reasons for the bank's failure and regarded the Bank's failure to step in at an earlier stage as 'inexplicable'. The episode left a long legacy of suspicion of the Bank in the Treasury.

As Burns recalls: 'We knew in 1997 that the lender of last resort question was a potential weakness of the new arrangements. So you [Davies] and I tried to resolve it. The Treasury focused on the issue of the Bank wanting to rescue a bank, when the Treasury did not. That was our assumption on how it would play out in practice. I asked what if the FSA and HMT wanted to mount a rescue, but the Bank did not? That question was not resolved. At the time Darling said, "We don't need to worry about that." But we failed to recognize that when the Bank was no longer the banking supervisor, it would not have the same institutional bias in favour of bank rescues to conceal supervision failings.'[11]

The original Treasury proposal was to put a numerical limit on the support the Bank could provide without explicit approval. For reasons no one can recall, the limit was to be set at £70 million, which George regarded as 'so low as to be almost useless in a crisis'. (He was surely right: £70 million would have funded 1.5% of the RBS bailout in 2008.) Furthermore, the Bank saw the imposition of a limit as striking at the heart of its status as an independent institution. An internal Bank memorandum concluded that 'the real heart of the issue in relation to the Bill . . . is whether we are to remain a central bank as that has been generally understood, or whether we are in effect to become something akin to a government department'.[12] On the idea of a limit on support, the Treasury backed down, but in other respects the Bill proceeded as Brown intended.

This lack of clarity on the responsibility for support operations was not the subject of much commentary at the time. The relations between the Bank and the supervisors who had moved to the FSA remained close. Most of the key people had worked together for a long time. The new Deputy Governor for financial stability, David Clementi, sat on the Board of the FSA, as did I on the Court of the Bank of England. Below board level, Michael Foot, a Bank 'lifer', was in charge of supervision. His Bank opposite number, Alistair Clark, was an old friend. They met weekly, at least, as did I with the Governor. But the problem was submerged, not resolved, and it emerged again when Northern Rock failed in 2007.

In the first decade of its existence, the principal criticisms of the FSA were quite different. During the passage of the Financial Services and Markets Act, the implementing legislation, the new authority's processes were regarded as 'unduly costly and burdensome', and it was argued that it 'will be able to act as prosecutor judge and jury'.[13] The move to statutory regulation of the securities markets, investment management and financial advice was controversial. There were dire warnings that the new regime would damage the City and its wealth-creating dynamic. Balls maintains that 'the reason why the Tories voted against the new legislation ... was because they argued that statutory regulation would hurt the City'.[14] But that criticism came not only from the Conservative side of the House. In 2005, Tony Blair as Prime Minister said in a speech to the Institute for Public Policy Research (which the Treasury did not see in advance) that the FSA 'is seen as hugely inhibiting of efficient business by perfectly respectable companies that have never defrauded anyone'.[15] The then Chairman of the FSA wrote a letter of protest, and the Chancellor was not pleased to find his creation attacked by his next-door neighbour. Blair was not alone in his criticisms. Indeed, according to Balls, 'all the grief in Parliament and the press came from complaints about too dirigiste a system'.[16]

Unfortunately, perhaps in response to that criticism, in a speech at Bloomberg in 2006 when City Minister, which came back to haunt him, Balls claimed: 'Today our system of light-touch and risk-based regulation is regularly cited ... as one of our chief attractions. It has provided us with a huge competitive advantage and is regarded as the best in the world.'[17]

There is no authoritative international ranking to substantiate that claim, but it is true that the FSA structure was copied around the world. Other countries had chosen single integrated regulators before the UK, notably in Scandinavia, but the number grew significantly after 1997, and indeed the letters FSA became a kind of quirky British global brand, like Barbour jackets or Frank Cooper's Oxford marmalade. In Europe one could find the E-FSA (Estonia), H-FSA (Hungary), I-FSA (Iceland), etc. Further afield, Japan and Indonesia operated a similar model. The number of integrated regulators grew from ten in 1997 to twenty-nine in 2004.[18] Part of the logic was that financial firms were themselves becoming supermarkets, no longer easy to categorize as either banks or insurers or stockbrokers, so regulators needed to combine to oversee them in a coherent way. There was also evidence that regulators outside the central bank were more rigorous in applying global banking standards.[19] While there remained no standard regulatory architecture for the finance industry around the globe, a model which involved the central bank focusing more narrowly on inflation, within an inflation targeting regime, and a separate regulator or regulators for other functions, gradually became more widespread.

The New Bank of England

The MOU left the Bank of England 'responsible for the overall stability of the financial system as a whole',[20] but in the period after the creation of the FSA the financial stability wing of the Bank was downgraded. By 2003 only 174 people worked in that area and, as Harold James notes in his history of the Bank from 1979 to 2003, 'there was a Financial Stability Committee, but it seemed like a very pale rival to the MPC'. And while the notion of regular consultation between the Treasury, the Bank and the FSA was maintained, as James notes, 'the three parts of the triune entity thus in practice moved away from each other, and there was less assessment of the policy spillovers than might have been desirable as financial risk built up in the 2000s'.[21]

Personnel changes played a part, too. Mervyn King replaced Eddie George in 2003, and at the same time my functions at the FSA were split between Callum McCarthy as Chairman, and John Tiner as CEO. The Treasury was opposed to the latter change, which painted a conventional corporate governance structure on the FSA, which had been constructed as a company purely to keep its spending out of the public expenditure totals and to give it more flexibility in paying its staff. A two-headed structure makes little sense for a regulatory body, and is almost unknown internationally. But the Treasury's hand was forced by Conservative opposition in the Lords, some of whose members continued to be concerned about the apparently excessive powers of the FSA and saw a nonexecutive chairman as a restraining hand. The change at the top led to the departure of the two most senior former Bank of England officials – Michael Foot and Carol Sergeant – the former to an overseas regulator and the latter to a UK bank. All these moves weakened the FSA–Bank relationship. And, as Alistair Darling explains, "the relationship between Callum McCarthy and Mervyn King was often strained, at times prickly'.[22]

But the more significant changes occurred at the Bank. King had not grown up in the financial markets, as George had done, and, as James says, he was 'critical of the multiple purposes of the Bank, and especially of any hint that it should continue in its old role as advocate of the City'.[23] The budget for the Financial Stability Wing was cut back[24] and staff numbers reduced from 174 to 120 during King's first term between 2003 and 2008. After the crash, these cuts were seen to have been highly significant, though they were little remarked on at the time. The MPC paid little attention to the banking system. From 1999 to 2007 the minutes show that around 1% or 2% of the committee's time was spent discussing banking. That escalated to 20% in late 2007,[25] but in evidence to the Treasury

Select Committee in 2010, Hector Sants, who took over from John Tiner as CEO of the FSA in 2007, said that 'the level of communication, and the level of interest, from the central bank in financial stability issues was recognised by all to have been very low, to say the least, in the pre-2007 period'.[26]

King's response was that under the terms of the MOU (which was redrafted, but not fundamentally changed, in 2006) the Bank 'was assumed to have responsibilities which it could not deliver because it had no powers or instruments to do so'.[27] He pointed out that the Bank had raised questions about the wisdom of the kind of wholesale funding strategy adopted by Northern Rock, and speculated that even had the Bank been endowed with the macroprudential powers it was given later, using them in the period before the crisis 'would have produced a chorus of complaints from banks, politicians and, dare I say, even the media about trying to restrain the extent to which our most successful industry wanted to expand'.[28]

The gathering storm

So the UK regulatory system approached the crisis in an ambiguous position. It was widely respected and emulated abroad, but – according to their subsequent testimonies at least – some of the participants were uncertain about the responsibilities for financial stability. As Darling put it: 'The whole system depended on the Chairman of the FSA, the Governor of the Bank and the Chancellor seeing things in exactly the same way. The problem was that, in September 2007, we simply did not see things in the same way.'[29] When he returned as Chancellor, ten years after the changes, Darling found 'that the Bank and the FSA were not talking to each other. It was not a structural problem. No one was looking at the system as a whole. The Governor would not meet the bankers. Had he met them he might have understood better what was going on.'[30]

What of the two other charges levelled at UK regulation subsequently – that the FSA had focused its concerns on conduct regulation and neglected prudential standards, and that the prevailing approach was one of 'light-touch' regulation, as asserted by Ed Balls?

There is some evidence that the FSA increased its relative emphasis on conduct of business after 2003, in response to a number of difficult episodes of mis-selling, of personal pensions and endowment mortgages in particular, where many customers were induced to move their pensions, or take up investment policies, which had damaged their finances and greatly enriched their advisers or providers. But was this at the expense of prudential supervision? In evidence to the Parliamentary Commission on Banking, Michael Foot said he 'had never felt this [the enhanced focus on conduct] had resulted in undue pressure on what was available for prudential purposes'.[31] He, however, left in 2004, just as the expansion of leverage, and utilization of wholesale funding in the banking sector, were beginning to accelerate.

The gross leverage of the UK banking sector grew from 2003 to 2007, as did the utilization of wholesale funding, which proved catastrophic in the case of Northern Rock. But how far was that the result of 'light-touch' regulation in the UK? The term was not used by regulators themselves. Where critics define it, they tend to refer to principles-based regulation, which the FSA did operate, as the legislation required it to do. When the idea was first introduced, by the SIB, the financial industry was critical. The risk they saw was that black letter rules could be easily interpreted, and breaches avoided through assiduous compliance departments, whereas principles could be interpreted after the event by regulators. Many firms thought that could be far more onerous than the previous regime. Principle 11 of the SIB rule book, for example, enjoined firms to be open with their regulators. But how to know what regulators would, after the event, consider to have been a material omission? So there is nothing necessarily 'light touch' about a principles-based regime. The objective is to ensure that firms cannot hide behind technical compliance with rules which may not have caught up with market practices.

It is perhaps more cogent to argue that the FSA used its enforcement powers more sparingly and levied far fewer fines on the industry than did the SEC. The SEC is pleased to describe itself as an enforcement-led regulator. The climate in which the FSA was established, where politicians of all parties revered the wealth-creating magic of the City, would have made that a hazardous strategy for the new regulator to adopt.

Arguably, though, that distinctiveness was not at the heart of the trends that led to the crisis. The big weakness was that the major banks were operating with too little capital, and some of what the regime said they had – tax credits for example – was not available to absorb losses when they were incurred. The capital rules originated in the Basel committee on Banking Supervision and, in the EU, were cascaded down into national legislation. The FSA applied those rules, typically with some national add-ons (some critics of the Bank and the FSA maintain simultaneously that they were light-touch regulators, and yet at the same time gold-plated European regulations). The problem, one can see in retrospect, was that the Basel requirements were too weak to cope with a sharp fall in the prices of financial assets, and a deep recession, whose impacts on banks were magnified by the use of exotic off-balance sheet instruments. That was a global problem, not a UK-specific issue.

As the markets roared ahead in the 2000s, house prices rose rapidly, and the traded volumes of new highly leveraged instruments grew exponentially. The Treasury did have some concerns – even though the IMF view was that securitization, and the risk transfers it facilitated, was making the system more robust and that the incidence of commercial bank failures was likely to be lower than in the past.[32] As City Minister, in 2006 Ed Balls sponsored a simulation exercise to assess the likely consequences of a bank failure in Britain. Brown asked Hank Paulson, then US Treasury Secretary, Ben Bernanke, Chairman of the Federal Reserve Board, and a gaggle of other US regulators to participate. Brown's recollection is that 'most who joined our financial "war game" started with the view that there would be moral hazard if a rescue was undertaken. After much discussion, most ended with the view that in at least some circumstances rescues would have to be undertaken. No one imagined that in our modern economy there would be queues around the block with runs on banks.'[33]

John Kingman, who chaired what was described as a Standing Committee deputies meeting, remembers the conclusions a little differently. The question put, he recalls, was 'Do the banks have enough capital?'. 'The unanimous conclusion was that they did. We all thought the banks were well-capitalized.'[34] Balls drew another conclusion from the exercise, which foreshadowed problems to come. 'There was a war game in 2006 which showed that Mervyn King and Callum McCarthy were living on different planets. We considered the case of a northern building society heavily dependent on wholesale funding of its mortgage book. The Bank was highly reluctant to intervene, while the FSA and Treasury could see that they might need to. It was unclear whether this was the Bank's institutional view, or just the Governor's. The Treasury wanted deputies also to be involved, but King flatly refused to allow the Deputy Governor for Financial Stability [at that time John Gieve] to attend.'[35]

It is not surprising that the exercise may be interpreted differently years after the event, especially refracted through the lens of the crisis which erupted in 2008. But all the participants agree that the 'war game', while not useless, did not address the interlinkages between banks, and between banks and the shadow banking system which was growing exponentially at the time. Furthermore, it did not result in any meaningful action. Balls notes that 'in 2012 Mervyn King claimed the Bank had looked at the issues and produced Financial Stability Reports, but did nothing as a result'. Andy Haldane of the Bank takes essentially the same view, but characteristically expresses it in more vivid language:

> The Bank, and others, spoke with increasing forcefulness about potential stresses in the system from 2003 onwards. We were dogs barking at the passing traffic. As the cars drove past at increasing speed, these barks grew louder. The drivers of some of the cars took notice, but they did not slow down. Why? Because they knew the dog's bark was worse than its bite.[36]

The Bank for International Settlements in Basel issued some of the strongest warnings, but in spite of its role as the central banks' central bank, it was largely ignored.

All hands to the pump

The participants all acknowledge that the 2006 'war game' was of some value when a real crisis hit in 2007, and the chosen scenario was not very far from the first actual casualty – Northern Rock. Its mortgage business had grown very rapidly in the 2000s, on the back of wholesale funding. The bank was run by an ambitious CEO with little awareness of the risks the bank was running, and chaired by Viscount Ridley, a local landowner and opinionated writer on environmental matters, whose qualifications to chair a bank were not obvious, apart for the fact that his father had held the same position. When the liquidity crisis of summer 2007 emerged, it was the most vulnerable of the large British banks, as much of its funding was short term, and needed to be rolled over frequently. Investors suspected that some banks would have a solvency problem, if asset prices fell sharply, and were therefore reluctant to supply liquidity, even at a high price.

The Treasury was not well-equipped to handle such a problem. As one senior official recalls: 'When Northern Rock erupted the financial stability area of the Treasury was tiny. No-one wanted to work there. There was just one junior person in the building who understood a bank's balance sheet.'[37] An Institute for Government report in 2019 found that between 2001 and 2008 there were seven different Directors General of Financial Services in the Treasury.[38] The policy staff numbered seventy to eighty, but few had financial sector experience. Sharon White's internal review of the Treasury's response to the crisis noted that it was not previously considered to be a high-profile area, and 'was not in the spotlight of ministers and top management'.[39]

So the Treasury was heavily dependent on advice from the FSA and the Bank. Unfortunately, that advice conflicted at times. The FSA was convinced that the Bank needed to supply liquidity, to prevent a systemic collapse. The Governor was not persuaded, and sent a memorandum to the Treasury Committee focusing on the moral hazard implications: 'The provision of large liquidity facilities penalises those financial institutions that sat out the dance, encourages herd behaviour, and increases the intensity of future crises.'[40] By this time Darling had concluded that it was necessary to provide funding, but the terms of the MOU meant that 'I could not in practice order the Bank to do what I wanted . . . The fact that we had given the Bank independence had a downside.'[41] Furthermore, the Treasury did not have the legal power to step in and force a sale, or take the bank over. That gap, which was also present in the US and elsewhere, was subsequently filled by the Special Resolution Scheme.

This stand-off did not last long. The Bank soon came to recognize that the position was critical. A rescue plan was devised, though not quickly enough to prevent an old-fashioned bank run, with people queuing in the street to take out their deposits following a leak of the imminent collapse to Robert Peston, then of the BBC. The rescue proceeded the following day, but the first significant bank failure in the UK since the closure of the City of Glasgow bank in 1878 attracted huge and unwelcome attention overseas and, in Darling's words, 'was disastrous for confidence in the government's ability to manage the growing crisis'.[42]

The Northern Rock rescue, in itself, did not turn out to be costly to the taxpayer. The quality of its mortgage book was relatively good, and it was eventually possible to dispose of the assets on reasonable terms. But it highlighted a significant difference of opinion between the Treasury and Gordon Brown. Brown was allergic to the idea of nationalization, and wanted to dispose of the bank as quickly as possible. As one senior official put it, 'he was petrified that it would turn into Railtrack all over again, and on the day of the rescue told us he was not sure he would survive the day'.[43] For a period, there were daily meetings in which Brown argued for a sale to Richard Branson's Virgin Group. 'Officials opposed the deal on the grounds that Branson would make a huge killing on the terms proposed.'

But Northern Rock was merely the overture before the main performance began. For the Treasury, as one official put it, 'it was a serious crash course in bank failure. There was not much to feel proud of in the way it was handled, but it was an unbelievably useful rehearsal. It meant we were geared up when we had to deal with Halifax Bank of Scotland and RBS. We had taken useful powers to deal with failing banks when we nationalised Northern Rock.'[44]

The broader consequences were not immediately apparent. For a time the failure seemed a one-off, and the other major banks appeared to be well capitalized. Indeed, the RBS acquisition of ABN-Amro was not completed until October 2007, after the Northern Rock collapse. The FSA did not object, even though the acquisition further stretched the bank's already thin capital base. But through the winter and into the spring of 2008 the strains in the financial system became more evident. Liquidity pressures grew. As Warren Buffett memorably remarked: 'You only learn who's been swimming naked when the tide goes out.'[45]

For the thinly staffed Treasury, the emerging crisis was a challenge. One side-effect of the 1997 reform, which the Treasury welcomed at the time, was that it allowed it to take political control of most aspects of financial regulation. Up to that point the Department of Trade and Industry (DTI) – as it then was – oversaw the regulation of securities markets and the insurance sector. The transfer of the SIB and its self-regulatory creatures, and of insurance regulation, to the FSA put them under the Treasury by a side wind. By 2008 this concentration of powers was seen as a mixed blessing, as the Treasury had no one else in government to blame, but it did facilitate the handling of the crisis.

The twists and turns of the global financial crisis, and its handling by the Treasury, have been described in some detail by Brown in two books of memoirs, and especially by Darling. After a slow start, the Treasury caught up rapidly, with some external assistance. Paul Myners, a bruiser with many years' experience of the City, was brought in as City Minister in September 2008. Shriti Vadera was closely involved, albeit from a position in another department, which at times caused tensions with the official Treasury, and with its ministers.

Vadera, who had been an investment banker at UBS, joined the Treasury as a member of the Council of Economic Advisers in 1999, but when Brown moved to Number 10 she was ennobled and became a minister in the Department of International Development, and later in the Business Department. She played a central role in managing the crisis. Her contacts in the City gave her early warnings of trouble ahead. They told her that the Treasury (and the Bank) were behind the game. 'That was true, but it was not their fault. Treasury people are very smart, but they are not commercial, and not negotiators. But once John Kingman was put in charge of bank rescues things started to improve, and in the heat of the crisis the Treasury executed well – though Nick MacPherson took a hair shirt approach to resourcing, which was a problem.'[46]

The decision-making process was unusual, and looked dysfunctional. The Treasury was formally responsible, and Darling worked well with Myners and with officials, who are almost unanimously positive about their Chancellor's calmness and discipline through an extraordinary period. But they acknowledge that all the key decisions were made in Number 10. Ed Balls, though he had by then become Secretary of State for Children, Schools and Families, was often involved. His wife, Yvette Cooper, was CST and ran her own press briefing operation, which added to the confusion. All that created, according to Jeremy Heywood, 'an unsustainable dynamic at the heart of government'.[47] Shortly after the European elections, Brown seriously contemplated appointing Balls as Chancellor and removing Darling, but finally told Heywood: 'It's the wrong time to do it, half way through an economic crisis.'

The key decision, to recapitalize the banks in the autumn of 2008, was so momentous and fraught with risk that the Prime Minister had to be centrally involved. The G20 summit in April 2009, which produced a huge coordinated global fiscal stimulus, could only be managed at the highest level. Downing Street was also involved in the detail of every bank rescue. In his memoirs, Darling records his frustrations at this way of working. But he generously acknowledges that a Chancellor who becomes Prime Minister is in a delicate position. 'The Prime Minister has only a small staff, and can often think s/he is not being told what is going on. That can be particularly the case if you have been Chancellor beforehand. Brown felt he was not given the information flow he had when in the Treasury, especially on bank rescues.'[48]

The bank recapitalization plan did turn out to be successful, and less costly than was feared at the time – though the government will probably lose more than £20 billion on its investment in RBS.[49] The plan was copied elsewhere, and drew a line under what could otherwise have been a far more damaging financial meltdown. In an unfortunate slip of the tongue in Parliament in December 2008,

Brown said: 'We not only saved the world . . . er . . . saved the banks . . .', which perhaps diminished the credit he deserved. Did he save the world? A senior official who lived through the period notes: 'Many people claimed the credit. Peter Sands of Standard Chartered implausibly maintained that his contribution was crucial. But Shriti was the intellectual driving force, and Tom Scholar (who ran the International and Finance Directorate) was next. That was the unsung story.'[50]

Financial regulation after the crisis

How did the other two legs of the Tripartite stool hold up in the crisis? We have seen that they differed in their view of what the Northern Rock problem was, and how it should be addressed. The Treasury Select Committee reviewed the way the authorities had handled the failure and were very critical. They rejected the arguments put forward to justify the way the system had operated, but concluded: 'We do not believe that the financial system in the United Kingdom would be well served by a dismantling of the Tripartite system. Instead, we want to see it reformed, with clearer leadership and stronger powers.'[51] In particular, they wanted stronger deposit protection arrangements, managed by the Bank of England, and new powers for the authorities to resolve failing institutions.

The conclusion that the system should not be fundamentally changed reflected the Treasury's view. As one senior official puts it: 'By 2008 the tripartite system was a strength not a weakness. Mervyn King had wanted to nationalize the whole British banking system, including HSBC. The Deputy Governors may well have had a different view, but were not allowed to express it. The culture of the Bank requires tight discipline and obedience to the Governor, whereas the Chairman of the FSA could express a different view openly in discussions with the Treasury. The debate was healthy. As it turned out, the Bank was more right than the FSA on the banks' capital needs. Tom Scholar split the difference between them.'[52] Vadera agrees: in her view the FSA's analysis was crucial. It was carefully structured and reflected close understanding of the individual businesses.

The Select Committee's conclusion proved to be only a stay of execution, for the FSA. As Shadow Chancellor, George Osborne had 'turned' one of Brown's former advisers, James Sassoon. For a time he was the personal interface with the Chairman of the FSA, then the Chancellor's Representative for Promotion of the City, but left the Treasury in 2008, and began to advise the Conservative Opposition, which was perhaps a more appropriate home for a man with his background and views. Osborne invited him to review the Tripartite system. His review was published in March 2009.[53] It recommended returning banking supervision to the Bank of England, with a new Financial Policy Committee in the Bank, as a parallel to the MPC. The FSA would be abolished, and be reborn as a conduct of business regulator, the Financial Conduct Authority (FCA). The proposals owed a lot to the ideas of Michael Taylor, who wrote a seminal paper on what he called 'Twin Peaks' (an echo of the David Lynch television series popular at the time).[54] The notion is that one regulator should be responsible for prudential standards and supervision across the financial sector, with a parallel body overseeing conduct of business standards. The eventual UK model did not follow that prescription precisely. While the Prudential Regulation Authority (PRA), part of the Bank of England, handles all the major institutions, the FCA is the prudential regulator for many smaller firms. But the principles are similar. The nearest international example for the new system could be found in the Netherlands, where De Nederlandsche Bank was the prudential supervisor, alongside a financial markets authority, the AFM. The Dutch banking system was the one other in Europe that proved to be even more vulnerable than the UK's when the crisis hit, so the precedents were unfavourable.

Sassoon was appointed Commercial Secretary to the Treasury in the Coalition government that took office in 2010, which gave him the opportunity to implement the ideas in his review.

Osborne recalls that when he took office relations between the Treasury and the Bank were very bad, no doubt partly as a result of the disputes involved in the management of the crisis. 'It was all very childish. I told them I didn't want to hear any sniping about Mervyn King. He was not on speaking terms with some of the senior Treasury officials. That had to stop.'[55] The principal arguments centred on the Bank's withdrawal of liquidity support from the banks, which the Treasury thought premature, and the Bank's refusal to move on credit easing, which meant the Treasury had to introduce the National Loan Guarantee Scheme. So granting the Bank new and far more extensive powers over the financial system might seem to be a curious response. 'Maybe the Bank was rewarded for failure? That was rough justice.'

Osborne's rationale for the change was that 'divorcing monetary policy from awareness of the position of the banks was a mistake'. There was a risk that giving the Bank responsibility for all prudential supervision made the Governor too powerful – the overmighty citizen argument. But 'the alternative is warring factions'. Also, 'there are few British institutions which have high status, authority and respect. The Bank has it, and the Treasury also. The Foreign Office has lost it. Where it exists it should be preserved and used effectively.' The Bank has the credibility to impose its will on the City in spite of the problems of the past. A downside of the change was that 'the FCA is the poor relation, and we made a bad choice of CEO with Martin Wheatley, but putting Andrew Bailey in there rescued it'.[56]

Others have a different interpretation of the motives for the change. One senior official describes the Osborne critique of the Tripartite arrangements as 'a red herring. It was simply a convenient line to take which allowed him

to blame Brown for the financial crisis.'[57] Vadera sees the
change as a mistake from the Treasury's perspective. In
future crises they will be entirely dependent on the Bank
for advice.

Brown continues to believe that the 1997 system was
the right one and that a Tripartite arrangement is necessary: 'The problem was that the Bank of England did not
take it seriously and the Treasury did not push it to do so.
Mervyn King did not want to have anything to do with the
financial sector.' Furthermore, he thinks the bank has now
'taken on far more than it should have done. It has too
much power over the financial system and the next time
there is trouble it will end in tears with the Bank taking
the blame.'[58]

Another Osborne banking reform is also controversial.
Under parliamentary pressure to do more to strengthen the
resilience of the UK banking system, in 2010 Osborne asked
John Vickers, Warden of All Souls College Oxford, and a
former Chief Economist of the Bank of England, to chair
an Independent Commission on Banking. At the time it was
not clear that the Basel Committee on Banking Supervision
would be able to agree bold measures to increase capital
in the global banking system. Vickers's principal recommendation was that large UK banks should be required to
ringfence their domestic retail and commercial operations
in a separate legal entity.[59] The ringfenced entity could
not offer financial support to the non-ringfenced parts of
the group (in practice mainly their investment banking
operations). The ring-fenced bank would be required to
maintain core tier one capital of at least 11%. Osborne
accepted the recommendations at once, and immediately
undertook to implement them through primary legislation,
rather than incorporating them in the prudential regulator's rulebook.

The proposals were strongly criticized at the time. Paul
Volcker, the former Chairman of the US Federal Reserve,
maintained that 'the concept that different subsidiaries of
a single commercial banking operation can maintain total

independence either in practice or in public perception is difficult to sustain. If you want to separate organizations clearly and decisively you put them in different organizations.'[60] Volcker's own solution to the problem was his eponymous 'rule', which prohibited banks from engaging in proprietary trading or investing in hedge funds. The EU also wrestled with the problem. The Liikanen Report for the European Commission recommended a kind of mirror image of the Vickers scheme, with a separate entity for some investment banking operations.[61] The Commission agreed to study the proposals, published in 2012. In the summer of 2021, it continues to study them, in theory, but there is no expectation that they will be taken forward. The French and Germans opposed them, largely on two grounds: that they would damage the competitiveness of European investment banks, and that the Basel capital requirements for all banks had become tougher, rendering separation redundant. By 2021, the average core tier one ratio for all UK banks was 15% compared to the 11% envisaged by Vickers for a ringfenced bank. The Vickers group did not expect that Basel standards would be very substantially raised for all banks. One member of the Committee told me that had he known how high the Basel requirements would turn out to be, he would not have signed the report.

A number of other countries examined the ringfencing idea, but to date all have decided not to proceed, through Australia is considering a weak-form version. Among global regulators, the UK system is regarded as mysterious and overcomplex, as well as damaging. Interpreting the legislation has involved writing around 400 rules governing transactions within banks and with clients, repapering many commercial contracts, and implementation costs of around £1 billion for a large bank.

MacPherson's view is that ringfencing has proved to be 'totally irrelevant to everyone except Barclay's. The only defence for it is that given the political mood at the time sometimes you have to do something stupid to avoid being pressured into doing something worse. The government might have been pushed into breaking up the banks. Something had to be done, and Osborne was a populist in that respect. If it damaged RBS, then so be it. Officials were more concerned not to do further damage to the bank's profitability, in the interests of getting their money back.'[62] (A review of the ringfencing regime was announced in late 2020.)

The Treasury has not repeated this direct intervention in financial regulation since. While the UK remained in the EU, most regulation emerged from directives drafted by the Commission and approved by the Parliament, or was developed by the PRA/FCA. In normal times, the Treasury's principal interest in the financial sector is in its contribution to the economy and especially to tax revenue. It does not consider itself to be a 'sponsoring department' in the way the DTI did in the past.

The tax take from finance dipped after the crisis of 2007–08, but recovered over the next decade, helped by additional levies on the banks. By 2019–20 the contribution was over £75 billion, around 10% of total tax receipts.[63] The banking sector alone contributed almost £40 billion. As the banks regularly pointed out, the total tax burden on banks in London was, at 47%, higher than in Frankfurt at 45% and well above New York at 33%.[64] But the politics of reducing taxation on banks, while the memories of the crash remained raw, were unattractive, and the City had proved remarkably resilient, without overt government assistance. Its share of the different elements of financially mobile business had remained stable or grown. Neither sitting outside the Eurozone, nor the well-publicized problems in the crisis itself, had made an impact.

Brexit and the City

But the EU referendum threatened a discontinuity. While the UK ran a sizeable deficit with the EU27 in trade in visible goods, the reverse was true for services. The City had benefited greatly from being part of the single financial market, with firms based in London, the great majority foreign-owned, using London as their base to access the whole European market. Governments elsewhere in Europe resented the dominance of London. They frequently railed against the apparent injustice of the principal financial centre of the Eurozone being outside it. When the European Banking Authority (itself based in London before Brexit) calculated the numbers of financiers in the EEA paid more than €500,000 – which triggered some regulatory controls – they found that 3,614 of the total of 4,938 were based in London.[65] The impact of that spending power on tax revenues and expenditure was a prize worth having. But the promotional efforts of organizations like Paris Europlace and Finanzplatz Frankfurt Main made little difference. The efforts made by the ECB to shift euro-denominated business into the Eurozone failed. The European Court of Justice (ECJ) ruled that the relevant jurisdiction was the single market, not the Eurozone.

The Brexit referendum changed that calculation. For a time it seemed possible that the UK would remain in the single market, or the customs union, but the approach to the negotiation taken by the May government summarily ruled out those intermediate solutions, without consultation with the affected businesses. So firms based in London would lose their 'passport' to operate across the EU unless a deal could be agreed with the 27.

City opinion, at least among the major international firms, broadly favoured trying to secure a deal which allowed continued access to European financial markets. There were some high-profile Brexit advocates, especially in the hedge-fund community which had been alienated by the Alternative Investment Fund Management Directive (AIFMD) of 2011, who helped to fund the Leave campaign. David Wright, a former Director General of Financial Markets in the Commission, argued, not entirely facetiously, that the AIFMD caused Brexit.[66] But majority opinion, in the larger firms at least, including those headquartered in France and Germany, had been in favour of remaining in the EU, and certainly wanted to maintain access to their clients in the 27. Dividing capital market operations, in particular, would be costly and inconvenient, and there was no single continental centre which could hope to rival London's regulatory expertise, and talent pool, in the short to medium term. That point of view was buttressed by early estimates of potential job losses in the Square Mile. An Oliver Wyman report for CityUK, a lobby group, argued that, with low access to EU markets, up to 75,000 jobs would be lost, as well as tax revenues of £10 billion.[67]

There were rival assessments, some of which argued that, while a few 'brass plates' might move to Dublin or Luxembourg, the job losses would be minimal. And over the lengthy period in which the Brexit deal was debated in Parliament the central estimates tended to fall. By early 2021 the City Corporation believed that the losses might be around 10% of the first Oliver Wyman estimate,[68] though that was based on possibly optimistic assumptions about future access. A detailed report by New Financial in April 2021 calculated that, by then, 7,400 jobs had been relocated.[69]

The Treasury was, however, concerned about the risks to its tax take in particular, and tried to protect City interests in the negotiations. The political climate was not favourable. Fishermen had much greater appeal, even on the Conservative benches, than financiers, even though the gross value added of the fishing industry was £784 million, compared to £132 billion for the financial sector.[70]

But while there was a broad Remain majority in the City, there was no consensus on what the post-Brexit arrangements should be. As Philip Hammond explained: 'The City was its own worst enemy. The lobbying was chaotic and tremendously unhelpful. They began by arguing for passporting, which was out of the question. The same was true of mutual recognition, another solution advanced by CityUK. The Treasury tried to push for something in the middle, but the EU always wanted something on freedom of movement in return, and Theresa May was reluctant to concede anything in that area.'[71]

There were also differences of view between the Treasury and the Bank of England. Hammond explains: 'The Bank of England was always keener on regulatory autonomy than the Treasury was. The Treasury was more focused on the hit to the financial services sector of losing passporting rights.'[72] In the Treasury view the Bank was in effect on the Brexit side of the argument, arguing that they could not accept any restriction on regulatory independence. The Treasury view was that an independent Bank constrained by the EU regulatory was fine, but they did not want Carney unchained. He might do things they did not like, on bank capital for example, where the Bank typically argued for requirements higher than the EU consensus. (After Brexit, the Bank's first autonomous decision was to remove the EU concession which allowed banks to capitalize software costs and count them as capital.)

In spite of these differences of view, the constraints imposed by the May government's 'red lines' and the reluctance of the EU27 to engage in an area where they saw that the UK was a *demandeur*, the Chancellor nonetheless thought that a deal which preserved a high degree of market access was possible. There were financial stability arguments which influenced the ECB. Fragmentation of liquidity could be costly for European firms. And the Capital Markets Union objective of the Commission would be far harder to achieve if the biggest and deepest European capital market was dismantled.

Hammond floated the idea of a deal based around 'enhanced equivalence'. Under the terms of certain directives, the EC can designate the rules of a third country as equivalent to EU regulation. US and Swiss regulation, among others, benefit from such a designation for the purposes of the Markets in Financial Instruments Directive. A designation facilitates cross-border business but, under the existing regime, it can be withdrawn unilaterally without notice, so is not a stable basis on which to establish a business focused largely on the EU market. And the EU negotiators took the view that while UK equivalence was by definition established at the point of departure, as we had been applying EU regulation throughout our membership, there was a need for assurance that the UK would not diverge in pursuit of competitive advantage. Some in the Treasury believed that it would be worth giving such an undertaking, to preserve single market access as far as possible. The approach came to be known as the High Alignment Model (HAM).

That was seen by the Bank, in particular, as putting the UK in the position of a 'rule-taker'. In one sense, of course, it had long been in that position, but as an EU member it had influenced the outcome. It is also the case that in many areas EU regulation originates in, for example, the Basel Committee or the International Organisation of Securities Commissions, where the UK is still represented. But once we were no longer in the Brussels drafting room, we could no longer be sure that what emerged from the EC would be to our liking. First drafts of EU Directives, before British regulators and officials had got at them, were often inimical to the City's interests. The Bank therefore produced an alternative acronym, B-DEM, which stood for a Bespoke Dynamic Equivalence Mechanism. B-DEM, devised by Deputy Governor Jon Cunliffe, not known for his euro enthusiasm, would have given the UK greater flexibility, and greater purchase on future regulations. It was logical, but not negotiable.

The underlying problem was that the two sides had very different objectives. The UK wished to retain as much inward business as possible, while the EU27, led in this case by the French, had the opposite ambition. In spite of these not inconsiderable difficulties, Hammond believes that 'if the City had coherently argued for enhanced equivalence with a committee to review divergence, and formal notice arrangements and a conciliation period if changes were proposed, that might have been achievable'.[73] Some kind of offer on free movement would have been necessary to close the deal, but 'we would continue to need EU labour so it would have been rational to offer an access deal, perhaps linked to automatic work permits for people above a certain earnings threshold, and a quota below that, with no access to benefits or right to permanent residence'. But CityUK continued to try to press for mutual recognition, which would never have been acceptable to the EU27, unless we remained subject to the ECJ. So by the time Hammond left office in July 2019, no agreement along those lines had been reached. And thereafter the interests of the financial sector fell down the list of priorities. As Hammond puts it: 'Dominic Cummings saw the City as part of a conspiracy of the elites in London and the South East. He wanted to break things, and that was one of them. There was an irony in that Boris Johnson had understood the importance of financial services to the economy when Mayor of London.'[74] But Johnson as Prime Minister had a different set of priorities. He regarded the City as full of 'moaning minnies' who consistently exaggerated the risks to jobs.

During the period of parliamentary turmoil in the autumn of 2019 there was little opportunity to pursue the financial services agenda, and the Treasury's approach to Brexit necessarily changed when Rishi Sunak became Chancellor in February 2020. He did not share Hammond's view that leaving the EU would seriously damage the interests of the City. He took little part in the fraught negotiations which ended in December, though he did intervene to knock out some French-drafted words in the Agreement, which would have outlawed delegation of portfolio management to London. There were other distractions which quite reasonably preoccupied him once the pandemic started in March 2020.

Senior officials say 'he is quite hard to read on Europe. In government he has credibility for being on the "right" side of the referendum, but on the details of Brexit has said the bare minimum he can get away with.'[75] On financial services he has not been dogmatic. The Treasury (and the Bank) took the view that it would make sense to grant unilateral equivalence to some EU regulations, to allow foreign firms to continue to operate in London, even if the EU would not reciprocate. So in November 2020 the Treasury launched the UK's Equivalence Framework for financial services. 'We thought he might be difficult about a unilateral move, but in fact he quickly accepted the logic.'

The Treasury therefore ceased to press for a financial services deal to be incorporated in the final EU–UK Trade and Cooperation Agreement, and it was not. The new instructions given to departments when Lord Frost took over the negotiations was that they should not ask for anything not in the Canada deal. As the *Financial Times* reported: 'While Theresa May saw Brexit as a problem to be managed – she unsuccessfully proposed a plan to stick to some EU rules in exchange for less border friction – Johnson insisted throughout that sovereignty was paramount, even if the economy took a hit.'[76]

After the event, Johnson acknowledged that the Treaty 'perhaps does not go as far as we would like' on financial services, though no negotiating capital had been expended on it. The consequences of that omission have yet to be seen. The EU seems intent on implementing a 'location policy', requiring specified activities to be undertaken within the Eurozone, which the UK always resisted. The Governor of the Bank of England has questioned the legality and effectiveness of efforts by the Commission and the ECB to force euro clearing activity to move into the EU.[77] There is no doubt that most firms established in London do not wish to relocate, but some may well now be forced to do so.

The Treasury's focus after Brexit has shifted, in two directions. First, it has commissioned a number of reviews to identify ways in which the UK's regulatory environment can be made more 'competitive', and attractive to international firms. There has been a review of the listing regime, for example, which recommended more flexible rules. Further reviews of Fintech regulation, insurance company solvency, etc. will follow. There may be changes which are beneficial and produce a better balance between innovation and stability. The EU regime is unlikely to be optimal in all cases: elements are an uneasy compromise between the views of countries with very different financial ancestries. But two consequences can be foreseen. The more that domestic changes are made, the less likely it is that the UK will secure equivalence designations by the EC, as the UK regime will inevitably diverge from European norms. Second, there will be tensions between political attempts to attract business to London, and the duties on regulators. The regulatory pendulum, which swung back sharply towards safety and soundness after the GFC, may be on the move again, with unpredictable consequences. Those who lived through the 2007–08 period are nervous.

The second shift is new. The Johnson government does not see the City of London and those who work in and around it as its natural constituency. Some even think that, as a consequence of Brexit, they have irrevocably lost a lot of the 'Anywhere' people, in David Goodhart's taxonomy.[78] Goodhart posits a social divide between 'Somewhere' people, rooted in a specific place or community, socially conservative and less well-educated, and 'Anywhere' people, footloose, mainly urban, socially liberal and university-educated. The Conservative heartlands are now the former Red Wall seats in the post-industrial North and Midlands, populated largely by the 'Somewheres'. That shift was confirmed in the local elections of May 2021. A policy which promotes the interests of mobile international capital does not appeal to those voters. So it is accepted that Brexit will result in a drift of business out of London. While the Treasury still wants the tax revenue, and needs it more than ever post-Covid, support for the financial sector may now come with a 'levelling-up' ticket attached. The Treasury is moving staff to Darlington and pressing the City firms to enhance their presence in the regions.

The Golden Age of London as Europe's undisputed financial centre is, as Golden Ages have a habit of doing, drawing to a close. As Nicolas Veron, one of the most acute observers of EU financial markets, put it: 'The medium term outlook for the City of London is unpromising . . . Once an onshore financial center for the entire EU single market, and a competitive offshore center for the rest of the world, the City has been reduced to an onshore center for the United Kingdom only and has become offshore centre for the European Union.'[79]

8

Climate Change and the Road to Net Zero

Jill Rutter, a former Treasury official now thinking in a tank, summed up the conventional view of the Treasury's interest in climate change at the end of 2020. She wrote:

> The Treasury has long been seen as the block on government progress on tackling climate change – focusing on short-term economic growth, sceptical about the UK getting ahead of competitors and burned with its forays into greening the tax system. Under the Coalition, George Osborne was seen as the brake by successive Lib Dem climate change secretaries.[1]

That reputation derives, to some extent at least, from the climate change scepticism espoused by at least one former Chancellor and a former Permanent Secretary. Nigel Lawson was one of the two founders of the Global Warming Policy Foundation in 2009, which describes itself as 'open-minded on the contested science of global warming . . . [and] deeply concerned about the costs and implications of many of the policies currently being advocated'.[2] It remains one of the most active proselytizers of an alternative view of climate change, sceptical about the impact of human activity. Andrew Turnbull, Permanent

Secretary from 1998 to 2002, was for some years a Trustee of the Foundation, and wrote a paper in 2011 arguing that the impact of man-made emissions has been exaggerated, and that 'the globe has been on a gentle warming trend since the end of the Little Ice Age around two hundred years ago'. On that basis he believed that 'the alarmism which characterises much of the current debate cannot be justified'.[3] Both Lawson and Turnbull had left the Treasury years before these developments, but they continue to be associated with HMT in the minds of climate policy thinkers.

On the other side of the ledger, one should include the Stern Review on the Economics of Climate Change, which was commissioned by Gordon Brown when Nicholas Stern was Head of the Government Economics Service, in the Treasury, and released in October 2006.[4] The genesis of the review was unusual. In early 2005, Stern had prepared a report on Africa for a G8 summit. The so-called 'Commission for Africa' which oversaw the work was chaired by Blair, rather than Brown. It had an impact and contributed to a global agreement on a sharp increase in aid to Africa. The second main topic at the 2005 summit was climate change. Tony Blair and French President Jacques Chirac took the subject seriously, but relations between them were poor, and the other leaders showed little interest, so little was achieved. In the summit postmortem, Brown and Stern decided to undertake a review of the economics of climate change in an attempt to generate more interest in the subject.[5] (It also had the side benefit of allowing Brown to seize the initiative from Blair, who had hitherto been in the lead in government – at a time when relations between the two men were at their lowest ebb.) Staffing the study was a challenge. There were very few economists in the Treasury with the relevant experience or expertise, so Stern supplemented the team with secondees from the Bank of England and elsewhere. The eventual result, only eighteen months later, was an impressive piece of work. By that time Blair had agreed to step down to make way for Brown, so relations had improved. The two of them walked to the Royal Society to launch it, with David Miliband – then widely seen as the next Prime Minister but two – in tow. It proved to be one of Treasury's most popular efforts, and for a time they promoted it actively. The reception in Europe was particularly positive.

Brown says curiously little about the Review in his memoirs – there is just one brief reference – but it had a great influence on opinion in the UK and, probably more so, around the world. When Director of the London School of Economics, I recruited Stern back to the School as a Professor on his retirement from the Treasury. There was little doubt that in global academic and policy circles he had acquired superstar status. But prophets are not always honoured immediately in their own country, and there was resistance in government, and especially in the Treasury, to some of his recommendations, especially in relation to the tax system. Brown did not welcome any report which threatened his prerogative in tax affairs.

Nonetheless, the Review was an important influence on government policy and was part of the background to the Climate Change Act 2008, which set out emission reduction targets with which the UK must legally comply. That was 'the first global legally binding climate change mitigation target set by a country'.[6] It also introduced the Committee on Climate Change (CCC), which has undoubtedly had a major impact on government policy in many areas. (My own review of airport policy, published in 2017, was heavily conditioned by the views of the Committee, and the recommendations had to be compatible with its carbon reduction targets.[7])

The Global Financial Crisis, perhaps inevitably, limited the Treasury's interest in the issue for a period. As Stern puts it, there was 'a bandwidth problem'. Alistair Darling refers to it only once in his memoirs, when he briefly discusses the unsuccessful Copenhagen summit in 2009. He notes that 'far too many finance ministers regard climate change as something for others', and blames China and India for the failure to make progress. There are no references to domestic policy.

The Coalition government promised to be 'the greenest ever', and David Cameron invited those electors who wanted to go green to vote blue. But Osborne was not keen to be in the vanguard:

> I want to provide for the country the cheapest energy possible, consistent with having it reliable, in other words as a steady supply, and consistent with us playing our part in an international effort to tackle climate change. But I don't want us to be the only people out there in front of the rest of the world. I certainly think we shouldn't be further ahead of our partners in Europe.[8]

He was firm in his view that climate change is happening, but his policy orientation was: 'Let's try to do this in as cheap a way as possible.'[9] He supported both nuclear power and shale gas as important elements in future electricity generation.

It would be wrong to characterize the Treasury at that time as climate change deniers in the Lawson mould. By 2013 the department published an annual Sustainability Report, though made little effort to promote it. The 2014–15 edition committed to 'ensuring all policies with long term implications developed within the department take into account the need to adapt to climate change'.[10] These commitments were welcomed by campaigners, but there were continued claims that in practice they were not a decisive influence on Treasury policy. In 2015, the Institution of Environmental Sciences argued: 'Recent policy decisions in which HM Treasury was a key participant give cause for serious concern, since environmental protection and climate change do not appear to be priorities at present.'[11] They instance decisions to cut renewable energy subsidies at short notice, to remove support for carbon capture and storage, and to cut grants to local authorities to tackle air pollution. Perhaps most significantly, the fuel price escalator introduced in 1993, designed to produce steady real increases in fuel prices, was suspended in 2000 and never reinstated. In Stern's view, the Treasury missed several opportunities to raise fuel duty, especially at times when a falling oil price has pushed down pump prices. The white van man clearly carries greater weight than climate scientists.

Nonetheless, Osborne's Treasury played a part in the work leading up to the COP21 in Paris at the end of 2015, which did stimulate important international arguments on emission reductions. Osborne did not champion climate policy in government, but nor did he get in the way except to demand rigour in assessing the result to be expected from tax expenditure. The Treasury argue that a commitment to address global warming does not mean that all projects targeted at offsetting climate change must be supported, and that their role in ensuring value for money in public spending, or forgone tax revenue, requires them to take a hard-nosed approach. A number of the schemes introduced to promote energy efficiency in homes have had a weak impact at a high cost. So in their view they are inevitably cast as the villain in this play.

Philip Hammond's approach differed little from Osborne's. By the time he was Chancellor the debate had moved on, driven by firmer scientific advice on the implications of failing to act soon enough to address the rise in average temperature. But the Treasury remained concerned by the potential costs of a commitment to reduce carbon emissions more, and more quickly. In the summer of 2019, Hammond wrote a letter to Prime Minister May on the costs of transitioning to a net zero economy. The CCC estimated that the cost would be £50 billion a year, but the Department of Business put it at £70 billion a year. 'On the basis of these estimates, the total cost of transitioning to a zero-carbon economy is likely to be well in excess of a trillion pounds.'[12] The LSE Grantham Research Institute, headed by Nick Stern, criticized the Chancellor strongly, on the grounds that his comments 'undermined this objective and raised the policy risk premium attached to decarbonisation investments'.[13]

Sajid Javid was not in office long enough to make an impact in this area of policy, but under Rishi Sunak the Treasury's tone changed markedly, no doubt influenced by the government's global ambition, in turn driven by the location of the COP 26 conference in Glasgow in November 2021. Boris Johnson's own record on climate change is perhaps best described as mixed. In past newspaper columns he flirted with the arguments presented by deniers, including Piers Corbyn, brother of Jeremy. In 2004 he asserted that 'there is no evidence that the planet is suffering from the extreme weather patterns associated with climate change'. In 2006, he argued that 'it would be an abomination to crucify our landscape with wind farms' and as late as 2016 he described worries about global warming as 'a primitive fear'.[14] As Prime Minister, he has referred to 'the devastating threat of climate change' and published a ten-point plan for a green industrial revolution, though Claire O'Neill, the first choice to lead the government's efforts on COP26, said on leaving the job: 'The Prime Minister has made incredibly weak statements about this over the years. He has also admitted to me he doesn't really understand it.'[15] But decisions taken on, for example, diesel- and petrol-fuelled cars, sales of which will be banned from 2030, suggest a change of heart.

In 2019 the government committed to a legally binding net zero target. The CCC recommended that the Treasury should undertake a review of the economic impact of the net zero target, including its fiscal consequences, and examine 'the full range of policy levers, including carbon pricing, taxes, financial incentives, public spending, regulation and information provision'.[16] An Interim Report was published in December 2020.[17] The tone was markedly different from the 2019 Hammond letter to May. Gone were the estimates of massive economic cost: the headline conclusion was that 'the combined effect of UK and global climate action on UK economic growth is likely to be small'. Some costs are recognized, but they are assumed to be offset by the new growth opportunities which would arise if the UK can be established 'as global leader across the low carbon economy'.

The body of the report is somewhat more sobering than the Executive Summary, which may have benefited from the attentions of political spin-doctors, or spin-paramedics at least. By the time of the report, the CCC had sharply reduced its estimate of the costs, from £50 billion a year to £16 billion. The Treasury does not produce a rival estimate, but the analysis is sceptical of the CCC's estimate, and warns that the transition to net zero will coincide with a period during which demographic trends will put greater pressure on the public finances. It also points to the risks to tax receipts over the period, notably from the expected decline in fuel duty as petrol and diesel consumption falls, concluding that the government will face tough decisions on 'whether or not to adjust taxes in order to maintain revenue in a low carbon economy, or to balance any loss of tax revenue with reductions in spending'.

Nonetheless, as Jill Rutter says, it is 'a significant change of approach . . . It is no longer a question of economy or climate change: the Treasury now accepts that economic performance is predicated on preventing serious climate change.' But the risks are spelled out, as are the likely differential impacts on different sectors and household types. There is a recognition, absent from other government assessments, that the government 'will have to help the people who are most exposed to those costs. That is a much better basis for developing policy than presenting everything as a win-win.'[18] The final report was due to be published in the first half of 2021, but the commitment was subsequently revised to promise publication before COP26 in November of that year.

In the 2021 Budget, the Chancellor sprang another surprise. Central banks around the world have been considering the role they should play in climate change. Should they, for example, consider the carbon emissions of companies whose bonds they buy in their quantitative easing programmes? Should they impose higher capital requirements on banks they regulate, if those banks are exposed to companies whose business models are at risk from global warming? These questions have divided the central banking world. In the US, the Federal Reserve has been reluctant to move in those directions, on the grounds that to do so would exceed their congressional mandate. The German Bundesbank has been similarly cautious, while the Bank of England, under Mark Carney, and the Banque de France have taken the lead, pressing for stronger disclosures of climate risks by banks and insurers, and establishing a Network (of central banks) for Greening the Financial System.[19] Brown sees it as a personal crusade by Carney: 'The Bank of England's enthusiasm relates to Mark Carney's special interest and some other central bankers are nothing like as focused on it.[20]

The more cautious central bankers argue that there is a risk, if they are seen to be campaigners on the issue, and to be acting outside the terms of their anti-inflation and financial stability mandates, that they may put their precious independence at risk. The first best answer to this problem is to change the bank's mandate. Sunak did so in March 2021, saying that in future monetary policy should 'also reflect the importance of environmental sustainability and the transition to net zero'.[21] In response, the Bank of England committed to changing its bond buying approach 'to account for the climate impact of the issuers of the bonds we hold'. That could be a very significant change in the longer term, as it seems likely that the central banks will be large-scale purchasers of bonds for some time to come. Other central banks around the world are looking with close interest at the implications.

The evolution of Treasury policy on climate change since 1997 has broadly paralleled the changes in opinion elsewhere. At times, as with the Stern Review, the Treasury has pushed the government's thinking forward. At other times it has applied the handbrake. Conversations with

Chancellors, and senior officials, do not spontaneously turn to climate change. It is not exactly an afterthought, but until very recently has not been seen as an area in which the Treasury should take the lead. The consequences of the Treasury adopting a more active approach could be very significant in the coming years, but doing so will pose a challenge to the organization. As Stern puts it: 'The Treasury believes that markets give the signals you need unless there is overwhelming evidence to the contrary, and it takes a narrow view of value for money.'[22] The economic system changes needed to arrest global warming cannot be well assessed using these methodologies. Climate change analysis is riddled with market failures and externalities which are not properly priced. Deaths from air pollution are a case in point. And there is growing evidence that relative asset prices are not adjusting rapidly enough, or at all. So the traditional Treasury approach is not well-suited to addressing the problem. Stern argues that 'radically different models of the economy need to be built to capture the impact of potentially immense and destabilising risks'.[23] He questions whether the Treasury, as currently staffed, is up to the challenge.

9

The Treasury's
Changing Shape

On the eve of the 1997 general election the Treasury was
at the peak of its powers. The breadth of its responsibilities was immense. In the US, monetary policy was run
by the Federal Reserve, and public expenditure control
by the Office of Management and Budget, The Treasury
Department is in charge of economic policy and international economic relations, and the Council of Economic
Advisers, in the White House, is also very influential. In
the UK, all those functions were brigaded in HM Treasury.
In continental Europe, the major countries had by then
made their central banks independent monetary authorities and typically divided the other tasks between a Finance
Ministry and a Ministry of the Economy. This Treasury
dominance was not a recent development. The classic
description of the department, by Lord Bridges in 1964,
traces its position at the centre of government back to 'the
Revolution of 1688 which marked the emergence of the
Treasury as a public department'.[1]

The Treasury was not all-powerful by choice. Successive
Chancellors – Howe, Lawson, Lamont and Clarke – had
all come to the view that interest rate policy should move
across to the east end of town. But as Kenneth Clarke

observed, 'the slight snag was that neither of the Prime Ministers we served was remotely interested in having an independent bank'.[2] Officials' opinions were mixed, but most had come to the view that central bank independence made sense. So the major change announced by Gordon Brown immediately after the election was widely welcomed (though in fact the Conservative Party subsequently opposed the legislation in Parliament).

Setting the Bank free

It is not surprising that the doubts about central bank independence were stronger in Number 10, than in Number 11 Downing Street. The Treasury remained in close touch with the Bank, but the direct influence on interest rate decisions wielded in the past by Prime Ministers was much reduced. When pressed by his next-door neighbour to relax policy, which has historically been the prevailing economic wind, the Chancellor could say he would love to help, but the decision was sadly out of his hands. And Prime Ministers were reluctant to be seen to be talking directly to the Governor.

Although the change did remove a lever of power, it was one the Treasury had found it hard to use sensibly, especially when elections were in the offing. And the staffing implications were modest. From 1980 to 1982 I was grandly entitled 'Principal, Monetary Policy', and was part of a division, known as Home Finance 3, of a dozen people under Andrew Turnbull, later Permanent Secretary. Until the Ken and Eddie Show began after the ERM debacle, interest rate decisions were made on an ad hoc basis, with Chancellor–Governor meetings convened usually when the Bank found it challenging to fund the deficit. At times it was necessary to raise rates to cut gilt prices and create the expectation of future capital gains as rates fell back – the so-called 'Duke of York' strategy. After 1997 these meetings ceased, but there remained a need to brief the Chancellor for his regular private meetings with the Governor, at which the interest rate prospect was discussed. And there was a Treasury observer at MPC meetings, giving the institution a ringside seat in the forum where the decisions were made. At the same time, another change was made, which has received less attention. Sales of government debt had been handled by the Bank, which guarded its independence fiercely. The Treasury could influence funding policy, and did so, for example, with the introduction of indexed gilts in 1982, which the Bank had vigorously opposed, as a step which would institutionalize inflation, but the relationship was always difficult. The Bank was in the markets every day, and the Treasury found it difficult to gainsay its advice.

For many years, the Treasury felt that the Bank overengineered and overcomplicated funding policy. So when the responsibility for interest rates was transferred, it took the opportunity to create the Debt Management Office (DMO). The principal justification was that it was wrong in principle for the monetary authority to be responsible for selling debt. Investors would be suspicious that the Bank, with inside knowledge of future interest rate moves, might have the incentive to sell them debt ahead of a rise in rates, leaving them nursing a loss. Brown's letter to the Governor in May 1997 said bluntly: 'The Bank's role as the government's agent for debt management, the sale of gilts, oversight of the gilts market and cash management will be transferred to the Treasury.'[3]

The Bank was unhappy with the loss of an important function but did not argue the point strongly. The responsibility was transferred in April 1998 to the new DMO, initially run by a Treasury official. It is constitutionally part of the Treasury, but constructed as an executive agency, operating to a funding remit set annually by the Chancellor. Since then, while the DMO has not avoided all criticism about its practices, the change has proved remarkably uncontroversial, and no subsequent Chancellor has considered any fundamental revision of the arrangements.

So the 1997 reforms removed a responsibility the Treasury no longer wanted, and gave it control over an area of policy which it had long thought in need of reform. And, as we have seen, the concentration of responsibility for all forms of financial regulation in the FSA gave the Treasury more direct oversight of the financial sector than it had had before. Balls now believes the changes gave the Bank too much responsibility, and argues for a new body, on top of the Bank, chaired by the Chancellor, along the lines of the US Financial Stability Oversight Council.[4] But so far no Chancellor has wanted to take that on.

Osborne, while accepting the 1997 settlement in its essentials, was concerned about one aspect of the impact on the Treasury. Its economic expertise had, in his view, become devalued. 'The Treasury had lost its capacity to challenge the Bank on macroeconomic policy. The Government Economic Service had been downgraded. Dave Ramsden (then the Chief Economic Adviser and joint Head of the Government Economic Service) was a good man, but not up to the task of arguing the toss with Mervyn King. So I tried to recruit an external adviser. The man I wanted was Ken Rogoff, who had been Chief Economist of the IMF. Both Nick MacPherson and Mervyn King helped to try to persuade him. Ken was keen, though in the end family problems got in the way.'[5] (5)". But in spite of that failure he had no regrets about the reforms he inherited.

Gus O'Donnell, Permanent Secretary from 2002 to 2005, accepts that there were too few economists in the Treasury, but does not see that as being a result of Bank of England independence. 'There were always few monetary economists in that area of the Treasury by comparison to the Bank', he points out. That certainly reflects my own experience when, in the Home Finance department, I was responsible for monetary advice in the early 1980s.

After this initial burst of reform, Brown did not propose further institutional changes. But the Treasury's policy responsibilities grew. He used Public Service Agreements with other departments to advance his agenda. The Treasury set up internal units on immigration policy and other areas not traditionally part of a Finance Ministry. Brown chaired the main economic committee of the Cabinet – a post historically occupied by the Prime Minister. Andrew Rawnsley described Blair as 'the Chairman and Brown the Chief Executive' of the government.[6] (6).

John Birt's teddy bear

These imperial ambitions on the part of the Chancellor eventually provoked a reaction in 10 Downing Street, as relations between the two principals deteriorated. John Birt, a former Director General of the BBC, who was appointed as a Strategy Adviser to the Prime Minister in 2001, devised a plan to cut the Treasury down to size. Almost forty years earlier, after Labour's victory in the 1964 election, Harold Wilson had similarly tried to break the Treasury's monopoly on economic policymaking. He created a Department of Economic Affairs, initially under George Brown, which prepared a National Plan for the economy. The impact was modest, partly because the Treasury largely ignored it, and the department was wound up in 1969. But there was an effect on the Treasury. According to Douglas Wass, Permanent Secretary from 1974 to 1983, 'as the attempt at the DEA failed . . . so it fell to the Treasury to fill that gap and to concern itself with the supply potential of the economy'.[7]

Birt's plan, known oddly as Project Teddy Bear, was different. As Jeremy Heywood, then Principal Private Secretary to Blair, recorded: 'John's new idea was to split the Treasury into two parts – a Ministry of Finance overseeing macroeconomic issues, taxation and financial services, and an office of Budget and Delivery that would manage departmental spending from the Cabinet Office.'[8] The clear purpose was to reduce the Chancellor's power: 'Number 10 advisers felt the Prime Minister needed to act and this was one way of doing it.' Unsurprisingly, Brown was totally opposed, though he says he 'had never seen a paper on Project Teddy Bear and was never completely clear what the proposal was'.[9] An attempt to sweeten the pill by moving competition policy into the Treasury from the DTI did not make the scheme any more acceptable to him. In one of a number of retreats from confrontation with his Chancellor, Blair gave the idea up in the winter of 2005. In his memoirs, Brown notes drily that 'all that came out of Lord Birt's review was the renaming of the DTI as the Department for Productivity, Energy and Industry, but that plan also went wrong. Within days of taking office it was revoked by the new Minister, Alan Johnson, when we realised that the initials could be pronounced DIPPY.'[10]

O'Donnell sees these periodic plans to cut the Treasury down to size as attempts by Number 10 to reduce the influence of the one major counterbalance to the power of the Prime Minister. 'In the UK system a Prime Minister with a working majority in the Commons is very powerful indeed. It can look like an elected dictatorship. A strong Treasury can be a useful check.'[11] So it is not a surprise that attacks on its range of functions have always come from above, whether from Harold Wilson in the 1960s, Blair and Birt in the late 1990s, or, more recently, Theresa May's Chief of Staff Nick Timothy.

It makes sense that the one Chancellor who became Prime Minister has a nuanced view. Brown now recognizes that 'people think the Treasury has been too powerful and resent it. Number 10 also resents it.' But for him the big question is the tension between an economic ministry and a finance ministry. 'I wanted the Treasury to be more of an economic ministry. Only the Treasury is in a position to lead the debate on growth and productivity. The idea of building on the business department and turning it into an economic strategy department is doomed to fail. The top civil servants in the business department are weak and most of them want to get into the Treasury if they can.'[12]

Structural changes

A more fruitful initiative came in the area of tax policy and administration. The separation of responsibility for VAT, which lay with HM Customs and Excise, and for the rest of the tax system, run by the Inland Revenue, had long been seen as an anachronism in the Treasury, and was increasingly out of line with international practice. The Inland Revenue had gradually been accruing new functions, for the Contributions Agency in 1999 and for the Child Benefit Office in 2003, which suggested it had the appetite to expand. At the same time, ministers and officials were increasingly frustrated by the weak capacity the Treasury had in the area of tax policy. At budget time they were heavily dependent on advice from Revenue and Customs, advice which they sometimes questioned.

So Brown commissioned a review from Gus O'Donnell. Typically, the outcomes of reviews commissioned by Brown as Chancellor were a foregone conclusion, resulting in more power to the Treasury, and O'Donnell did not disappoint. He recommended a merger of the Revenue and Customs Departments into a new single department called Her Majesty's Revenue and Customs, reporting to the Chancellor.[13] Introducing the report, Brown said his conclusion was that 'the Treasury should lead tax policy development and strengthen its capability for high-level analysis of the tax regime, and the new Department should lead policy maintenance and delivery'.[14] The proposed change was welcomed by the Treasury Select Committee and implemented quickly. A number of tax policy people moved across to HMT. Nick Stern worked on the project and, in his words, 'smuggled in an extra 100 people' to strengthen the Treasury's capacity.[15]

It is difficult to assess whether the reform has fully met the desired objectives. Treasury officials are positive and believe it has strengthened their ability to advise ministers on tax proposals. O'Donnell himself still thinks it was the right move. 'The way the Treasury ran the budget process beforehand was a scandal. The Treasury did not have the needed expertise on tax, while HMRC was not capable of serious policy thinking.'[16]

External assessments have been less favourable. One academic paper describes it as an example of 'a dangerous tendency to view the practice of politics as a predominantly technical activity'.[17] Another argues that 'centralising authority with the Treasury has left technical knowledge undervalued by consigning it to policy maintenance'.[18] And a more recent review by the Institute for Government concluded that 'the balance of responsibilities between the two departments has created a distance between policy and the operational front line, which is exacerbated by problems engaging external expertise'.[19] HMRC people have been reluctant to move to the Treasury for a number of reasons, including working hours and pay. They point out that the age and grade structures of the two departments are so different that to expect frequent interchanges between them is unrealistic. Staff at the Treasury are far younger on average, with much more rapid turnover. The incidence of failed or withdrawn tax measures has not fallen and, in the Institute for Government's view, 'the government fails to set out and follow a direction of travel for specific areas of tax policy or the system as a whole'. (Tax reform was discussed in Chapter 4.)

A more obviously successful example of institutional reform was the establishment of the Office of Budget Responsibility by George Osborne in 2010. Osborne recalls that during his five years as Shadow Chancellor he had the unwanted leisure to work up policy ideas in some detail. The OBR was one such. 'The OBR was not an intrinsically Conservative idea. The IMF had suggested something similar. Andrew Tyrie [Chair of the TSC] worked on the idea too. I was also influenced by something Denis Healey said (in *The Chancellor's Tales*) about the problem of being held responsible for the Treasury's forecasts. It seemed sensible to have someone else produce those forecasts so the Chancellor could not be blamed for them. But there was also a political incentive, in that Gordon Brown was widely thought to have fiddled the budgetary figures and could not be trusted.'[20]

The plan was well developed by the time of the election. Osborne continued: 'Alan Budd had worked on the OBR idea while we were in opposition and had agreed to be its first head. There were a lot of discussions with Treasury officials too. It was the fifth year of the Parliament so we knew an election was coming, and contacts between Treasury officials and the opposition are routine. Officials were not at all defensive about it, and the arguments they had been involved in between Number 10 and Number 11 on the Treasury's forecasts had scarred them. So the idea ticked a lot of boxes. It is important to remember that after Black Wednesday in 1992 the Conservatives had been behind Labour in the polls on economic competence for some years, so we needed something which would help to level the score.'

Alistair Darling himself agrees that the OBR was a good idea, and would not advise a future Labour Chancellor to change it. 'In fact I explored the idea of setting up something similar, but Gordon would not agree to it. His argument was that if I introduced an independent entity to produce a forecast, I would effectively be accusing Gordon of not telling the truth in the past.'[21] Labour's attitude has since changed. Brown now acknowledges that 'we could have done it ourselves'.[22] As Shadow Chancellor, Ed Balls asked the OBR to audit the Labour manifesto.[23] Osborne did not fall for that.

The three heads so far, Alan Budd, Robert Chote and Richard Hughes, have managed the role skilfully, retaining their independence, but being careful not to exceed their brief.

Officials do not regret the increased discipline on Chancellors to make realistic assumptions about the future growth rate. Chancellors may sometimes wish they had more flexibility, but do not say so. It is more difficult to make late changes to taxation in the run-up to the budget. The OBR reasonably insists on being given time to assess the impact of new proposals. That makes for a more considered process. As Hammond puts it: 'It makes it hard to change your mind at a late stage as the OBR does not have the capacity to make late adjustments. It also makes it difficult for the Prime Minister to ask for late changes, which is a big advantage.'[24]

Feeble threats

Under Ed Miliband, the Labour Party in opposition did give serious consideration to reform. *The End of the Treasury*, published in September 2014, was what is known in the journalism trade as 'a searing indictment' of the institution and all its works. 'The Treasury's own ideological biases and rules of thumb . . . constitute a political actor in their own right, and instil government as a whole with a chilling pessimism.' If one replaced 'pessimism' with 'realism', there are many officials who would be proud to be thought of in that way, and some Chancellors too. The authors charged the Treasury with 'government by accountant', and 'over-centralization', among a long list of crimes. The proposed remedy was to break it up, 'moving budgetary powers into a significantly enlarged Prime Minister's department, and economic policy into a genuine department of growth (which would be merged with the Business Department), leaving a much smaller finance ministry to deal with taxation and macroeconomics.'[25] There were strong echoes of John Birt's Teddy Bear in this prescription.

The proposal was never formally adopted by Miliband, and we cannot know if it would have been taken forward. Three years later, after the Corbyn takeover, Shadow Chancellor John McDonnell commissioned another review, from Bob (now Lord) Kerslake, who had been Head of the Home Civil Service under the Coalition government. Kerslake took a different tack, perhaps reflecting his own experience at the centre of government. He noted that the Treasury had played an increasing role in 'arbitrating and even initiating domestic policy', especially under Gordon Brown, and welcomed 'the more recent move of the Treasury back to its underlying role'. The culture of the department he characterized as 'arrogant, overbearing and negative towards other departments'. He noted that "'the standing and credibility of the Treasury was damaged by the widespread rejection of its warnings' in the EU referendum (see Chapter 6) and that its role in the Brexit debate had been weakened. His assessment was that 'we may have reached the high water mark of an expansionist Treasury'.[26]

The body of the Kerslake Review included an extremely critical assessment of the department's performance in its core areas of responsibility. It scored very poorly on financial regulation, and on taxation it 'has contributed to creating one of the most complex and hard to operate tax systems in the world'. It did not prepare for Brexit. Its culture and capability were found wanting. So it is not surprising that the review team explored the option of a break-up and the creation of a separate finance ministry. What is more of a surprise is that they rejected it, largely on the practical grounds 'that the disruption caused by such a reorganisation outweighed the benefits'. The only conditions attached to the Treasury continuing in its present form were that it should stick to its core roles and that "'the disciplines of good economic and financial management were given equal weighting, which they clearly are not at present'. So once again the Treasury escaped the threat of dismemberment, even on the basis of a very dirty bill of health.

The referendum result, the departure of Cameron and Osborne and the arrival in Downing Street of Theresa May produced another attack on Treasury dominance, from the usual quarter: Number 10. May herself was no friend, after many bruising spending arguments during her long stint at the Home Office. Nick Timothy was especially hostile. His attitude was toughened when it became clear that her appointee as Chancellor, Philip Hammond, was determined to argue for a soft Brexit. He also suspected the Treasury of being institutionally committed to austerity, which was inimical to his concept of blue-collar Toryism. One official describes May's first year as one of the worst in Treasury history.

Timothy wanted what would in effect have been a version of the 1960s Department of Economic Affairs, based in the Department for Business, Energy and Industrial Strategy (BEIS). That department was asked to produce a new industrial strategy. When Treasury officials asked to see a draft, they were told they could not. Hammond had to intervene personally. Relations were at a low ebb when May called an election over Easter in 2017. Hammond mentally packed his bags: he did not expect to be reappointed after her expected victory, and the Treasury braced for a post-election attack. But the election went badly. Timothy was seen as one of the key architects with his imprudent manifesto language about the costs of social care, and the idea of cutting HMT down to size left government with him.

Lionel Barber, former editor of the *Financial Times*, summed up a widely held view in 2021 in an article in *Prospect* magazine, 'The Treasury Today: A Devalued Currency'.[27] He rehearses the arguments about the Treasury and Brexit: it 'inflicted damage on many UK institutions, but few more than the Treasury'. The Covid-19 episode has been 'a chastening experience'. But the Treasury still 'enjoys a pedigree and clarity of mission unmatched in Whitehall', in spite of its 'extraordinary, at times infuriating, attention to financial minutiae'. The problem Barber identifies, though, is 'the decline of economics as the determining factor in Whitehall policy-making' and the indifference of the Johnson government to economic arguments. If that persists, however brilliant Treasury officials may be, the influence of their department will be less, unless and until an economic crisis intervenes.

In the meantime, the Chancellor should 'aim to stay in the driving seat of a re-modelled Treasury car: less the effortlessly superior Rolls-Royce of old, which was never quite as good as it was thought. More a sleek, environmentally sensitive, high-tech Tesla – with a more realistic valuation.'

That view of the Treasury's diminished status is, however well supported by the commentariat, almost certainly wrong. The Covid pandemic put the Treasury back in centre stage. It devised support programmes for businesses and jobs in very quick order, under a Chancellor who exuded competence in an otherwise chaotic administration. Johnson, who had seen the Treasury as a hotbed of Remainers during his time at the Foreign Office, realized that it was the only institution that could save his government, and quickly became a strong supporter. So the wheel turned full circle. In March 2021 the Industrial Strategy Committee, set up by Theresa May under the Business Department and chaired by Andy Haldane of the Bank of England, was summarily dismissed. The Treasury assumed charge of the government's Plan for Growth, which incorporates initiatives which had been under the aegis of BEIS.

Does size matter?

There is one point, however, on which almost all these external commentators agree: the Treasury is very thinly staffed for the range of functions it performs.

Time series comparisons are difficult, given the changing suite of responsibilities over the period since 1997. A simple analysis would show that the Treasury employed 1,000 people in 1997, which fell to 850 at the turn of the millennium.[28] The headline number rose to 1,400 in 2009, after 200 additional civil servants were recruited to handle the financial crisis,[29] before falling back to little over 1,000 in 2014. By 2020 the number had risen again, to 1,700 (with another 1,000 in agencies like the Debt Management Office), but most of the increase came in the four years after the EU referendum, driven first by the demands of Brexit, and then by the Covid crisis. Staff numbers have risen by almost 50% since the summer of 2016.[30] These late additions are something of an exception to the rule over the past fifty years. For most of that period the Treasury has adopted a hair-shirt approach to staffing levels, to the pay of its staff, and to expenditure in general. To encourage other departments to control their spending and headcount, it has behaved as the Caesar's wife of Whitehall, sometimes to a fault. As Kerslake says: 'The Treasury was inclined to offer up budget and staff cuts in spending reviews to set an example to other Departments. Whilst laudable in its intent, the effect of this when combined with below average rates of pay by Whitehall standards, raised real capacity issues.'[31] O'Donnell agrees: 'The hair shirt idea has always been taken too seriously. There are too few people overall, but it does mean the Treasury is the most efficient Whitehall department, with the highest productivity.'[32]

The intellectual ability of Treasury civil servants is rarely questioned. (As a former official, I am unlikely to prove an exception to that rule.) Denis Healey as Chancellor said, in a phrase reminiscent of the current Prime Minister's propensity to claim world-beating capacity in the UK: 'The Treasury commands the best brains in a civil service which has no intellectual superior in the world.'[33] But there are doubts about three things:

1. Do they have the right skills and experience?
2. Do they stay long enough in post?
3. Is the structure appropriate for all the different Treasury responsibilities?

Kerslake responds negatively to the first question. In 2017, according to his review, the average age of Treasury officials was twenty-seven. Respondents to his review argued furthermore that the department had too few qualified finance staff, 'which was felt to reflect a view that finance work was less glamorous or important than economics-based policy advice to Ministers'. In her review of the Treasury's response to the financial crisis in 2012, Sharon White had made essentially the same point.[34] There were efforts to fill the gap after her paper, but it is hard to see that the Treasury changed fundamentally as a result. In any event, staffing up to cope with a once-in-a-century event would hardly be a rational deployment of resources.

John Kingman, a Second Permanent Secretary in the Treasury until 2016, returned to the topic at the end of 2020. He modestly accepted that senior civil servants were usually blessed with outstanding intellect and ingenuity at finding solutions for tricky problems, as well as the ability to work well with ministers. But 'what is wrong is what is missing . . . a track record of ever having made anything happen, as opposed to successfully keeping the plates spinning, is still – at most – seen as a "nice to have". And, perhaps most oddly of all, substantial or deep domain knowledge and experience is still not really particularly valued – at any rate in the higher reaches of the policymaking civil service.'[35] He recalled that he was asked in 2003 to lead a review of the Treasury. In it, he 'suggested there might be certain topics – corporate tax, say, or pensions, or the energy market – which were core business but which were also ferociously complex and technical, and perhaps not ideally suited to even brilliant 24-year-old generalists'. Gus O'Donnell accepted the recommendation, but it proved 'just too weird and counter-cultural. It died a quiet death'.[36]

So there are powerful arguments, espoused by some in the Treasury itself, suggesting that it is short of some important skills. What of the second, linked charge, that officials move too frequently and therefore do not build up domain knowledge? Furthermore, that partly as a result of rapid moves, their training is neglected.

Michael Gove, famously suspicious of experts, nonetheless would like to see a civil service where officials stayed in post long enough to develop deep knowledge. His diagnosis is that 'the current structure of the Civil Service career ladder means that promotion comes from switching roles, and departments, with determined regularity'.[37] He acknowledges that ministers move too rapidly, but is especially critical of 'the whirligig of Civil Service transfers and promotions'. He is scathing about current civil service training efforts and calls for 'a properly-resourced campus for training those in government'. Kingman agrees, referring to 'the almost comic lack of serious attention to training' in the upper reaches of the civil service, and a 'disdain for knowledge and expertise'.[38] Gove's recommendations involve slowing down the whirligig, requiring officials to build up real knowledge and experience, more expertise in mathematics, statistics and probability, more commercial experience and greater exposure to the world outside Westminster and Whitehall. Kingman notes that 'Gove echoes, surprisingly directly, the Fulton report, commissioned more than 50 years ago by Harold Wilson', which suggests that 'changing the civil service is a lot easier to advocate than to achieve'.

These points all apply to the Treasury. It is able to recruit highly talented staff more easily than are other departments, because of the high interest and significance of the work. Working for the Treasury has a certain cachet in the London job market outside the civil service. I moved from a monetary policy job in HMT to McKinsey in 1982. That move would have been far harder to engineer from the DHSS, as it then was, or DWP today. The Treasury's high reputation helped enormously. So there is more than average movement in and out, which leads to the remarkably low average age. Turnover in the Treasury in 2017–18 was about 20%, the third highest in Whitehall, behind only the Cabinet Office, a special case, and the Ministry of Communities, Housing and Local Government, not the favourite billet for aspiring civil servants.[39]

Cheap but cheerful?

That is associated with another problem, which ministers do not acknowledge, but Kingman does: pay. He points out that in 2020 the starting salary of a fast-stream graduate civil servant was £28,000. In management consulting the rate was at least £45,000 and a good first-year graduate in a top investment bank would earn, including bonus, more like £80,000. Those differentials become wider as one's career develops. A successful 30-year-old civil servant may be earning £75,000. In consulting, the figure would be between twice and four times as high, and probably six times in an investment bank. The average FTSE100 CEO now earns around twenty-five times the Permanent Secretary rate. These differentials have worsened over time in two ways. The remarkable success of the financial City has meant a growth in the number of competing, high-wage jobs. (That may change post-Brexit to some extent, but gradually.) And frequent public sector pay freezes have held down civil service pay.

There are few novels in which Treasury officials play a leading role. But Alec Waugh's *A Spy in the Family*, set in the 1960s, centres on a middle-ranking official in his thirties. He lives in Kensington, lunches every day at his club, the Athenaeum, and shops in Jermyn Street.[40] Every other Friday he is manicured at Simpson's. That is no longer the way of things. Treasury officials have been priced out of the inner London property market. Kingman calculates that 'in 1970 the average London house price was 1.2 times the median grade 6/7 pay. That ratio is now 8.4 times.' In the late 1970s, I bought a two-bedroom flat in Islington on my Treasury grade 7 salary, close enough to run, slowly, to the office. That would be inconceivable today. No one joins the Treasury to get rich, but, as Kingman says, 'high-quality STEM graduates are simply a lot more employable in higher-paying jobs in the rest of the economy. Is it any surprise that the civil service is left with the less high-earning humanities graduates, whose skills (conveniently) happen to be quite well-suited to a career which is mainly about the skilful use of words?'[41] One slightly odd consequence, according to him, is that the Treasury has become more middle class than before. Data are hard to come by, but there is anecdotal evidence to suggest that a growing number of senior officials have partners in more highly paid jobs in the law or the City, allowing them to work for a low salary in government.

That is a pessimistic conclusion, and neither Gove nor Kingman hold out the prospect of improvements in the foreseeable future. Another post-Covid public sector pay freeze is likely to make the differential problem worse. The removal of a number of senior officials whose faces didn't fit with the Johnson government has not helped morale either. A further development, whose consequences are unpredictable, is the announcement in the 2021 Budget that a group of staff will move to Darlington. That will help the housing cost problem, but may reduce the attraction of working close to the seat of power, unless ministers spend time there.

Is there a structural solution, my third question? When, following the O'Donnell report, some tax policy people were moved into the Treasury, there was, as we have seen, a significant mismatch between the structures of the two departments, HMRC and HMT. In HMRC there is a premium on people with a deep understanding of the tax system; in HMT a premium on fast-moving, adaptable staff, strong on problem-solving and drafting. So perhaps the Treasury needs a more varied approach to staffing. Tax policy is one area where deep domain knowledge is needed, and financial regulation may be another now that the responsibility for legislation has passed back to Whitehall from the European Commission.

It would be an exaggeration to say that the Treasury faces a crisis. And another serving senior official, with private sector experience, believes the criticisms are overstated. 'I have consistently been positively surprised by the quality of the teams who work for me, and there has been no diminution of quality over the last decade.'[42] But as Kingman says 'there is only so far you can stretch the elastic', and we are moving towards a position more like the US one, where public servants are very poorly paid and depend on a rapidly revolving door between the civil service and the financial and commercial sectors, or on their partners. That may prove to be the only workable model in the future, but it is not one the country has explicitly chosen.

Call a spad a spad

There is another dimension of the Treasury's staffing, which has waxed and waned over the decades – the role of special advisers. They have existed, in one form or another, since 1964. In the early years they were funded by the Rowntree Foundation and known charmingly as chocolate soldiers.[43] Their numbers grew under Labour in the 1970s, then declined under Margaret Thatcher, though in other ways their importance grew. John Redwood, David Willetts and Oliver Letwin all played significant roles in Downing Street. Thatcher allowed only one spad, as they were not then called, per department, but the Treasury had a special dispensation and employed three. For a time, I was one, by accident. The Brighton bomb created a parliamentary opening for Michael Portillo, then one of Nigel Lawson's entourage, and I was invited to fill the gap for a year, on secondment from McKinsey.

At that time, the Treasury team of advisers were not principal drivers of policy. It would be wrong to say we were wholly irrelevant. My colleagues were close to party thinking, and I took on the role of speechwriter. Nigel Lawson affected to believe we were useful, though in one meeting he complained forcefully that we are 'all supporters of the bloody SDP'. But it would not be false modesty to assert that our influence did not compare with that of some of our successors in the period under review.

Ed Balls became Chief Economic Adviser after a time as a special adviser. His role in Bank of England independence was crucial, and he and Ed Miliband carried out much of the liaison between the Chancellor and Treasury officials. Shriti Vadera was also a crucial actor in the financial crisis, as we have seen, from within the Treasury or from outside it, though technically she was never a spad. Darling's method of working was rather different. His memoirs show that spads were not insignificant, especially on policy presentation, but there was no one of the stature of Balls, Miliband or Vadera. Osborne, however, depended heavily on Rupert Harrison, an economist of some distinction and who had been an adviser to Osborne in opposition. Harrison was respected by Treasury officials and his strong working relationship with Osborne made him an especially valuable conduit. Hammond ran a team of half a dozen, of varying stature and roles, none of whom achieved high public profile. Javid was not in office long enough for his advisers to achieve prominence for their views or what they did, but they were significant in his departure. After his election victory in December 2019, Johnson insisted, as a condition of Javid's reappointment, that his team should be managed by Dominic Cummings in Downing Street. Javid declined, and was rapidly replaced by Rishi Sunak. Does that mark the end of the Treasury's own advisory team? To an extent yes, but after the departure of Cummings 'the joint unit means nothing at all' according to one official.[44] It was not a totally new idea, as Harrison had advised both Cameron and Osborne in opposition. But, in any event, it did not last. 'There is a vacuum at Number 10 and we have reverted to the old-fashioned way of doing business with the Chancellor and the PM negotiating between themselves.'

Culture

After a few years working on the control of defence expenditure, in 1979 I was released to spend a year at Stanford Business School in California. On my return, having learnt a lot about business strategy and finance, I was posted to the Home Finance division as Principal, Monetary Policy, a subject not offered in the MBA programme. But I was excited to return to the centre of policymaking, in the midst of what came to be known as Thatcher's sado-monetarist phase, when short-term interest rates were raised to 16 per cent.

On my first day back, I picked up a pass at the front door and made my way to my new office on the inner circle. En route I passed three colleagues I knew quite well: none acknowledged my existence. I immediately felt I had come back home.

The Treasury does not cultivate a warm and cuddly working environment. You may well not know if your immediate boss has a spouse or partner, and would certainly never meet them if they exist. Social events are at a premium. But it is not hierarchical. If a junior official has an opinion worth hearing, it will be heard. The contrast with the Foreign Office, from which I had moved, could have been more stark, in both respects. The Treasury's own description of its culture declares that 'we value intellectual honestly, regularly question assumptions'.[45] That is a fair description. People work very hard: heavy individual workloads are driven by the 'Caesar's wife' approach to spending and staffing levels. But in spite of salary levels that are low in market terms, it achieves a high rating of 4.3 on Glassdoor (a website where employees anonymously review employers), compared to 3.9 for the more highly paid Bank of England.[46]

In his early days as Permanent Secretary, Burns asked me (at the time I ran the Audit Commission) to review the Treasury's culture and working approaches and, by interviewing those who interacted with it from other departments and the private sector, to paint a picture of how it was viewed by others.[47] The conclusions were mixed. Officials believed in what they were doing and saw themselves as a 'respected elite corps' but thought the department cultivated an ascetic, self-denying culture. Its assumption was that anyone who approached the department from the outside was after money. That may have been a safe assumption in the case of David Cameron and Lex Greensill in 2021 (where the Treasury was firm in rejecting pleas for special treatment), but it applied to other Whitehall departments too, which made it difficult to develop collaborative relations with them. Brown identified that weakness, and believed he had done something about it, but as Prime Minister worried that it was 'shifting away from being the activist department that said "yes" to innovation and reform and reverting to its traditional role as the finance department that specialised in saying "No"'.[48] Darling was also frustrated at the poor relationship he observed between the Treasury and the Bank. The former's view of the latter has long been that it is over-staffed, overpaid and over there (in the City). (That type of relationship between the Finance Ministry and Central Bank is not unknown elsewhere.)

My 1992 review also highlighted the department's poor reputation with the private sector. 'Outsiders see it as a remote, arrogant, out-of-touch organisation engaged in many insignificant – and some positively harmful – activities, while failing in its main task of providing strategic guidance to the economy.' They noted that 'charm is an undervalued characteristic', that 'the dismissive and lofty tone taken with other departments and the outside world harms the Treasury's reputation', and that 'only a certain sort of woman can succeed.' So there was remarkable divergence between how the Treasury saw itself and how others saw it, but also a willingness to face up to the problem. The strongest critic was an internal interviewee who described it as 'an institutional shambles'.

Much has happened since 1992, though some of the criticisms of the tone the Treasury adopts with other departments still ring true today. The department has made strenuous efforts to update its practices. It set and achieved targets for 50% representation of women in its senior grades, where it ranks among the leading departments of state on that measure.[49] The mean gender pay gap, at 14.6%, is below the national median.[50] But it is one of only six departments where women are in a minority overall, and there has never been a female Permanent Secretary, which is increasingly rare in Whitehall.[51] Treasury women have moved to senior positions elsewhere, like Rachel Lomax who became a Deputy Governor of the Bank of England, or Sharon White who became Chief Executive of Ofcom, and is now in the chair at the John Lewis Partnership, but none has made it to the top job internally.

At political level the same is true. There has never been a female Chancellor, and since 1997 that is the only Cabinet position (aside from the intermittent role of Deputy Prime Minister) which has not been held by a woman.[52] It seems unlikely that that can continue, given the gender profile in Parliament of the two main parties, but when recent appointments to the position have been made there has not been an obvious woman candidate, except perhaps Liz Truss, who is now in another major office of state at the Foreign, Commonwealth and Development Office (FCDO).

10
Leadership

By comparison with most other government departments the Treasury benefited, through most of the period, from strong political leadership. Chancellors typically spend longer in office than is the case elsewhere in the Cabinet. The ministerial merry-go-round whirls less rapidly in Horse Guards Road. In the forty-seven years since Denis Healey took office, there have been only twelve holders of the Chancellor's office, only ten if one discounts the short interregnums of John Major and Sajid Javid. Sunak is early into what could well be a lengthy term.

As we have seen, the character of the individuals who held office has at times had a major impact on the way the department worked, as well as on policy. How are the Chancellors during the period viewed by the officials they oversaw?

Gordon Brown

Gordon Brown came as a shock to the Treasury system, and not only because he arrived with well-developed, and non-negotiable, plans to grant independence to the Bank and restructure financial regulation. His working methods were quite different from anything officials had known before. The previous five Chancellors were all men with strong convictions and, in the case of Howe and Lawson, clear views on how they believed economic policy should be constructed. But they all worked with the grain of the policymaking machine.

Brown took a different approach. He was not interested in convening large meetings and hearing a range of official views. His instinct was not to hold a meeting until he knew what he wanted. In set-pieces, he was almost always on transmit, not receive.

Brown made no secret of his dislike of the way the Treasury was run. In his memoir he said: 'The way the Treasury then worked was, in my view, unmanageable – gatherings of countless officials assembled around this massive oval table. It was also a waste of valuable time for senior officials, since only one or two of them were ever expected to speak.'[1] It did not concern him that junior officials learnt a great deal from hearing the debate, which allowed them to tailor their analysis and advice appropriately.

He gradually allowed a small number of officials to influence policy, notably Nigel Wicks on the international side and Steve Robson on finance and industry, but that number did not include Terry Burns, his first Permanent Secretary, who was soon squeezed out. Officials' views were transmitted through 'the two Eds' (Balls and Miliband). That unusual way of operating worked tolerably well, and important business was transacted efficiently, through there were many occasions on which needed decisions languished unmade in his private office, as Brown was not sufficiently engaged to address them.

Though they saw less of their master then they would have liked, officials respected his intellect and welcomed his high standing in the government. He had 'a lateral way of thinking', said one.[2] Decision-making was more fraught and complicated than it had been under Kenneth Clarke, whose sunny disposition and cheerful ability to dismiss counter-arguments with a wave of the hand won grudging respect. But officials thought Brown could normally be relied on to reach a sensible view, once all the possible alternatives had been explored.

One aspect of the Brown operation did jar with the Treasury, however. Brown 'used thugs to do his dirty work', men like Ian Austin, Charlie Whelan and Damian McBride. They 'were seriously unpleasant people', said one official. When challenged about using them, or about any other bad behaviour, Brown would 'begin to talk about his father, to suggest that no son of such a righteous man could possibly do wrong'. At times the leaking and hostile briefing of colleagues made the working environment very disagreeable. Some excellent officials, like Jill Rutter, left rather than continue working in that climate.

The Treasury understood Brown's strategy on spending. He wanted to gain credibility for fiscal continence in the early years, to gain the room for manoeuvre to implement bigger spending plans later. The aim of a bigger state, eventually, was understood, as was the declared policy aim of ending, or at least minimizing, child poverty. His regular interference in the business of other departments was also welcomed. The Treasury tends to believe it can do other people's jobs better than they can. (In late 2000 Brown asked me to review enterprise education in schools. I agreed, but asked if the Education Department was on board. 'I must tell Estelle [Morris, then the Secretary of State] we are doing it', he replied.)

As for the euro, officials quickly appreciated that his aim was to keep Britain out. Balls had made no secret of that ambition. Most Treasury officials were sympathetic. The ERM experience had scarred them deeply. The work on the five tests (see Chapter 6) generally reflected the views of most Treasury economists, though the output of the exercise was weaponized by Ed Balls and created bad blood between the Treasury and Number 10 which made other business harder to transact for a time.

In an interview with the *Financial Times* in 2007, as Brown neared the end of his long tenure as Chancellor, which may not have been intended for publication, Andrew Turnbull delivered his verdict:

> He cannot allow (his colleagues) any serious discussion about priorities. His view is that it is just not worth it and 'they will get what I decide'. And that is a very insulting process. Do those ends justify the means? It has enhanced Treasury control, but at the expense of any government cohesion and any assessment of strategy. You can choose whether you are impressed or depressed by that, but you cannot help admire the sheer Stalinist ruthlessness of it all.[3]

Turnbull is at the negative end of the spectrum. Steve Robson admired Brown, but nonetheless noted that 'Gordon would take an opposing view simply to bugger up Tony. Arguments would go on and on and on.'[4] The debate on Brown's suitability as Prime Minister similarly goes on and on. He was far more suited to the Finance Director role. As chairman of a company, you do not want your chief financial officer to be on warm terms with every executive, particularly not with those who are not meeting their financial targets. So the verdict of those who served in the Treasury with him is positive overall. He was clearly a better Chancellor than Prime Minister. He could master a brief, and left the Treasury stronger than he found it.

Alistair Darling

Of all Chancellors in this period, Alistair Darling elicits the most positive opinions from his officials. 'The nearest thing to a human being to have done the job in recent years', as one put it.[5] He reverted to the more traditional way of doing business, stylistically similar to Lawson and Lamont. There were meetings at which competing views were presented and argued, and a conclusion was reached, then implemented. After the Brown era, that way of doing business came as a pleasant change. The atmosphere in the building improved. Treasury officials are not prone to spontaneous outbursts of emotion, but some came close.

Unfortunately, Darling's Treasury honeymoon was short. He took office on 28 June 2007. On 8 August 2007 BNP suspended the calculation of the net asset value of three of its funds – an event generally seen as the starting gun of the GFC. From then on, he was consumed by its demand. He also had another handicap: his next-door neighbour. Brown found it difficult to relinquish control of the department, and at times did not try very hard to do so. He ran a kind of Shadow Treasury in Number 10, using Ed Balls, Shriti Vadera and others. Darling explains the difficulty of operating in that unconventional way in his memoirs *Back from the Brink*.[6] On Brown, he comments: 'Something changed after he became Prime Minister and suddenly I was definitely outside the tent . . . I wasn't privy to thinking or discussion on policy issues within a close team.' The problem persisted throughout his Chancellorship.

That division became crystallized around the question of the appropriate fiscal stance in the run-up to the 2010 election. It was caricatured, only a little, as a conflict between Darling's preference for deficit reduction (albeit not on the scale subsequently pursued by Osborne) and Brown's bias towards investment. In 2009, Brown told Darling he planned to move him. Darling acknowledged that the PM would be better off with a Chancellor he could get on with and who was in the same place as him in policy terms. But after James Purnell's resignation from the government, and other intra-Cabinet disputes, Brown backed off and Darling remained in office, albeit now in the knowledge that his boss did not want him there.

This lack of understanding with Brown proved to be a serious handicap. Nonetheless, after a difficult start Darling is widely seen to have handled the crisis as well as could be expected. As we have seen, the Treasury was not well-prepared for the Northern Rock failure, but quickly equipped itself with greater expertise. Darling proved a

sure-footed operator when tough decisions were needed
in the autumn of 2008. Officials admired his calmness
under fire, and his reluctance to shoot messengers or blame
his staff – a failing often seen in Brown. He also had the
admirable quality of reading his briefing: 'An Edinburgh
lawyer, he has the capacity to absorb information and
make decisions', said one. Brown would have been much
worse in the Treasury during the financial crisis. He was
better in Downing Street calling up other global leaders.
Brown and Balls were critical of Darling for not being
political enough, and for being too cautious. 'In particular
he made good decisions in the late stages as he thought
they would lose and wanted to leave with the reputation
for doing the right thing.'[7]

He was never a charismatic media presenter, which
could be a handicap when it was important to explain dramatic and costly interventions, but he retained the respect
of the House of Commons, and many in the media, for his
doggedness under fire. The Treasury was sorry to see him
go in the 2010 election.

George Osborne

Officials knew a lot about George Osborne before he
took office. He had been Shadow Chancellor since 2005,
initially appointed by Michael Howard, but retained by
David Cameron. He was very critical of Brown in his early
years, describing him in 2005 as 'a Chancellor past his
sell-by date', a jibe not forgotten by its victim, and as
'brutal and unpleasant'.[8] He was never similarly abusive
to Alistair Darling, perhaps recognizing that he would be
difficult to demonize.

Osborne divides opinion in the Treasury. All witnesses
described him as a very political Chancellor, but some
regard that as a positive trait, suggestive of a minister who
knows which policies are deliverable, while others think
it betrays a lack of principle and a tendency to be blown

by the erratic winds of public opinion. Oliver Letwin, a political colleague rather than an official, reconciles the two thoughts, praising his ability to 'combine robust and meticulous attention to detail with a capacity to abstract from it and see the big picture historically, politically and economically'.[9]

He began with a strength denied to Darling, in the form of a generally positive relationship with the Prime Minister. Cameron did intervene in economic decision-making at times, usually foolishly, but for the most part left his Chancellor alone. Political decision- making in the coalition government could have been complex and dysfunctional, but Osborne handled his relationship with Danny Alexander (Lib Dem MP and CST) sensitively and well, which contributed greatly to the effectiveness of 'the Quad'.

Osborne was comfortable with the Treasury's ways of working. As one official put it: 'He had been a special advisor and was a historian and had thought about how he would work. He wanted challenge and we were happy to provide it. Overall his relationship with the Treasury was good.'[10] Like Darling, he was very capable of understanding complex briefs, and like Brown he relied heavily on a special adviser, Rupert Harrison, who was well respected by officials and regarded as a reliable conduit to his boss. In the end, another official concludes, 'he would always put the party's political interest first, but he was at least interested in the arguments and would not take offence if people disagreed with him. With Brown policy debate was also a loyalty test.'[11]

There were differences of view within the Treasury about the composition, if not the overall direction, of the austerity programme. And in retrospect, officials resent the politicization of official advice around the Scottish and European referendums, which damaged the institution. But Osborne's ultimate failure cannot be ascribed principally to his own actions or inactions. He personally opposed the 2016 referendum and came close to resigning over it. His strategy to win it, by focusing on the economic case, was ultimately overwhelmed by other factors. So he left the Treasury in unfortunate circumstances, and left frontline politics entirely soon afterwards, leaving a curate's-egg legacy behind him.

Philip Hammond

Unlike Osborne, but like Darling, Hammond had spent several years as a Cabinet Minister before taking on the Chancellor role. So he was familiar with the ways of Whitehall and had fought his own battles with the Treasury. His working methods were conventional. There were special advisers, but none with the weight or influence of Balls or Harrison. His style was relaxed and courteous and his successful private sector business experience was an asset none of his recent predecessors had had. Not for several decades had a Chancellor run his own business before taking the job.

But relations with Number 10, which had been relatively harmonious under Osborne, reverted to a posture of mutual suspicion reminiscent of the Darling era. Teresa May was not close to Hammond (or indeed to many others of her colleagues) and appointed him without enthusiasm. Her two closest advisors, Nick Timothy and Fiona Hill, were particularly hostile, in good part because Hammond had been a cogent and clear, if not outspoken, Remain supporter in the referendum campaign. In that respect his views coincided with those of most Treasury officials, but he reached them independently.

As the debates on the nature of Brexit continued, from 2016 until he left office, Hammond became more isolated. He doggedly pursued the objective of some form of 'soft Brexit' which would preserve as much access to EU markets as possible for London-based financial services businesses, and at times promoted a 'rule-taker' scheme which Treasury officials, and the Bank of England, did not favour. After the 2017 election his position was weakened in one sense: it was widely known that had May won a larger majority she would have replaced him. But the failed election strategy instead led to the departure of Timothy and Hill, his principal antagonists in Downing Street. Parliamentary arithmetic, and the failure of the Remain majority in Parliament to coalesce around any particular version of Brexit, led to May's replacement by Johnson as Prime Minister and Hammond's moves to the backbenches first, and eventually out of Parliament altogether in December 2019.

In those circumstances it would be difficult to describe his term of office as an unalloyed success. But he did fight off the threat from Timothy to create a rival centre of economic strategy-making. Officials speak well of his ability to operate in challenging circumstances. He preserved his dignity throughout and made one move which was widely welcomed in the building: a return to the earlier practice of holding only one fiscal event each year. He was much less of a fiscal tinkerer than Osborne, which the Treasury regard as a Good Thing.

Sajid Javid

In July 2019 Hammond was replaced by Sajid Javid, who had finished in fourth place, just off the podium, in the leadership election campaign.

He was known to the Treasury. Unlike his four predecessors, he had served for eighteen months as a junior minister in the department from 2012 to 2014, initially as Economic, then as Financial Secretary under George Osborne. That short apprenticeship might have proved an advantage in office, but he held the top job for only 200 days, and did not deliver a budget, so we shall (probably) never know. He did, however, steer through the appointment of Andrew Bailey as the next Governor against opposition from Dominic Cummings, who ran a slate of more politically congenial but not obviously qualified rival candidates.

His short time was marked by another flurry of rumours about plans to create another economic ministry to rival the Treasury. They were driven by Leave-supporting Conservatives, who resented the department's activist role in the referendum debate and sought revenge. The gossip had it that Rishi Sunak, then Chief Secretary, might lead a 'Leaver' rival to the dead hand of Great George Street.

It was not to be. Relations between Javid and his noisy neighbours deteriorated shortly after his appointment, when one of his advisers was dismissed by Cummings and escorted off the premises by an armed policeman. And immediately after the December 2019 election, when a victorious Boris Johnson remade his Cabinet in his image, Javid was told that a condition of keeping the job was that his special advisers would be managed from Number 10 as part of a joint team. Javid resigned, saying that 'no self-respecting minister would accept those terms'.[12]

Javid's 200 days were politically turbulent, but apart from promulgating some unachievable fiscal rules he did little of note. He won some admiration for his principled stand at the end of his term, but otherwise left only a faint impression. To paraphrase Malcolm's verdict on Macbeth after his death in battle, 'nothing in his life became him like the leaving of it'.

Rishi Sunak

There are Chancellors who left office under a pall, whose reputations subsequently recovered. We might see Norman Lamont and Alistair Darling in that category. For others, the reverse is true. So it is foolhardy to attempt a judgement on a serving Chancellor, especially one who has been obliged to respond to the deepest recession for 300 years.

Sunak was appointed CST in July 2019, after a short period as a junior minister for local government. He stepped into the Chancellor's shoes on Javid's resignation. The reason for that resignation quickly became seen as a red herring. Cummings was preoccupied by other matters as soon as Covid-19 appeared. In practice, there was only one spad of any significance: Liam Booth-Smith, who had worked with Cummings on the Vote Leave campaign and was sent to the Treasury to prevent the Chancellor and Permanent Secretary from meeting without him in the room. Once the reality of handling a pandemic sank in, this cloak-and-dagger agenda became irrelevant.

Sunak voted Leave in the referendum. Before entering politics he had worked for Goldman Sachs and a couple of hedge funds. Many hedge-fund managers were instinctively anti-EU as the Alternative Investment Fund Management Directive was a regulatory nuisance. His view was that in global markets the EU was a tiresome irrelevance at best. He played a low-key role in the negotiations on the Brexit terms. On that issue he was outside the mainstream of Treasury thinking.

In the event, that mattered much less than it might have done. From March 2020 Brexit took a back seat to Covid, and Sunak was admired for his hard work, willingness to take advice, knowledge of financial markets and ability to move fast and communicate well. Officials looked with some bemusement at his personalization of some complex business support schemes and the development of 'Brand Rishi'.[13] He was even filmed in front of a Treasury flag, whose origins were obscure. But it seemed a harmless hobby. The only risk was of rekindling Downing Street warfare, but Johnson's concerns were elsewhere through 2020 and 2021, as Sunak quickly emerged as a strong succession candidate. That had the positive side-effect of neutralizing any threat to the Treasury's economic monopoly. He quickly saw off moves to develop an industrial strategy in the business department.

A question-mark hovers over Sunak, however. It is easy to be popular when handing out money, whether through guaranteed loans, furlough schemes or direct grants to the arts and other favoured causes. At some point this process will need to stop and eventually go into reverse. Sunak claims to be a fiscal conservative, but he is Chancellor in a government committed to costly 'levelling-up' schemes and dependent on the votes of MPs from former Labour constituencies whose voters have a bias towards more public spending. His first 2021 Budget warned that the jam would one day run out and that the bill for the jars eaten so far would have to be paid. Businesses are on notice that they will pay higher Corporation Tax, but not for a while. The NHS and Social Care Levy has been legislated but has yet to hit pay packets, and that may not be the end of the tax increases. Public spending, outside the health budget, will also suffer cuts. If he can remain popular until the next election, Sunak will prove himself to be an outstanding politician.

Other ministers

As a government department, the Treasury is unusual in three ways. First, since 1961 it has been endowed with a second Cabinet Minister, the CST; second, the other junior ministers enjoy special titles – Financial Secretary, Economic Secretary and so on, which tends to suggest that they are a cut above the average minister of state or Parliamentary Secretary, even though their ranks and salaries are the same; third, the Treasury does not normally employ a Lords minister, as finance bills – the main legislation for which it is responsible – are not voted on in the upper house.

Junior ministerial roles in the Treasury are often given to rising stars. In recent times, four Chief Secretaries – Major, Lamont, Darling and Sunak – have become Chancellors. Stephen Barclay climbed from Economic Secretary to Chief Secretary. Sajid Javid served as both Economic and Financial Secretary before getting the top job. Many other Cabinet Ministers have cut their teeth there. Of the 2021

Cabinet, in addition to Javid, Liz Truss, Robert Jenrick and Priti Patel had all held junior Treasury posts. In principle, the Treasury regards it as a good thing that some spending ministers appreciate that there are two sides to an income and expenditure statement.

But there is a long distance between the Chancellor and the rest of the team, and the importance of the junior jobs depends heavily on the confidence the Chancellor has in them. Nigel Lawson spent more time than most with his juniors, assembling them on three mornings a week, but the meetings focused largely on parliamentary and party management, rather than on policy.

The CST position is by far the most significant of the 'other ranks', though the position has had far higher turn-over than the Chancellor, with seventeen appointees from 1998 to 2021. The postholder was a full Cabinet member from 1961 to 2015, when it was downgraded – apparently to accommodate additional Cabinet positions – to the status of a minister 'also attending the Cabinet'. That change has not altered the role in practice. Under the Labour governments from 1997 to 2010, Darling was the most significant, as he was given responsibility for the reform of financial regulation from 1997 to 1998, as well as steering several tight public spending rounds through the Cabinet. From month to month, the core diet of a CST is a series of negotiations with department ministers on their spending proposals, but within a spending umbrella set by the Chancellor and Prime Minister. So the key skill is to beat up cabinet colleagues, leaving the minimum visible bruising, a tactic deployed in the interview rooms of police stations the world over.

The other Labour CST whose profile was higher than the norm was Liam Byrne, who famously left a note for his successor, David Laws, in 2010, reading: 'I'm afraid there is no money' – a message he came to regret.[14] Laws made shameless political use of what might by another minister have been seen as a friendly, personal communication.

Laws did not survive long to enjoy his moment in the sun, as he was felled by an expenses scandal. He resigned after sixteen days, to be replaced by Danny Alexander, who became the second Liberal Democrat member of the 'Quad', which steered policy throughout the coalition government. Cameron, Clegg, Osborne and Alexander proved effective at making decisions, though the quality of the decisions, especially on spending, is heavily contested. The new status of the CST had important implications across government. As Alexander correctly observed later, 'decision-making in the Treasury is oriented towards the Chancellor, and it took a long time for officials to realise that both Ministers had to agree'.[15] I was made aware of that when I chaired the Airports Commission. Osborne was a longstanding supporter of Heathrow expansion, but I was 'encouraged' to make a visit to Alexander's constituency to buy his support for a plan which the Liberal Democrats had long opposed.

Since the end of the coalition agreement the role has returned to its traditional public spending roots, with a corresponding reduction in its profile. When spending rounds become tougher, as the need to reassert control over the fiscal deficit imposes itself, it will be an unenviable position to hold.

There is less to say about the more junior positions. Traditionally, the Financial Secretary handles tax matters, which involves steering the annual (at least) finance bill through Parliament. That unsung task requires concentration and attention to detail. There is also a relentless flow of tax cases involving HMRC rules, the most contentious of which land on the FST's desk. There were eighteen FSTs during the period: ambitious ministers see it as a sometimes tiresome, but necessary rung on the political ladder. There were also eighteen Economic Secretaries. The EST's portfolio is less straightforward to define. He or she often deputizes for more senior ministers across the full range of Treasury business. Recent incumbents have also carried the courtesy title of 'City Minister'.

That role has a short history. Gordon Brown invented the position, formally known as Financial Services Secretary to the Treasury, in October 2008 to bring Paul, later Lord, Myners into the Treasury to help handle the developing financial crisis. As Myners put it later: 'I was brought in, in Gordon Brown's words, to be able to speak with the bankers eye to eye.'[16] His reflection on the roles of junior ministers in the department, from a man with extensive business experience, are instructive:

> I wouldn't say getting to know the other ministers in the department was particularly pressing, as they are here today, gone tomorrow ... We need to have what were called 'ministerials', which were weekly meetings with the Chancellor, in which we sat around in his office and we told the Chancellor what we were doing. He never told us what he was doing, and that was the only time the six Treasury Ministers would get together, and the meeting was frequently cancelled ... We had one junior minister whose name the Permanent Secretary could never remember.[17]

The effectiveness of the department was also influenced by its official leadership, especially at Permanent Secretary level. Here again the Treasury benefited from a high degree of continuity, and a series of calm and predictable transitions.

Permanent Secretaries

Over the twenty-four-year period under review there were just five Permanent Secretaries and the first, Terry Burns, served for a year only.

Burns and Brown did not get on. They set off on the wrong foot when Burns urged delay in reforming banking supervision. Brown believed the resulting confusion with Governor Eddie George on what was proposed was Burns's fault. The latter also refused to confirm that he had approved an offshore trust of which Geoffrey Robinson, then Paymaster General, was the beneficiary. In his memoir, Robinson addresses a number of other reasons for removing Burns: the Treasury's poor forecasting record, a confused plan to remodel the Treasury's offices (which did go ahead later), his eighteen-year residence on the same corridor, the collapse of 'the monetarist experiment, of which he was a principal architect'.[18]

These are half-truths and posterior rationalizations. When he left in June 1998, Burns had had enough of the fraught working atmosphere of Brown's Treasury, and has had an outstandingly successful third career in the private sector and the House of Lords. His tenure from 1991 to 1998 had its ups and downs, notably the ERM failure, but he devoted a deal of energy to improving the way the Treasury was run, opening up career opportunities for more junior staff, and addressing the cultural issues which had left the Treasury with very low morale in the early 90s.

Andrew Turnbull, who took over from Brown in 1998, had been one of the last two candidates for the Cabinet Secretary job in the same year, and went on to that job in 2002. In an interview in 2013, he told Peter Hennessy that 'I don't regret not getting it at all as it gave me four years in the Treasury'.[19] Brown made the appointment – Turnbull was then the obvious candidate and personal relations at the top of the house improved. Turnbull was another grammar school boy with an intellect as powerful as Brown's.

It is notable, though, that in spite of four years together in harness, Brown omits any mention whatsoever of Turnbull in his memoir, suggesting that the latter's 'Stalinist' jibe had not been forgotten or forgiven. Balls and Robinson, too, make only passing reference to him. Turnbull's assessment that 'the Brown/Balls regime had enhanced Treasury control but at the expense of any government cohesion' was too accurate for comfort.[20]

Turnbull describes his own style as 'functional: get things done, make things happen, make them work effectively, get people to come together, rather than very overt extrovert leadership. . . On the introvert or extrovert scale

I am quite hard over to the "I".'[21] One consequence of that style was that he gave considerable latitude to his key lieutenants, Robert Culpin on public expenditure and Steve Robson on finance, regulation and industry.

But although Turnbull's style was self-effacing, and Brown now seems not to recall his presence, the public perception was of a powerful official pulling on the strings of power. A 'power list' compiled in 1998 by a panel chaired by Roy Hattersley ranked him as the 150th most powerful person in the UK, one above Delia Smith, though twelve places below Mick Jagger.[22]

Burns and Turnbull are both 'boys' boys' whose conversation is dotted with references to their respective football teams, Queens Park Rangers and Tottenham Hotspur. Gus O'Donnell, who took over in 2002, is another such, though with a difference. From south London, O'Donnell chose nonetheless to hitch his fortunes to the Manchester United bandwagon, which has proved a less reliable vehicle in recent years. He was a congenial colleague for the New Labour leadership. As Bill Keegan notes, Brown and Balls got on so well with O'Donnell that he was brought back from the Treasury Embassy/IMF job in Washington to become a trusted and valued member of 'the team'.[23]

Of all the incumbents, before and after him, O'Donnell has benefited from the most positive, even fawning, media treatment. He spent time as the Treasury's and John Major's spokesman, which helped. His GOD initials acronym is a gift for headline-writers, but his approachable style has helped too. A *New Statesman* profile paid tribute to his 'wondrous interpersonal gifts'.[24] It helped that he so obviously loved the job: 'I was like a bear in a honey pot in the Treasury'.[25] But that did not prevent him applying for the Cabinet Secretary job after three years, when Turnbull hit the retirement age of sixty, which was still policed scrupulously at the time.

GOD left the Treasury in 2005 and was replaced by Nick MacPherson, who showed greater staying power and served until 2016. MacPherson had been the Chancellor's

Private Secretary when Brown came into office in 1997, so understood the New Labour regime as well as anyone. But his term almost came to a premature end. Brown recognized that MacPherson had become 'a popular leader of a department that was often thought of as difficult to lead, despite (or perhaps because of) having some of the best brains in the country'.[26] Nonetheless, by 2007 he had reached the view that the Treasury had reverted to its traditional role as the finance department that specialized in saying 'no'. So Brown proposed an unusual plan which would have put GOD back in charge of a joint Cabinet Office/Treasury operation, with MacPherson as Cabinet Secretary. O'Donnell and MacPherson together scuppered his plan.'

So MacPherson lived on and chose his own departure date in 2016. He was unusually forthright in his external communications. As we have seen, his advice on the economics of Scottish independence was published in 2014, and he delivered several public lectures. He became closely associated with the Coalition's spending plans and was a powerful advocate of fiscal responsibility both during and after his period in charge. In 2007 he maintained that, under Osborne, 'Britain never experienced austerity' and warned that the electorate is falling out of love with fiscal consolidation just at the moment that a rigorous approach to public spending is likely to become more necessary.[27]

Both Darling and Osborne relied heavily on MacPherson. Darling's pen-picture rings true. He describes him as 'engaging and somewhat idiosyncratic. Nick, unstuffy and about as unlike someone out of C. P. Snow's *Corridors of Power* as could be imagined, is intellectively self-confident. He always had an opinion which I valued but he was intensely relaxed when I didn't follow his advice, as came to happen.'[28]

In 2016 the apostolic succession delivered Tom Scholar as his replacement. His father Michael was a senior Treasury official. Tom joined in 1992 and become the Principal Private Secretary to the Chancellor in 1997. After a Washington posting, he served briefly as Brown's Private Secretary in 10 Downing Street before returning to the Treasury, then bouncing back next door where he was Cameron's man in the EU renegotiations before replacing MacPherson just before the referendum. He could not have been better prepared for the role, and the transition was smooth. It would probably have been the same had the main alternative candidate, John Kingman, got the nod instead.

More conventional than MacPherson, and slightly lugubrious in manner, Scholar was just as on top of his brief. Under Hammond, relationships at the top of the Treasury were mainly calm and constructive, but that had seemed likely to change when Johnson became Prime Minister in July 2019 and Hammond went into internal exile. In February 2020 a well-sourced article in the *Sunday Telegraph* reported that Scholar featured on a hit list of Permanent Secretaries carded for the chop.[29] Scholar was identified as being 'offside completely on Brexit'. The other two names on the list, Simon McDonald at the Foreign Office and Philip Rutnam at the Home Office, were duly dispatched, but Scholar survived and was reappointed to a second five-year term in 2021. By that time, Cummings had left Downing Street and the Johnson Terror was over.[30] The Treasury could again relax as one of their own remained in charge.

So, pace John Kingman's jeremiad about Treasury staffing, discussed in Chapter 10, the Treasury has benefited from stable and consistent top management through the period, without the disruption and beheadings that have affected many parts of the civil service machine. Ministers of both parties have toyed with the idea of radical change, or the appointment of potentially rebellious heads, but in the case of the Treasury (and the Bank of England) have concluded that the risk of disrupting such a vital part of the edifice was too dangerous to take.

It has also been possible to recruit some high-class people from the private sector, such as Edward Troup on tax policy, James Sassoon on financial markets, James Leigh-Pemberton at UK Financial Investments and Charles Roxburgh from McKinsey. It may be, as Kingman suggests, that there is a risk of degradation, as relative pay continues to fall, but that has not happened yet.

11

Trouble Ahead

The period from 1997 to 2021 was tumultuous for the Treasury. It began with the dramatic change to the status of the Bank of England and the consequential loss of responsibility for monetary policy. Ten years later, the storm of the global financial crisis blew through the corridors of Horse Guards Road. The worst financial crisis for eighty years devastated the British financial system. Then, in 2020, when the recovery was still incomplete, the Covid-19 pandemic produced the biggest drop in UK GDP for over 300 years.

So to note that, on average, economic performance was moderately satisfactory, is, while broadly true, an observation that conceals a multitude of sins. Taking the period as a whole, growth was generally in line with comparable EU countries, though the trend rate was lower after the GFC than before it, and there were signs of even weaker relative performance after the EU referendum. The UK suffered a deeper Covid recession than other G7 economies, and it is too early to say how robust the post-pandemic rebound will be. Supply bottlenecks, some the result of Brexit, have slowed the recovery.

The Treasury, as an institution, suffered some blows to its authority, and its reputation. Bank of England independence reduced its scope, though in a way that Treasury officials and Chancellors had recommended for some time, and which matched international best practice. The OBR imposed constraints on its freedom of action, but they were constraints which, again, Treasury officials welcomed. And the boundary between it and HMRC was shifted in its favour, with a stronger tax policy function in Horse Guards Road

The financial crisis certainly damaged the Treasury's reputation in the short term. The handling of Northern Rock was uncertain and at times chaotic. But the handling of the second, more severe phase in the autumn of 2008 was more sure-footed. Though Brown feared it might cost him his job, the bank rescue and recapitalization exercise became a model for others to follow, and for a time the UK commanded a leadership position internationally. In spite of the scale of the crisis, the Labour government came closer than many expected to winning the 2010 election.

Osborne's austerity programme damaged the Treasury's reputation in much of the economics profession, which saw the hair shirt as unsuitable attire at a time of con-sistently high unemployment, with its echoes of the 1981 budget. It was seen primarily as a political choice driven in part by Osborne's desire to see a smaller state, but officials, notably Nick MacPherson, were accused of having bought into the project with too much enthusiasm.

Osborne and MacPherson did, however, score a per-sonal and institutional success with their campaign against Scottish independence in the 2014 referendum. The eco-nomic and constitutional case they advanced seemed to have a decisive impact on voting intentions. The Treasury's reputation was enhanced, outside the membership of the Scottish National Party, at least.

But Osborne's attempt to repeat the trick in the EU referendum campaign ended in humiliating failure, and left the Treasury with many enemies in the Brexit branch of the Conservative Party.

For a period it seemed possible that an anti-Treasury coalition, in Number 10 and other departments, might develop and lead to structural change. The Treasury had successfully fought off attempts by Blair to reduce its authority, but the campaign by Brexiteers developed greater momentum for a time. The parliamentary chaos of 2019 ended the May government. Johnson and Dominic Cummings won a victory of sorts in removing Sajid Javid from office. But that 'victory' proved inconsequential and wholly insignificant when Cummings himself left Downing Street, in the midst of the Covid crisis, and Javid returned to government. While the dominant policy response to the GFC was monetary, with central banks in the lead, the Covid pandemic required strong fiscal action. Support schemes were devised and implemented in very short order, and the effect was powerful. Chancellor Sunak quickly personalized the initiative, but that led to less tension than might have been expected, with a Prime Minister widely seen as having little interest in, or knowledge of, economic policy. The latter could see, however, that his political future depended on softening the economic impact of the pandemic on the electorate, and the Treasury was the only body which could deliver that.

So at the end of the period the Treasury was as powerful as it was at the start. Attempts to create a rival centre of economic policymaking had failed. The Business Department had been through several acronymical makeovers yet remained as weak as ever. The same was true of the Department of Work and Pensions. The other 'spending departments' continued to do as they were told. The Cabinet Office has been weakened by scandal, intrigue and downgrading of the Cabinet Secretary.

The Foreign Office, now brigaded with Overseas Development, found itself condemned to the status of a bystander in the Brexit drama, and its reputation was further tarnished by the Afghanistan debacle. Only the Bank of England retains a comparable status and the Treasury maintains a privileged relationship with the Old Lady.

But the Treasury now faces a number of challenges, which will test it severely, and to which it is not well-equipped to respond. I identify seven.

1. The Treasury View

The phase is, in my experience, not much used in the Treasury itself. Conventionally the term referred to the impact of government borrowing on the economy. In his 1929 Budget speech, Churchill said: 'The orthodox Treasury view . . . is that when the Government borrows in the money market it becomes a new competitor with industry and engrosses to itself resources which would otherwise have been employed by private enterprise, and in the process raised the rent of money to all who have need of it.'[1]

More recently, Nick MacPherson has advanced a somewhat broader definition of the way the Treasury sees the world. In a 2014 speech entitled 'The Treasury View: A Testament of Experience', he identified a series of propositions which he saw as the bedrock of officials views. They included 'a belief in free trade', and opposition to 'protectionism and mercantilism'. He noted that 'historically, the Treasury opposed bilateral trade deals, which it saw as "commercial sin"'. In that sense, the current Cabinet is full of sinners. The Treasury's failure to sway voters in the EU referendum kicked away this fundamental underpinning of the 'Treasury view'.[2]

MacPherson's second proposition is that 'markets generally work'. That applies both to product and labour markets. While some saw the financial crisis as demonstrating the limitations of their belief in markets, for him 'the lesson of the financial crisis is not that we had too much competition but that we did not have enough'. The provision of sound money is his third proposition, while his fourth is 'that there are limits to what the state can do to regulate demand'. Monetary policy is the first port of call in that area. 'That does not mean the Treasury denies a role for fiscal policy', but he sees that as operating primarily through the automatic stabilizers, the areas of spending and income that tend to vary with the economic cycle. He notes that 'the Treasury has tended to be sceptical about the efficacy of fiscal fine-tuning' and that boosts to public investment are hard to achieve, partly because 'the mythical shovel ready infrastructure project is precisely that – a myth'. Furthermore, he is also sceptical about the government's ability to raise additional revenue when needed. In spite of many different tax rates 'the share of national income accounted for by taxes and national insurance contributions has remained stubbornly stable'.

That convenient restatement of the Treasury view captures the essence of officials' thinking over the last quarter of a century, yet now much of it is challenged. Brexit was a retreat from a large free trade area with a robust competition policy. Membership of the single market is being replaced by a series of bilateral deals, anathema to the Treasury view. And there are other signs of creeping protectionism. The National Security and Investment Act strengthens the government's ability to intervene in mergers and acquisitions in the defence industry. 'Project Birch' is a Treasury plan to save strategically important companies which must have former Treasury officials turning in their graves.

On the public finances, Covid has pushed government debt up to an unprecedented level in peacetime, without any impact on interest rates so far, and majority opinion on the Conservative parliamentary benches is a long way from any previous formulation of the Treasury view.

So MacPherson's successor could not make the same speech today. But what speech could he make? There is no sign yet of any reformulation of the department's core beliefs in the new world in which it finds itself. That is politically prudent in current circumstances, no doubt, but it leaves the department dangerously exposed to heretical policy proposals advanced elsewhere in government, especially on public spending.

2. Monetary and fiscal policy

For MacPherson, 'the provision of price stability is tantamount to a moral issue, it goes to the heart of the fundamental duties of the state'. Since 1997, his morals have been in the safe keeping of the Bank of England. The Bank's performance against the inflation target has been good: excellent since 2010. And the separation of powers agreed in 1997 has been stable.

Now, after two waves of quantitative easing, following the financial and Covid crises, the position is different. The Bank's massive purchases of gilts have the effect of shortening the maturity of the debt, which is now down from seven to only four years, making the public finances more sensitive to interest rate changes. The risk of fiscal dominance of monetary policy, with the Bank reluctant to raise rates for fear of the consequences for public spending, is clear. Greater coordination of monetary and fiscal policy will be required, but how can that be achieved without destabilizing the 1997 settlement and putting the credibility gains achieved from Central Bank independence at risk? So far, the response to question on this issue has been 'nothing to see here', and the settlement is unchanged. I doubt that response will suffice for long. The Balls plan for more fiscal and monetary policy coordination, or something like it, may come onto the agenda.

3. Public finance post-Covid

The economic consensus on public debt has been changing over the years since the GFC. That is less true in Germany, where there remain strong supporters of a commitment to balanced budgets through the cycle. But in the UK, and the US, the centre of economic gravity has shifted. The IMF, which used to be a temple of fiscal rectitude, advising governments across the globe to balance their books, has changed tack, and now acknowledges that governments can reasonably run large deficits when private sector demand is weak, and that public austerity at a time of weak private demand can make a bad situation worse. And while interest rates remain very low, the government's debt servicing costs are manageable.

But how far can this new approach run? The Treasury is by no means converted to modern monetary theory. Officials share Mervyn King's view that it is 'neither modern, nor monetary, nor theory'.[3] At some point, interest rates will rise and the debt burden will need to be reduced. Precisely when that trap will be set is hard to judge. But the Treasury will need to plan ahead. So far, the projected changes to corporation tax look quite inadequate, and the new Social Care Levy is to pay for additional NHS spending and the public costs of social care, not to reduce the deficit. The main positive feature of that change is that the government is prepared to find ways around its unwise electoral commitments not to raise any taxes. But there is a fundamental incompatibility between the desire for more spending on public services, and more public investment, and a commitment not to raise the main tax rates. Something will have to give.

4. Tax policy

Chapter 4 showed that attempts to construct a more economically rational approach to taxation have foundered on political rocks. As Edward Troup pointed out, ministers – though some like Osborne began with good intentions – have baulked at the risk of creating silent winners and noisy losers. While the revenues have continued to roll in at a roughly acceptable rate, the incentive for radical reform has been low. That will now change. As we have seen, some existing sources of revenue are highly likely to decline in the next few years. So a revenue gap will open up, at the worst possible time. Benign neglect, from which tax policy has long suffered, will no longer be an option.

5. Levelling up

The Treasury is deeply sceptical about levelling up, a policy with strong political impetus not yet matched by intellectual clarity. A senior Cabinet Office official was quoted in May 2021 as saying 'it's a slogan without a purpose', and that there was 'widespread cluelessness' about what it meant.[4]

Officials see a serious risk of wasting money on an epic scale. Active regional policies have rarely been successful in the UK. The government's lack of confidence in the Treasury's enthusiasm – beyond sending a few staff to Darlington – was demonstrated when Johnson appointed Andy Haldane as an auxiliary Permanent Secretary, working for Michael Gove, to take control of that agenda. Haldane is unsentimental, and logical, but the government sees the need for eye-catching initiatives, which the Treasury will find it hard to support. If more funding is to be channelled to infrastructure projects in deprived areas, they will need to change their approach to public investment decisions. Critics argue that 'the official methodology (in the Green Book) has reinforced the regional imbalance of the UK economy (and that) infrastructure investments also need to be based on a strategic view about economic development for the whole of the UK'.[5] The existing approach tends to reinforce areas of strength, where the additional economic input of investment is likely to be greatest. The Treasury has long resisted major changes to the methodology, though some tweaks have been made, but the political pressure for a radically different approach will be powerful.

6. Climate change

The government has made strong commitments to achieve net zero, through the detail promised by the Treasury in spring 2021 has (in September 2021) still not emerged. Critics argued that the interim report in December 2020 'lacks detail or an overall systematised approach to finance, which is needed now to frontload investment for net-zero this decade'.[6]

Nick Stern believes the Treasury will struggle to deal with a fundamental change to the economic system that an effective response to climate change requires, and that a major revision of the 'Treasury view' will be required. 'Climate change analysis requires a radically different approach to market failures, which the Treasury is ill-equipped to deliver.'[7] There is, in his view, simply not the depth of economic expertise in the department that is needed to produce a comprehensive and rational response.

7. Productivity

All these challenges will be easier to deal with if the economy returns to healthy growth. That, in turn, requires an improvement in the rate of productivity increases. There were signs of a very modest uptick in the difficult years of 2020–21 after more than a decade during which output per hour stagnated. Economists are divided on the role played by weak demand. They are more aligned in supporting extra investment in infrastructure and education and training, as remedies. There are signs of increased infrastructure investment (much of it on the very expensive high-speed train (HST) project) but the education budget will struggle to match the appeal of the NHS and social care in a constrained post-Covid environment. And there are those who think efforts to enhance productivity are unlikely to be successful. Brexit will be a handicap if the

Treasury's analysis is correct. And Dietrich Vollrath of the University of Houston has argued that consumers in developed countries have turned to new forms of production and consumption that increase well-being but do not contribute to growth in GDP.[8]

These challenges together will test the Treasury more than the crisis of the last fifteen years. It is hard not to conclude that, if the department is to maintain its full range of functions, it will need a significant increase in resources. To try to respond to those threats with a skeleton staff, recruited cheaply, would be a costly mistake, for the Treasury hair shirts are easier to put on than take off, but the alternative is to allow space for a rival centre of economic policymaking to emerge, which the Treasury will surely continue to resist.

Notes

Introduction

1   *The Chancellors' Tales*, ed. Howard Davies. Polity, 2006.
2   Lionel Barber, The Treasury today: A devalued currency? *Prospect*, January/February 2021. https://www.prospectm agazine.co.uk/magazine/the-treasury-today-a-devalued-cur rency-lionel-barber-rishi-sunak.

Chapter 1: Economic Performance

1   Gus O'Donnell, Angus Deaton, Martine Durand, David Halpern and Richard Layard, *Wellbeing and Policy*. Legatum Institute, 2014. https://li.com/wp-content/uploads/2019/03 /commission-on-wellbeing-and-policy-report-march-2014 -pdf.pdf. The Kennedy speech can be found at https://en.wi kipedia.org/wiki/Robert_F._Kennedy%27s_remarks_at_the _University_of_Kansas.
2   Nicholas Crafts, The impact of EU membership on UK economic performance. *The Political Quarterly*, 18 May 2016. https://doi.org/10.1111/1467-923X.12261.
3   Dan Corry, Anna Valero and John Van Reenen, UK economic performance since 1997: Growth, productivity and

jobs. Centre for Economic Performance, LSE. December 2011. http://eprints.lse.ac.uk/47521/1/CEPSP24.pdf.

4 Nicholas Bloom and John Van Reenen. Why do management practices differ across firms and countries? *Journal of Economic Perspectives* 24/1, 2010, pp. 203–224.

5 Nicholas Sowels, From prudence to profligacy: How Gordon Brown undermined Britain's public finances. *Observatoire de la société britannique*, 2011, pp. 77–93. https://doi.org /10.4000/osb.1136.

6 Jonathan Portes. The Coalition's confidence trick. *The New Statesman*, 2011.

7 Gordon Brown, *My Life, Our Times*. Bodley Head, 2017, p. 350.

8 Howard Davies, *The Financial Crisis: Who's to Blame?* Polity, 2010.

9 Jonathan Cribb and Paul Johnson, 10 years on: Have we recovered from the financial crisis? Institute for Fiscal Studies, 12 September 2018. https://ifs.org.uk/publications /13302.

10 Ibid.

11 Benjamin Nabarro and Christian Schulz, Recent trends to the UK economy. IFS Green Budget, October 2019. https:// ifs.org.uk/uploads/GB2019-Chapter-2-Recent-trends-to-the -UK-economy.pdf.

12 Jonathan Portes, ed., The economic record of the Coalition government. *National Institute Economic Review* 231, February 2015. https://www.cambridge.org/core/journals /national-institute-economic-review/article/abs/economic-re cord-of-the-coalition-government-introduction/8015174E2 D750BB262797CB54D544413.

13 Jennifer Castle, David Hendry and Andrew Martinez, The paradox of stagnant real wages yet rising 'living standards' in the UK. VoxEU, 21 January 2020. https://voxeu.org/artic le/paradox-stagnant-real-wages-yet-rising-living-standards -uk.

14 Paul Krugman, *The Age of Diminished Expectations: US Economic Policy in the 1990s*, 3rd edn. MIT Press, 1997, p. 11.

15 Martin Wolf, Why once successful countries like the UK get left behind. *Financial Times*, 21 February 2021.

16 Nabarro and Schulz, Recent trends to the UK economy, p. 66.

17 David Sainsbury, *Windows of Opportunity: How Nations Create Wealth*. Profile Books, 2021.

18 Abigail Haddow, Chris Hare, John Hooley and Tamarah Shakir, Macroeconomic uncertainty: What is it, how can we measure it and why does it matter? Bank of England Quarterly Bulletin, 2013 Q2. https://www.bankofengland .co.uk/quarterly-bulletin/2013/q2/macroeconomic-uncertai nty-what-is-it-how-can-we-measure-it-and-why-does-it-mat ter.

19 Impact of the Brexit trade agreement on our economy fore- cast. Office for Budget Responsibility, 3 March 2021.

20 Torsten Bell et al., The UK's decisive decade. The launch report of 'The Economy 2030 Inquiry'. Resolution Foundation. May 2021. https://economy2030.resolutionfo undation.org/reports/the-uks-decisive-decade/

21 Sascha Becker, Peter Egger and Maximilian von Ehrlich, Absorptive capacity and the growth and investment effects of regional transfers: A regression discontinuity design with heterogeneous treatment effects. *American Economic Journal: Economic Policy* 5/4, November 2013, pp. 29–77.

22 Diane Coyle, Sam Warner, Dave Richards and Martin Smith, Budget ditches industrial strategy for centralised levelling up. Bennett Institute for Public Policy, 10 March 2021. https:// www.bennettinstitute.cam.ac.uk/blog/budget-ditches-indust rial-strategy-centralised-lev/.

23 Bell et al., The UK's Decisive Decade.

24 Gregory Claeys, Zsolt Darvas, Maria Demertzis and Guntram Wolff, The great COVID-19 divergence: Managing a sustain- able recovery in the European Union. *Policy Contribution* 11 2021, Bruegel. w https://www.bruegel.org/wp-content/up loads/2021/05/PC-2021-11-ecofin-210521-1.pdf.

Chapter 2: Macroeconomic Policy

1   Interview with the author, August 2021

2   ECB's governing council approves its new monetary policy strategy. 8 July 2021. https://publications.banque-france .fr/sites/default/files/medias/documents/2021-07-08_-_ecbs _governing_council_approves_its_new_monetary_policy_str ategy.pdf.

3 Quoted in Camilla Hodgson, Bank of England given new mandate to buy 'green' bonds. *Financial Times*, 3 March 2021. https://www.ft.com/content/f436d69b-2bf0-48cd-bb34-644856fba17f.

4 John Cochrane, Central banks and climate: A case of mission creep. Hoover Institution, 13 November 2020. https://www.hoover.org/research/central-banks-and-climate-case-mission-creep.

5 Mervyn King and Dan Katz, Central banks are risking their independence. Bloomberg Opinion. 23 August 2021. https://www.bloomberg.com/opinion/articles/2021-08-23/central-banks-are-risking-their-independence-mervyn-king-dan-katz.

6 Interview with the author, March 2021

7 Daniel Harari and Matthew Ward, Quantitative easing. House of Commons Library. CDP 2016/0166, 14 September 2016. https://researchbriefings.files.parliament.uk/documents/CDP-2016-0166/CDP-2016-0166.pdf.

8 Quoted in James Dorn, Maintaining distance between monetary and fiscal policy. Cato Institute, 18 November 2020. https://www.cato.org/publications/pandemics-policy/maintaining-distance-between-monetary-fiscal-policy#.

9 HM Treasury and the Bank of England announce temporary extension of Ways and Means facility. 9 April 2020. https://www.bankofengland.co.uk/news/2020/april/hmt-and-boe-announce-temporary-extension-to-ways-and-means-facility.

10 Chris Papadopoullos, The Bank of England nearly financed the deficit. Does it matter? OMFIF, 21 January 2020. https://www.omfif.org/2021/01/the-bank-of-england-nearly-financed-the-deficit-does-it-matter/.

11 Andrew Bailey, Bank of England is not doing 'monetary financing'. *Financial Times*, 5 April 2020. https://www.ft.com/content/3a33c7fe-75a6-11ea-95fe-fcd274e920ca.

12 Tommy Stubbington and Chris Giles, Investors sceptical over Bank of England's QE programme. *Financial Times*, 5 January 2021. https://www.ft.com/content/f92b6c67-15ef-460f-8655-e458f2fe2487.

13 Andy Haldane, What has central bank independence ever done for us? UCL Economists' Society Economics Conference, 28 November 2020. https://www.bankofengland.co.uk/-/media/boe/files/speech/2020/what-has-central-ba

nk-independence-ever-done-for-us-speech-by-andy-haldane
.pdf?la=en&hash=E89B59B9A236C37F6DCE94CDC567B
38A52835813.

14 Charles Goodhart and Manoj Pradhan, Future imperfect
after Coronavirus. VoxEU, 27 March 2020. https://voxeu
.org/article/future-imperfect-after-coronavirus.

15 Inflation: A tiger by the tail? Speech by Andy Haldane, 26
February 2021. https://www.bankofengland.co.uk/speech
/2021/february/andy-haldane-recorded-mini-speech-on-infl
ation-outlook.

16 Letter from Governor Andrew Bailey to the Chancellor, 23
September 2021. https://www.bankofengland.co.uk/-/media
/boe/files/letter/2021/september/chancellor-cpi-letter-septem
ber-2021.pdf?la=en&hash=12662A8C1907065B9C02D88
F8A46FB3EA7B52458.

17 Quantitative easing: A dangerous addiction? House of Lords
Economics Affairs Committee, 1st Report of Session 2019–
21. 16 July 2021. https://publications.parliament.uk/pa/ld58
02/ldselect/ldeconaf/42/4203.htm.

18 Ed Balls, James Howat and Anna Stansbury, Central bank
independence revisited: After the financial crisis, what should
a model central bank look like? M-RCBG Associate Working
Paper No. 87. Harvard University, 2018. https://www.hks
.harvard.edu/centers/mrcbg/publications/awp/awp87.

19 Simon Wren-Lewis, Macroeconomic policy beyond Brexit.
The Political Quarterly, 21 February 2019. https://onlinelib
rary.wiley.com/doi/full/10.1111/1467-923X.12647.

20 New economic challenges and the Fed's monetary policy
review. Federal Reserve Speech by Jerome H. Powell at
Jackson Hole, Wyoming symposium, 27 August 2020.
https://www.federalreserve.gov/newsevents/speech/powell20
200827a.htm.

21 Balls et al., Central bank independence revisited.

22 Rethinking fiscal and monetary policy, post-Covid.
Bendheim Center for Finance, Princeton University, 2 June
2021. https://bcf.princeton.edu/events/olivier-blanchard-on
-rethinking-fiscal-and-monetary-policy-post-covid/.

Chapter 3: Public Expenditure

1 Labour's macroeconomic framework. Speech by Gordon Brown to the Labour Finance and Industry Group, 17 May 1995.
2 William Keegan, *The Prudence of Mr Gordon Brown*. Wiley, 2004, p. 243.
3 Interview with the author, March 2021.
4 Interview with the author, January 2021.
5 David Butler and Denis Kavanagh, *The British General Election of 2001*. Palgrave Macmillan, 2002.
6 Interview with the author, February 2021
7 Gordon Brown, *My Life, Our Times*. Bodley Head, 2017, p. 135.
8 Keegan, *The Prudence of Mr Gordon Brown*, p. 244.
9 David Piachaud and Holly Sutherland, Changing poverty post-1997. CASE paper 63. London School of Economics, 2002. https://www.researchgate.net/publication/4929043_Changing_Poverty_Post-1997.
10 Nicholas Timmins, Projects seek partners. *Financial Times*, 24 February 2009.
11 Brown, *My Life, Our Times*, p. 136.
12 BBC Breakfast with Frost. Tony Blair interview. 16 January 2000. http://news.bbc.co.uk/hi/english/static/audio_video/programmes/breakfast_with_frost/transcripts/blair16.jan.txt.
13 Interview with the author, March 2021
14 Brown, *My Life, Our Times*, pp. 349–350.
15 Interview with the author, August 2021
16 Nicholas Sowels, From prudence to profligacy: How Gordon Brown undermined Britain's public finances. *Observatoire de la société britannique*, 2011, pp. 77–93. https://doi.org/10.4000/osb.1136.
17 Robert Chote, Rowena Crawford, Carl Emmerson and Gemma Tetlow, The public finances: 1997–2010. Institute for Fiscal Studies Election Briefing Note No. 6, 2010. https://ifs.org.uk/publications/4822.
18 Interview with the author, January 2021.
19 Interview with the author, November 2020.
20 Interview with the author, March 2021.
21 Jonathan Cribb and Paul Johnson, 10 years on – have we

recovered from the financial crisis? 12 September 2018. Institute for Fiscal Studies. https://ifs.org.uk/publications /13302.

22 Chote et al., The public finances: 1997–2010.

23 The Code for Fiscal Stability. HM Treasury, November 1998. https://www.internationalbudget.org/wp-content/up loads/UnitedKingdom-CodeOfFiscalStaiblity1998-English .pdf.

24 The government's fiscal framework. HM Treasury, November 2008. http://news.bbc.co.uk/2/shared/bsp/hi/pdfs /24_11_08_pbr_fiscalframework.pdf.

25 Interview with the author, January 2021.

26 Brown, My Life, Our Times, p. 351.

27 Inflation Report – May 2010. Bank of England, 12 May 2012. https://www.bankofengland.co.uk/inflation-report/20 10/may-2010.

28 Alistair Darling, Back from the Brink: 1,000 Days at Number 11. Atlantic Books, 2011, p. 4266 (Kindle edition).

29 Robert Chote, Rowena Crawford, Carl Emmerson and Gemma Tetlow, Filling the hole: How do the three main UK parties plan to repair the public finances? Institute of Fiscal Studies, 27 April 2010. https://ifs.org.uk/publications/48 48.

30 Ibid.

31 Interview with the author, January 2021.

32 Janan Ganes, George Osborne: The Austerity Chancellor. Biteback Publishing, 2012, p. xi.

33 Interview with the author, January 2021.

34 George Osborne, Chancellor speech on the economy, 9 September 2013. https://www.gov.uk/government/speeches /chancellor-speech-on-the-economy.

35 Martin Wolf, Osborne has now been proved wrong on aus- terity. Financial Times, 26 September 2013. https://www.ft .com/content/c2fc7352-25de-11e3-aee8-00144feab7de.

36 Spencer Dale and James Talbot, Forward guidance in the UK. VoxEU, 13 September 2013. https://voxeu.org/article /forward-guidance-uk.

37 Alan Taylor, When is the time for austerity? VoxEU, 20 July 2013. https://voxeu.org/article/when-time-austerity.

38 Wolf, Osborne has now been proved wrong on austerity.

39 Paul Johnson and Daniel Chandler, The Coalition and

the economy. In Anthony Seldon and Mike Finn, eds, *The Coalition Effect 2010–2015*. Cambridge University Press.

40 Thiemo Fetzer, Did austerity cause Brexit? Working paper no. 381. Centre for Competitive Advantage in the Global Economy, 22 July 2018. https://econpapers.repec.org/paper/wrkwarwec/1170.htm.

41 Interview with the author, February 2021

42 Ministers reflect: Philip Hammond interviewed by Tim Durrant and Gemma Tetlow. Institute for Government, 4 November 2019. https://www.instituteforgovernment.org.uk/ministers-reflect/person/philip-hammond/.

43 Ibid.

44 Interview with the author, February 2021

45 Ibid.

46 Ministers reflect: Philip Hammond.

47 Interview with the author, February 2021.

48 James Forsyth and Katy Balls, Austerity was not the way forward. *The Spectator*, 30 November 2019. https://www.spectator.co.uk/article/-austerity-was-not-the-way-forward-.

49 They work for you. https://www.theyworkforyou.com/mp/10999/boris_johnson/uxbridge_and_south_ruislip/votes#welfare.

50 Interview with the author, February 2021.

51 Torsten Bell, Jack Leslie, Cara Pacitti and Matt Whittaker, Rewriting the rules. Assessing Conservative and Labour's new fiscal frameworks. Resolution Foundation, 7 November 2019. https://www.resolutionfoundation.org/app/uploads/2019/11/Rewriting-the-rules-1.pdf.

52 Richard Hughes, Jack Leslie, Cara Pacitti and James Smith, Playing by their own rules? Resolution Foundation, 28 November 2019. https://www.resolutionfoundation.org/publications/playing-by-their-own-rules/.

53 Ibid.

54 Interview with the author, January 2021

55 Martin Wolf, Sunak's budget: A spending spree to get the job done. *Financial Times*, 11 March 2020.

56 10 March 2021. Twitter, @nickmacpherson2.

57 Ben Zaranko, The Chancellor's spending plans are even tighter than they seem. Institute for Fiscal Studies, 18 March 2021. https://ifs.org.uk/publications/15365.

58 Paul Johnson, Spring Budget 2021. Institute for Fiscal Studies. https://ifs.org.uk/spring-budget-2021.

59 Fiscal monitor: Policies for the recovery. International Monetary Fund, October 2020. www.imf.org.

60 Commentary on the Public Sector Finances. 1 July 2021. 20 August 2021. Office for Budget Responsibility. https://obr .uk/docs/dlm_uploads/August-2021-PSF-commentary.pdf.

61 Overview of the March 2021 economic and fiscal outlook. Office for Budget Responsibility, 3 March 2021. https://obr .uk/overview-of-the-march-2021-economic-and-fiscal-out look/.

62 Interviews with the author, January to March 2021.

63 Ibid.

64 Sunak rules out austerity and denies rift with PM. *Daily Telegraph*. 12 August 2021. https://www.pressreader.com /uk/the-daily-telegraph/20210813/281573768761010.

65 Interviews with the author, January to March 2021.

66 Ibid.

67 Ibid.

68 Ibid.

69 Building back better: Our plan for health and social care. Command Paper 506, 7 September 2021. https://www.gov .uk/government/publications/build-back-better-our-plan-for -health-and-social-care.

70 Paul Johnson et al., An initial response to the Prime Minister's announcement on health, social care and National Insurance. Institute for Fiscal Studies, 7 September 2021. https://ifs.org .uk/publications/15597.

71 The Treasury view: A testament of experience. Speech to the Mile End Group by Nicholas MacPherson, 17 January 2014. https://www.gov.uk/government/speeches/speech-by-the-per manent-secretary-to-the-treasury-the-treasury-view-a-testa ment-of-experience.

Chapter 4: Tax Policy

1 David Cameron income tax law promise 'made up on the hoof'. 29 October 2016. https://www.bbc.com/news/uk-poli tics-37797134.

2 James Mirrlees et al., Tax by design. Institute for Fiscal

Studies, September 2011, p. 503. https://ifs.org.uk/docs/taxb ydesign.pdf.

3 Paul Johnson, Tax without design: Recent developments in UK tax policy. Institute for Fiscal Studies, May 2014, p. 1. https://ifs.org.uk/wps/wp201409.pdf.

4 www.sharefound.org.

5 Gordon Brown, *My Life, Our Times*. Bodley Head, 2017, p. 149.

6 Ibid., p. 150.

7 Alistair Darling, Overcoming barriers to tax reform. Institute for Government, 4 October 2019. Interviewed by Gemma Tetlow and Thomas Pope. https://www.instituteforgovern ment.org.uk/sites/default/files/alistair-darling-tax-interview .pdf.

8 Ibid.

9 The principles of tax reform. Speech by George Osborne at Policy Exchange, 15 February 2008. https://conservative-spe eches.sayit.mysociety.org/speech/599703.

10 Tax matters: Reforming the Tax System. Report of the Tax Reform Commission, October 2006. www.taxreformcom mission.com.

11 Osborne, The principles of tax reform.

12 Ibid.

13 Tom Welsh, George Osborne's tinkering has made the UK tax system more complicated than ever. City A.M., 18 March 2016. https://www.cityam.com/george-osbornes-tin kering-has-made-the-uk-tax-system-more-complicated-than -ever/.

14 Evidence to the Treasury Select Committee: Tax after Coronavirus, HC664. House of Commons, 1 September 2020. https://committees.parliament.uk/oralevidence/788/pdf/.

15 David Gauke, The corporate tax road map. HM Treasury, 29 November 2010. www.gov.uk/the-corporate-tax-road -map.

16 Evidence to the Treasury Select Committee. 1 September 2020.

17 George Osborne hits out at Sunak's 'unenterprising' corpo-ration tax hike. CityAm. Stefan Boscia. 9 March 2021. www .cityam.com.

18 Evidence to the Treasury Select Committee: Tax after Coronavirus, HC664.

19 Treasury Committee, Tax after Coronavirus. House of Commons, 1 March 2021. https://committees.parliament.uk /publications/4865/documents/50796/default/.

20 Mirrlees et al., Tax by design.

21 As summarized in Brown, *My Life, Our Times*, pp. 494–5.

22 Jill Rutter et al., *Better Budgets: Making Tax Policy Better*. Institute for Government, January 2017, p. 6. https:// www.instituteforgovernment.org.uk/sites/default/files/publications /Better_Budgets_report_WEB.pdf.

23 Gemma Tetlow and Joe Marshall, *Taxing Times: The Need to Reform the UK Tax System*. Institute for Government, July 2019. https://www.instituteforgovernment.org.uk/sites /default/files/publications/taxing-times-final.pdf

24 Gemma Tetlow et al., *Overcoming the Barriers to Tax Reform*. Institute for Government, April 2020. https:// www.instituteforgovernment.org.uk/sites/default/files/pub lications/overcoming-barriers-tax-reform.pdf.

25 Interview with Edward Troup, 2 July 2019. In Gemma Tetlow et al., *Overcoming Barriers to Tax Reform*. https:// www.instituteforgovernment.org.uk/sites/default/files/edwa rd-troup-tax-interview.pdf.

26 Interview with the author, August 2021.

27 Interview with Nicholas MacPherson, 6 August 2019. In Gemma Tetlow et al., *Overcoming Barriers to Tax Reform*. https://www.instituteforgovernment.org.uk/sites/default/fi les/lord-macpherson-tax-interview.pdf.

28 Tetlow et al., *Overcoming the Barriers to Tax Reform*, p. 34.

29 Interview with Nicholas MacPherson, 6 August 2019.

30 Interview with Gus O'Donnell, 24 April 2019. In Gemma Tetlow et al., *Overcoming the Barriers to Tax Reform*, p. 48.

31 Interview with the author, March 2021.

32 Bronwen Maddox, Tax policy in the real world: In conversation with former Chancellors. Institute for Government, 9 March 2021. https://www.instituteforgovernment.org.uk /events/tax-policy.

33 Interview with Terry Burns, 10 July 2019. In Gemma Tetlow et al., *Overcoming the Barriers to Tax Reform*. https://www .instituteforgovernment.org.uk/sites/default/files/lord-burns -tax-interview.pdf.

34 Interview with Andrew Turnbull. 12 September 2019. In Gemma Tetlow et al., *Overcoming the Barriers to Tax*

Reform. https://www.instituteforgovernment.org.uk/sites/de
fault/files/lord-turnbull-tax-interview.pdf.

35 Interview with Alistair Darling. 4 October 2019. In Gemma
Tetlow et al., *Overcoming the Barriers to Tax Reform*.
https://www.instituteforgovernment.org.uk/sites/default/fi
les/alistair-darling-tax-interview.pdf.

36 Interview with Edward Troup, 2 July 2019.

37 G7 Finance Ministers agree historic global tax agreement.
HM Treasury, 5 June 2021. https://www.g7uk.org/g7-finan
ce-ministers-agree-historic-global-tax-agreement/.

38 Interview with Alistair Darling, 4 October 2019.

39 Arun Advani, Emma Chamberlain and Andy Summers, A
wealth tax for the UK. Final Report of the Wealth Tax
Commission, 9 December 2020. https://www.wealthandpo
licy.com/wp/WealthTaxFinalReport.html.

40 Interview with the author, February 2021.

41 Paul Johnson et al., An initial response to the Prime Minister's
announcement on health, social care and National Insurance.
Institute for Fiscal Studies, 7 September 2021. https://ifs.org
.uk/publications/15619.

Chapter 5: Scotland: Saving the Union

1 The Treasury and the Union. Speech by Nicholas MacPherson
to the Strand Group, 19 January 2015. Published 21 January
2015.   https://www.gov.uk/government/speeches/speech-by
-the-permanent-secretary-to-the-treasury-the-treasury-and
-the-union.

2 Interview with the author, January 2021

3 The original formulation was 'most large financial institutions are global – at least in life if not in death': Banking
– from Bagehot to Basel, and back again. Speech by Mervyn
King at the Second Bagehot Lecture, Buttonwood Gathering,
New York, 25 October 2010. https://www.bis.org/review/r1
01028a.pdf.

4 Fiscal Commission Working Group, *First Report – Macroeconomic Framework*. The Scottish Government, February
2013. http://www.realinstitutoelcano.org/wps/wcm/connect/
a53335004ec4137faa27eeb5284b5e68/GovScotland_Fiscal

CWGReport.pdf?MOD=AJPERES&CACHEID=a53335004ec4
137faa27eeb5284b5e68.

5   MacPherson, The Treasury and the Union.
6   Fiscal Commission Working Group, *First Report*.
7   Scottish Government, *Scotland's Future: Your Guide to an Independent Scotland*. November 2013. https://www.gov.sc
ot/binaries/content/documents/govscot/publications/strategy
-plan/2013/11/scotlands-future/documents/scotlands-future
-guide-independent-scotland/scotlands-future-guide-indepen
dent-scotland/govscot%3Adocument/00439021.pdf.
8   The economics of currency unions. Speech by Mark Carney
at a lunch hosted by the Scottish Council for Development
and Industry, Edinburgh, 29 January 2014. https://www
.bankofengland.co.uk/-/media/boe/files/speech/2014/the-eco
nomics-of-currency-unions.pdf?la=en&hash=6BF118868A0
F396FA4987D31B05B71435E3AD16C.
9   Speech by Chancellor of the Exchequer on the prospect of
a currency union between an independent Scotland and the
rest of the UK, 13 February 2014. https://www.gov.uk/gover
nment/speeches/chancellor-on-the-prospect-of-a-currency-u
nion-with-an-independent-scotland.
10 Interview with the author, January 2021.
11 MacPherson: The Treasury and the Union.
12 Interview with the author, February 2021.
13 Interview with the author, January 2021.
14 Post-Referendum Scotland Poll, 18–19 September 2014.
https://lordashcroftpolls.com/wp-content/uploads/2014/09
/Lord-Ashcroft-Polls-Referendum-day-poll-summary-14091
91.pdf.
15 Gordon Brown, *My Life, Our Times*. Bodley Head, 2017,
p. 406.
16 Interview with the author, July 2021.
17 Post-Referendum Scotland Poll.
18 Interview with the author, January 2021

Chapter 6: Europe: The Ins and Outs

1   Chris Giles, How a Eurosceptic Treasury became Remain's
anti-Brexit champion. *Financial Times*, 31 May 2016.

https://www.ft.com/content/dc838140-23f0-11e6-9d4d-c11
776a5124d.

2 Philip Stephens, *Britain Alone: The Path from Suez to Brexit.*
Faber and Faber, 2021, p. 273.

3 Interview with *Prospect Magazine*, 30 January 2017. https://
www.prospectmagazine.co.uk/politics/interview-jacob-rees
-mogg-brexit-wonderful-liberation-economy.

4 Peter Oborne, Brexit, and the return of political lying. *The
Spectator*, 28 May 2016. https://www.spectator.co.uk/artic
le/brexit-and-the-return-of-political-lying.

5 Interview with the author, January 2021.

6 Conversation with the author.

7 Quoted in David Marsh, *The Euro: The Politics of the New
Global Currency.* Yale University Press, 2009, p. 161.

8 New Labour because Britain deserves better. Labour Party
Manifesto, 1997. http://www.labour-party.org.uk/manif
estos/1997/1997-labour-manifesto.shtml.

9 Key quotes from Blair on the euro, May 15 2002. https://
www.theguardian.com/world/2002/may/16/euro.eu

10 The UK and Preparations for Stage Three of Economic
and Monetary Union. Select Committee on Treasury Fifth
Report, 1998. https://publications.parliament.uk/pa/cm199
798/cmselect/cmtreasy/503v/ts0503.htm#a2.

11 Ed Balls, *Speaking Out: Lessons in Life and Politics.* Arrow
Books. 2016, pp. 160–162.

12 Ed Balls, *Euro-Monetarism: Why Britain Was Ensnared and
How It Should Escape.* Fabian Society, 1992.

13 Suzanne Heywood, *What Does Jeremy Think? Jeremy
Heywood and the Making of Modern Britain.* William
Collins, 2020.

14 Government policy on EMU and the five economic tests.
HM Treasury 2003. https://www.elibrary.imf.org/download
pdf/journals/001/2004/116/article-A001-en.xml.

15 Ibid.

16 Quoted in John Rentoul, How the Blair government decided
against adopting the euro. *Independent*, 18 March 2016.
https://www.independent.co.uk/voices/comment/how-the-bl
air-government-decided-against-adopting-the-euro-a69377
36.html.

17 Ibid.

18 Government policy on EMU and the five economic tests.

19 Quoted in John Rentoul, How the Blair government decided against adopting.

20 Robert Peston, *Brown's Britain*. Short Books, 2005, p. 244.

21 Balls, *Speaking Out*, p. 171.

22 Interview with the author, March 2021

23 Johnny Runge, EU migrants contribute to public finances, but the money hasn't gone where it's needed. National Institute of Economic and Social Research, 29 May 2019. https://blogs.lse.ac.uk/brexit/2019/05/29/eu-migrants-cont ribute-to-uk-public-finances-but-the-money-hasnt-gone-wh ere-its-needed/.

24 Philip Hammond interview with UK in a Changing Europe. Brexit Witness Archive, November 2020. https://ukandeu.ac .uk/interview-pdf/?personid=42190.

25 Stephens, *Britain Alone*, pp. 336–7.

26 Interview with the author, January 2021.

27 Howard Davies, Royal Bank of Scotland and the Financial Crisis: Ten Years On. The Strand Group, 12 September 2018. https://thestrandgroup.kcl.ac.uk/event/rbs-the-finan cial-crisis-ten-years-on/.

28 Interview with the author, March 2021.

29 HM Treasury analysis: The long-term economic impact of EU membership and the alternatives. Command Paper 9250, April 2016. https://assets.publishing.service.gov.uk/gover nment/uploads/system/uploads/attachment_data/file/5174 15/treasury_analysis_economic_impact_of_eu_membership _web.pdf.

30 Nicholas Crafts, The impact of EU membership on UK economic performance. *The Political Quarterly*, 18 May 2016, pp. 262–268. https://doi.org/10.1111/1467-923X.12261

31 Thomas Sampson, Swati Dhingra, Gianmarco Ottaviano and John Van Reenen, Economists for Brexit: A critique. Centre for Economic Performance, 2016. https://cep.lse.ac .uk/pubs/download/brexit06.pdf.

32 Ken Coutts, Graham Gudgin and Jordan Buchanan, How the economics profession got it wrong on Brexit. Working Paper 493. Centre for Business Research. University of Cambridge, January 2018. https://www.cbr.cam.ac.uk/wp-content/uploa ds/2020/08/wp493.pdf.

33 HM Treasury analysis: The immediate economic impact of leaving the EU. Command 9292, May 2016. https://www

.gov.uk/government/publications/hm-treasury-analysis-the-i mmediate-economic-impact-of-leaving-the-eu.

34 EU referendum: Osborne warns of Brexit budget cuts. 15 June 2016. www.bbc.co.uk.

35 Interview with the author, March 2021.

36 Interview with the author, January 2021.

37 Interview with the author, March 2021.

38 Interview with the author, February 2021.

39 Interviews with the author, January/February 2021.

40 Interview with the author, January 2021.

41 Interviews with the author, February 2021.

42 Quoted in the *Guardian*, 23 May 2016. https://www.thegu ardian.com/politics/2016/may/23/tory-grandees-dismiss-tre asury-brexit-report-inaccurate-propaganda-former-chancel lors.

43 George Parker, Conservative party infighting on Europe referendum escalates. *Financial Times*, 13 May 2016. https:// www.ft.com/content/10fe75d6-1859-11e6-bb7d-ee563a5a 1cc1.

44 Mark Carney, *Value(s): Building a Better World for All*. William Collins, 2021, p. 188.

45 Interview with the author, January 2021.

46 Hammond interview with UK in a Changing Europe.

47 Simon McDonald interview with UK in a Changing Europe. Brexit Witness Archive, 26 March 2021. https://ukandeu.ac .uk/brexit-witness-archive/simon-mcdonald/.

48 Hammond interview with UK in a Changing Europe, 13 and 20 November.

49 Ibid.

50 Sajid Javid. On my watch the Treasury is ready to play a full role in delivering Brexit. *Sunday Telegraph*, 27 July 2019. https://www.telegraph.co.uk/politics/2019/07/27/watch-trea sury-ready-play-full-role-delivering-brexit/.

51 Rishi Sunak explains EU decision 'toughest' of his career. *Yorkshire Post*, 26 February 2016. https://www.yorkshirep ost.co.uk/news/politics/rishi-sunak-mp-explains-eu-decision -toughest-his-career-1803236.

52 Interview with the author, January 2021.

53 Alex Stojanovic, Trade: Freeports and free zones. Institute for government, 10 February 2020. https://www.institutefor government.org.uk/explainers/trade-freeports-free-zones.

54 Holger Breinlich, Elsa Leromain, Dennis Novy and Thomas Sampson, The Brexit vote, inflation and UK living standards. *International Economic Review*, 3 September 2021. https://onlinelibrary.wiley.com/doi/full/10.1111/iere.125 41.

Chapter 7: Financial Regulation and the City of London

1   Interview with the author, January 2021.
2   Report into the collapse of Barings Bank. Board of Banking Supervision, 18 July 1995. https://www.gov.uk/government /publications/report-into-the-collapse-of-barings-bank.
3   *Financial Stability Review*. Issue One, Autumn 1996. https:// www.bankofengland.co.uk/-/media/boe/files/financial-stabil ity-report/1996/autumn-1996.pdf.
4   Martin Cihák, Sonia Munoz, Shakira Teh Sharifuddin and Kalin Tintchev, Financial stability reports: What are they good for? Working paper 12/1. International Monetary Fund, January 2012. https://www.imf.org/external/pubs/ft /wp/2012/wp1201.pdf.
5   William Keegan, *The Prudence of Mr Gordon Brown*. Wiley, 2003, pp. 178ff.
6   Gordon Brown, *My Life, Our Times*. Bodley Head, 2017, p. 120.
7   Geoffrey Robinson, *The Unconventional Minister: My Life Inside New Labour*. Michael Joseph, 2000, p. 42.
8   Quoted in Harold James, *Making a Modern Central Bank. The Bank of England 1979–2003*. Cambridge University Press, 2020, p. 420.
9   Memorandum of understanding between HM Treasury, the Bank of England and the Financial Services Authority, 1997. www.bankofengland.co.uk.
10 Nigel Lawson, *The View from No. 11: Memoirs of a Tory Radical*. Bantam Press, 1992, p. 404.
11 Interview with the author, January 2021.
12 Quoted in David Kynaston, *Till Time's Last Sand: A History of the Bank of England 1694–2013*. Bloomsbury, 2017, p. 726.
13 Joint Committee on Financial Services and Markets First

Report, 29 April 1999. https://publications.parliament.uk
/pa/jt199899/jtselect/jtfinser/328/32802.htm.

14 Ed Balls, *Speaking Out*. Penguin, 2016, p. 302.

15 Speech by Tony Blair to the Institute of Public Policy and
Research, London, 26 May 2005. https://www.theguardian
.com/politics/2005/may/26/speeches.media.

16 Ed Balls interview with the author. January 2021.

17 Speech by Ed Balls at Bloomberg London offices, September
2006.

18 Martin Cihák and Richard Podpiera, Is one watchdog better
than three? International experience with integrated financial sector supervision. Working paper 06/57. International
Monetary Fund, March 2006. https://www.imf.org/external
/pubs/ft/wp/2006/wp0657.pdf.

19 Barry Eichengreen and Nergiz Dincer, Who should super-
vise? The structure of bank supervision and the performance
of the financial system. Working paper 17401. National
Bureau of Economic Research, September 2011. https://
www.nber.org/papers/w17401.

20 Memorandum of understanding between HM Treasury, the
Bank of England and the Financial Services Authority.

21 James, *Making a Modern Central Bank*, pp. 426, 427.

22 Alistair Darling, *Back from the Brink: 1000 Days at Number
11*. Atlantic Books, 2011.

23 James, *Making a Modern Central Bank*, p. 427.

24 Kynaston, *Till Time's Last Sand*, p. 738.

25 Central bank psychology. Speech by Andrew Haldane, 17
November 2014. https://www.bankofengland.co.uk/-/media
/boe/files/speech/2014/central-bank-psychology.pdf?la=en
&hash=ADB06E35C7569B61D94BFF7E86C7F86343A0
6838.

26 Evidence from Hector Sants to the Treasury Select
Committee, 23 November 2010. https://publications.parli
ament.uk/pa/cm201011/cmselect/cmtreasy/430/10112302
.htm.

27 Evidence from Mervyn King to the Treasury Select
Committee, 29 April 2008. https://publications.parliament
.uk/pa/cm200708/cmselect/cmtreasy/524/8042903.htm.

28 History man believes that posterity will give him credit he
deserves. *The Times*, 15 March 2012. https://www.thetim

es.co.uk/article/history-man-believes-that-posterity-will-give-him-credit-he-deserves-r0n5x897872

29 Darling, *Back from the Brink*.
30 Interview with the author, February 2021
31 Evidence from Michael Foot to the Parliamentary Commission on Banking Standards, 27 November 2012. https://publications.parliament.uk/pa/jt201213/jtselect/jtpcbs/144/144we08.htm
32 Global Financial Stability Report. International Monetary Fund, April 2006. https://www.imf.org/en/Publications/GFSR/Issues/2016/12/31/Global-Financial-Stability-Report-April-2006-Market-Developments-and-Issues-18690.
33 Gordon Brown, *Beyond the Crash: Overcoming the First Crisis of Globalization*. Simon and Schuster, 2010, p. 18.
34 Interview with the author, January 2021.
35 Interview with the author, January 2021.
36 Andy Haldane, interviewed by Robert Pringle. Quoted in Kynaston, *Till Time's Last Sand*, pp. 740–1.
37 Interview with the author, January 2021
38 Tom Sasse and Emma Norris, Moving on: The costs of high staff turnover in the civil service. Institute for Government, 16 January 2019. https://www.instituteforgovernment.org.uk/sites/default/files/publications/IfG_staff_turnover_WEB.pdf.
39 Sharon White, Review of HM Treasury's management response to the financial crisis. HM Treasury, March 2012. https://assets.publishing.service.gov.uk/government/uploads/system/uploads/attachment_data/file/220506/review_fincrisis_response_290312.pdf.
40 Mervyn King, letter to Treasury Select Committee, 12 September 2007. https://publications.parliament.uk/pa/cm200708/cmselect/cmtreasy/56/56ii.pdf.
41 Darling, *Back from the Brink*.
42 Ibid.
43 Interview with the author, January 2021
44 Ibid.
45 Warren Buffett, letter to Berkshire Hathaway shareholders, February 2008. https://www.berkshirehathaway.com/letters/2007ltr.pdf.
46 Interview with the author, January 2021

47 Suzanne Heywood, *What Does Jeremy Think? Jeremy Heywood and the Making of Modern Britain*. William Collins, 2020.

48 Interview with the author, February 2021.

49 Howard Davies, Royal Bank of Scotland and the Financial Crisis: Ten Years On. The Strand Group, 12 September 2018. https://thestrandgroup.kcl.ac.uk/event/rbs-the-financial-crisis-ten-years-on/.

50 Interview with the author, February 2021.

51 The run on the Rock. House of Commons Treasury Committee. Fifth Report of Session 2007–08, Volume 1, 24 January 2008. https://publications.parliament.uk/pa/cm200708/cmselect/cmtreasy/56/56i.pdf.

52 Interview with the author, January 2021

53 Sir James Sassoon, Review of the tripartite structure of financial regulation, 9 March 2009. https://www.conservativehome.com/thetorydiary/2009/03/george-osborn-1-3.html.

54 Michael Taylor, 'Twin Peaks': A regulatory structure for the new century. Centre for the Study of Financial Innovation, December 1995. https://static1.squarespace.com/static/54d620fce4b049bf4cd5be9b/t/55241159e4b0c8f3afe1d11e/1428427097907/Twin+Peaks+A+regulatory+structure+for+the+new+century.pdf.

55 Interview with the author, February 2021.

56 Ibid.

57 Interview with the author, February 2021

58 Interview with the author, July 2021.

59 Independent Commission on Banking: final report. 12 September 2011. https://webarchive.nationalarchives.gov.uk/ukgwa/20120827143059/http://bankingcommission.independent.gov.uk///.

60 Paul Volcker, Evidence to the Parliamentary Commission on Banking Standards, 17 October 2012. https://publications.parliament.uk/pa/jt201314/jtselect/jtpcbs/27/121017.htm.

61 High-level expert group on reforming the structure of the EU banking sector. Liikanen Report, 2 October 2012. https://ec.europa.eu/info/sites/default/files/liikanen-report-02102012_en.pdf.

62 Interview with the author, February 2021.

63 The Total tax contribution of UK financial services in 2020, 13th edn. PriceWaterhouseCoopers for the City of London,

February 2021. https://www.cityoflondon.gov.uk/assets/Bu
siness/total-tax-contribution-2020.pdf.

64 2019 Total tax contribution of the UK banking sector.
PriceWaterhouseCoopers for UK Finance, October 2019.
https://www.ukfinance.org.uk/system/files/2019%20-%20T
otal%20Tax%20Contribution%20of%20the%20UK%20
banking%20sector.pdf.

65 European Banking Authority Report: Benchmarking of
remuneration practices at the European Union level and data
on high earners. https://www.eba.europa.eu/sites/default/do
cuments/files/document_library/Publications/Reports/2020
/897301/Report%20on%20remuneration%20benchmar
king%20and%20High%20Earners.pdf.

66 Conversation with the author, June 2019.

67 Oliver Wyman, The impact of the UK's exit from the EU on
the UK-based financial services sector. TheCityUK, 2016.
https://www.oliverwyman.com/content/dam/oliver-wyman
/global/en/2016/oct/OW%20report_Brexit%20impact%20
on%20Uk-based%20FS.pdf.

68 Catherine McGuinness, quoted in Guy Faulconbridge and
Huw Jones, No Brexit bonfire for City of London, 27
January 2021. https://www.reuters.com/article/uk-britain-eu
-london-idUSKBN29W0OV.

69 Eivind Hamre and William Wright, Brexit and the City: The
impact so far. New Financial, April 2021. https://newfinan
cial.org/brexit-the-city-the-impact-so-far/.

70 Henry Goodwin, Why fishing does, and doesn't, matter for
post-Brexit Britain. The London Economic, 8 December
2020. https://www.thelondoneconomic.com/politics/why-fish
ing-does-and-doesnt-matter-for-post-brexit-britain-212262/.

71 Interview with the author, January 2021.

72 Philip Hammond interview with UK in a Changing Europe.
Brexit Witness Archive, 13 and 20 November 2020. https://
ukandeu.ac.uk/brexit-witness-archive/philip-hammond/.

73 Interview with the author, January 2021.

74 Ibid.

75 Interviews with the author, February 2021

76 George Parker, Peter Foster, Sam Fleming and Jim Brunsden,
Inside the Brexit deal: The agreement and the aftermath.
Financial Times, 22 January 2021. https://www.ft.com/con
tent/cc6b0d9a-d8cc-4ddb-8c57-726df018c10e.

77 Evidence from Andrew Bailey to the Treasury Select Committee, 24 February 2021. https://committees.parlia ment.uk/oralevidence/1789/pdf/.

78 David Goodhart, *The Road to Somewhere: The Populist Revolt and the Future of Politics*. Hurst, 2017.

79 Nicolas Véron, After orderly Brexit, a new European financial landscape starts to emerge. Peterson Institute for International Economics, 19 March 2021. https://www.piie .com/blogs/realtime-economic-issues-watch/after-orderly-br exit-new-european-financial-landscape-starts.

Chapter 8: Climate Change and the Road to Net Zero

1 Jill Rutter, The Treasury's interim review is a major step on the path to net zero. Institute for Government, 24 December 2020. https://www.instituteforgovernment.org.uk/blog/trea sury-interim-review-net-zero.

2 The Global Warming Policy Foundation: History and mission. www.thegwpf.org.

3 Andrew Turnbull, The really inconvenient truth or 'it ain't necessarily so'. Briefing Paper No. 1. The Global Warming Policy Foundation., July 2011. https://www.thegwpf.org /images/stories/gwpf-reports/lord-turnbull.pdf.

4 Nicholas Stern, *The Economics of Climate Change: The Stern Review*. Cambridge University Press, 2007.

5 Interview with Gordon Brown, August 2021.

6 What is the 2008 Climate Change Act? Grantham Research Institute, 30 April 2020. https://www.lse.ac.uk/granthamins titute/explainers/what-is-the-2008-climate-change-act/.

7 Airports Commission: Final report. July 2016. www.assets .publishing.service.gov.uk.

8 I don't want UK to be at forefront of tackling climate change, says Osborne. 28 September 2013. https://www.theguardian .com/environment/2013/sep/28/climate-change-energy-bills -george-osborne.

9 George Osborne wants climate change tackled as cheaply as possible. 20 February 2014. https://www.theguardian.com /politics/2014/feb/20/george-osborne-climate-change-che aply.

10 Annex B: Sustainability Report, in HM Treasury, *Annual Report and Accounts 2014–15*. https://assets.publishing.ser vice.gov.uk/government/uploads/system/uploads/attachme nt_data/file/446730/50601_HC_34_HMT_Annual_Report _WEB.pdf.

11 Written evidence to the Environmental Audit Committee – Sustainability and HM Treasury. The Institution of Environmental Sciences, 2015. https://www.the-ies.org/sites /default/files/policy/Sustainability-HM-Treasury_IES_web .pdf.

12 Jim Pickard, UK net zero emissions plans will 'cost more than £1tn'. *Financial Times*, 5 June 2019. https://www.ft .com/content/036a5596-87a7-11e9-a028-86cea8523dc2.

13 Dimitri Zengheli, Why the Chancellor's statement on the cost of a net-zero transition in the UK could imperil the country's climate ambitions. Grantham Research Institute, 6 June 2019. https://www.lse.ac.uk/granthaminstitute/news /why-the-chancellors-statement-on-the-cost-of-a-net-zero-t ransition-in-the-uk-could-imperil-the-countrys-climate-am bitions/.

14 Dave Keatin, Four years ago, Boris Johnson said climate concern was 'without foundation'. Forbes, 5 February 2020. https://www.forbes.com/sites/davekeating/2020/02/05/four -years-ago-boris-johnson-said-climate-concern-was-without -foundation/.

15 Roger Harrabin, COP26: PM 'doesn't get' climate change, says sacked president. BBC News, 4 February 2020. https:// www.bbc.com/news/science-environment-51368799.

16 Net zero: The UK's contribution to stopping global warm- ing. Climate Change Committee, 2 May 2019. Page 196. https://www.theccc.org.uk/publication/net-zero-the-uks-con tribution-to-stopping-global-warming/.

17 Net zero review: Interim report. HM Treasury, 17 December 2020.   https://www.gov.uk/government/publications/net-ze ro-review-interim-report.

18 Rutter, The Treasury's interim review is a major step on the path to net zero.

19 Howard Davies, Central banks' green goals are raising red flags. Project Syndicate, 2 March 2021. https://www.project -syndicate.org/commentary/central-bank-green-goals-raising -red-flags-by-howard-davies-2021-03.

20 Interview with the author, July 2021.
21 Interview with the author, August 2021.
22 Nicholas Stern, Public economics as if time matters: Climate change and the dynamics of policy. *Journal of Public Economics* 162, June 2018, pp. 4–17.
23 Interview with the author, July 2021.

Chapter 9: The Treasury's Changing Shape

1   Lord Bridges, *The Treasury*. Allen and Unwin, 1964, p. 17.
2   Kenneth Clarke, in Howard Davies, ed., *The Chancellors' Tales*. Polity, 2006, p. 194.
3   Quoted in David Kynaston, *Till Time's Last Sand: A History of the Bank of England 1694–2013*. Bloomsbury, 2017, p. 719.
4   Ed Balls, James Howat and Anna Stansbury, Central bank independence revisited: After the financial crisis what should a model central bank look like? Working paper 67. M-RBCG Associates, 2016. https://www.hks.harvard.edu/centers/mrc bg/publications/awp/awp67.
5   Interview with the author, February 2021
6   Andrew Rawnsley, *Servants of the People: The Inside Story of New Labour*. Penguin, 2001, p. 143.
7   Quoted in The origins of Treasury control. Speech by Sir Nicholas MacPherson, 16 January 2013. https://www.gov .uk/government/speeches/speech-by-the-permanent-secreta ry-to-the-treasury-sir-nicholas-macpherson-the-origins-of-tr easury-control.
8   Suzanne Heywood, *What Does Jeremy Think? Jeremy Heywood and the Making of Modern Britain*. William Collins, 2020, pp. 178–179.
9   Interview with the author, August 2021
10 Gordon Brown, *My Life, Our Times*. Bodley Head, 2017, p. 188.
11 Interview with the author, March 2021.
12 Interview with the author, July 2021
13 Gus O'Donnell, Financing Britain's future: Review of the revenue departments. Command paper 6163, March 2004. https://webarchive.nationalarchives.gov.uk/ukgwa/+/htt

p:/www.hm-treasury.gov.uk/media/FBAA7/odonnell_fore
_ch1_245.pdf.

14 Foreword by Gordon Brown, in O'Donnell, Financing
    Britain's future.

15 Interview with the author, August 2021

16 Interview with the author, March 2021.

17 Penelope Tuck, Dominic De Cogan and John Snape, A tale
    of the merger between the Inland Revenue and HM Customs
    and Excise. University of Birmingham, 2019. https://core.ac
    .uk/download/pdf/188666659.pdf.

18 Christopher John Wales and Christopher Peter Wales,
    Structures, processes and governance in tax policy-making:
    An initial report. Saïd Business School, University of Oxford,
    December 2012. https://wayback.archive-it.org/org-467/202
    00808151828/http://eureka.sbs.ox.ac.uk/7340/1/Structures
    %20and%20processes%20in%20tax%20policy%20ma
    king.pdf.

19 Jill Rutter et al., *Better Budgets: Making Tax Policy Better*.
    Institute for Government, January 2017. https://www.insti
    tuteforgovernment.org.uk/sites/default/files/publications/Bet
    ter_Budgets_report_WEB.pdf.

20 Interview with the author, February 2021

21 Interview with the author, January 2021

22 Interview with the author, July 2021

23 Ed Balls, *Speaking Out*. Arrow Books, 2016, p. 336,

24 Interview with the author, January 2021

25 Giles Wilkes and Stian Westlake, The end of the Treasury:
    Breaking up the UK's finance ministry. Nesta, 3 September
    2014. https://media.nesta.org.uk/documents/end_of_treasu
    ry.pdf

26 Lord Kerslake, Rethinking the Treasury. Kerslake review
    of the Treasury, February 2017. http://www.industry-forum
    .org/wp-content/uploads/2017/03/9076_17-Kerslake-Revi
    ew-of-the-Treasury-_-final_v2.pdf.

27 Lionel Barber, The Treasury today: A devalued currency?
    Prospect, January/February 2021. https://www.prospectm
    agazine.co.uk/magazine/the-treasury-today-a-devalued-cur
    rency-lionel-barber-rishi-sunak

28 Civil Service Statistics 2000. https://www.civilservant.org.uk
    /library/cs%20stats%202000.pdf.

29 Sharon White, Review of HM Treasury's management

response to the financial crisis. HM Treasury, March 2012. https://assets.publishing.service.gov.uk/government/uploads /system/uploads/attachment_data/file/220506/review_fincri sis_response_290312.pdf.

30 Civil service staff numbers. Institute for government, 2020. https://www.instituteforgovernment.org.uk/explainers/civil -service-staff-numbers.

31 Kerslake, Rethinking the Treasury

32 Quoted in Barber, The Treasury today.

33 Healey, in Davies, ed., *The Chancellors' Tales*.

34 White, Review of HM Treasury's management response to the financial crisis.

35 Why is civil service reform so hard? John Kingman in conversation with Bronwen Maddox. Institute for Government, 16 December 2020. https://www.instituteforgovernment.org .uk/events/civil-service-reform-john-kingman.

36 Interview with the author [DATE??]

37 Michael Gove, The privilege of public service. Ditchley Annual Lecture, 1 July 2020. https://www.gov.uk/govern ment/speeches/the-privilege-of-public-service-given-as-the-di tchley-annual-lecture.

38 Why is civil service reform so hard? John Kingman in conversation with Bronwen Maddox

39 Moving On. The costs of high turnover in the civil service. Tom Sasse and Emma Norris. Institute for Government. 2019. www.instituteforgovernment.org.uk

40 Alec Waugh, *A Spy in the Family: An Erotic Comedy*. W.H. Allen, 1970.

41 Why is civil service reform so hard?

42 Interview with the author, March 2021

43 Peter Cardwell, *The Secret Life of Special Advisers*. Biteback, 2020.

44 Interview with the author, January 2021

45 HM Treasury Careers: Our Values. https://www.hmtreasury careers.co.uk/about-us/our-culture-values/.

46 www.glassdoor.co.uk.

47 Howard Davies and Joanna Howard, HM Treasury: How others see it. March 1992, unpublished.

48 Brown, *My Life, Our Times*, p. 351.

49 Women in Finance Charter. HM Treasury, September 2019.

https://www.gov.uk/government/publications/women-in-fi
nance-charter.

50 Gender pay gap report 2019. HM Treasury, 23 January
2020.   https://assets.publishing.service.gov.uk/government
/uploads/system/uploads/attachment_data/file/860302/Gen
der_Pay_Gap_report_-_2018_19.pdf.

51 Gender balance in the civil service. Institute for Government,
31 March 2020. https://www.instituteforgovernment.org.uk
/publication/gender/civil-service.

52 Catherine Haddon, How have cabinet posts changed by
gender? Institute for Government, 16 September 2021.
https://www.instituteforgovernment.org.uk/blog/governme
nt-reshuffle-september-2021?page=3.

Chapter 10: Leadership

1   Gordon Brown, *My Life, Our Times*. Bodley Head, 2017,
p. 114.

2   Interview with the author, February 2021

3   Quoted in Nicholas Timmins, UK Chancellor accused of
'Stalinist' style. *Financial Times*, 20 March 2007. https://
www.ft.com/content/ec849680-d6eb-11db-98da-000b5df1
0621.

4   Quoted in Andrew Rawnsley, Moody, angry, naive: Yes, he
was flawed but Gordon Brown did save the world. *Observer*,
7 December 2014. https://www.theguardian.com/politics/20
14/dec/07/gordon-brown-moody-complex-angry-naive-sa
ved-world.

5   Interview with the author, February 2021

6   Alistair Darling, *Back from the Brink: 1000 days at Number
11*. Atlantic Books, 2011.

7   Interview with the author, February 2021

8   Cathy Newman, Shadow Chancellor attacks 'brutal' Brown.
Financial Times, 5 December 2005. https://www.ft.com/con
tent/3dbad21e-6378-11da-be11-0000779e2340

9   Quoted in Janan Ganesh, *The Austerity Chancellor*.
Biteback, 2012, p. 196.

10 Interview with the author, January 2021

11 Interview with the author, February 2021

12 Rowena Manson, Sajid Javid resigns as Chancellor amid Johnson's reshuffle. *Guardian*, 13 February 2020. https://www.theguardian.com/politics/2020/feb/13/sajid-javid-resigns-as-chancellor-amid-boris-johnson-reshuffle.

13 Isabel Hardman, The rise of brand Rishi. *The Spectator*, 9 July 2020. https://www.spectator.co.uk/article/the-rise-of-brand-rishi.

14 Liam Byrne, 'I'm afraid there is no money.' The letter I will regret for ever. *Guardian*, 9 May 2015. https://www.theguardian.com/commentisfree/2015/may/09/liam-byrne-apology-letter-there-is-no-money-labour-general-election.

15 John Rentoul, Danny Alexander on the role of the Chief Secretary to the Treasury. *Independent*, 8 December 2015. https://www.independent.co.uk/voices/comment/daily-catch-danny-alexander-role-chief-secretary-treasury-a6764161.html.

16 Ministers reflect. Lord Myners interviewed by Nicola Hughes and Peter Riddell. Institute for Government, 7 June 2016. https://www.instituteforgovernment.org.uk/ministers-reflect/person/lord-myners/.

17 Ibid.

18 Geoffrey Robinson, *The Unconventional Minister: My Life Inside New Labour*. Penguin, 2001, p. 48.

19 Lord Turnbull interview with Lord Hennessy. 14 January 2012. https://history.blog.gov.uk/2013/07/11/lord-turnbull/.

20 Quoted in Lionel Barber, *The Powerful and the Damned*. W.H. Allen, 2020, p. 48.

21 Turnbull interview with Hennessy

22 Kevin Theakston, *Permanent Secretaries: Comparative Biography and Leadership in Whitehall in Transforming British Government*. Palgrave Macmillan, 2000.

23 William Keegan, *The Prudence of Mr Gordon Brown*. John Wiley, 2004, pp. 175–176.

24 George Lucas, New Statesman Profile: Gus O'Donnell. *New Statesman*, 27 November 1998.

25 Lord O'Donnell interview with Lord Hennessy. 30 [*sic*] February 2013. https://www.civilservant.org.uk/library/Cabinet_Secretary_Interviews/2013-Gus_O%27Donnell-Interview.pdf.

26 Brown, *My Life, Our Times*, p. 351.

27 Nicholas MacPherson, Now is not the time to fall out of love with austerity. *Financial Times*, 16 June 2017. https://www.ft.com/content/48b2f6f8-5270-11e7-a1f2-db19572361bb.

28 Darling, *Back from the Brink*.

29 Edward Malnick, Top civil servants on Tories 'hit list'. *Sunday Telegraph*, 22 February 2020. https://www.telegraph.co.uk/politics/2020/02/22/top-civil-servants-tories-hit-list/.

30 Sebastian Payne, New term for Tom Scholar signals end to 'war' on Whitehall. *Financial Times*. 7 January 2021. https://www.ft.com/content/ac4ad04f-f416-4301-aa7b-1ab7b13bc443.

Chapter 11: Trouble Ahead

1 Winston Churchill, Budget speech 1929. https://hansard.parliament.uk/Commons/1929-04-15/debates/b8e883c6-b582-4112-bbf4-64c103edb29e/OrdersOfTheDay.

2 The Treasury view: A testament of experience. Speech to the Mile End Group by Nicholas MacPherson, 17 January 2014. https://www.gov.uk/government/speeches/speech-by-the-permanent-secretary-to-the-treasury-the-treasury-view-a-testament-of-experience.

3 Mervyn King, The ideological bankruptcy of modern monetary theory. *The Spectator*, 19 December 2020. https://www.spectator.co.uk/article/the-ideological-bankruptcy-of-modern-monetary-theory.

4 Sebastian Payne and Chris Giles, Confusion over UK 'levelling-up' plan prompts Boris Johnson to hire new adviser. *Financial Times*. 3 May 2021. https://www.ft.com/content/22c5a8ed-e5be-4616-a944-ba2550faea78.

5 Diane Coyle and Marianne Sensier, The imperial Treasury: Appraisal methodology and regional economic performance in the UK. Bennett Institute for Public Policy, University of Cambridge, July 2018. https://www.bennettinstitute.cam.ac.uk/media/uploads/files/The_Imperial_Treasury_appraisal_methodology_and_regional_economic_performance_in_the_UK.pdf.

6 The Treasury's Net Zero Review: Bedrock of a just transition.

Grantham Research Institute, 16 February 2021. https://www.lse.ac.uk/granthaminstitute/news/the-treasurys-net-zero-review-bedrock-of-a-just-transition/.
7   Interview with the author, August 2021
8   Dietrich Vollrath, *Fully Grown: Why a Stagnant Economy Is a Sign of Success*. University of Chicago Press, 2020.